THE POLITICAL THOUGHT OF ANEURIN BEVAN

THE POLITICAL THOUGHT OF ANEURIN BEVAN

Nye Davies

UNIVERSITY OF WALES PRESS
2024

www.uwp.co.uk

British Library Cataloguing-in-Publication Data

A catalogue record for this book is available from the British Library.

ISBN 978-1-83772-141-2
e-ISBN 978-1-83772-142-9

The University of Wales Press gratefully acknowledges the funding support of HEFCW and Cardiff University in publication of this book.

Typeset by Geethik Technologies
Printed by CPI Antony Rowe, Melksham

CONTENTS

ACKNOWLEDGEMENTS

THIS BOOK emerged from my PhD thesis, which began in 2015. I have several people to thank, both from during that period and since. First, I would like to express my sincere thanks to my PhD supervisors Richard Wyn Jones and Peri Roberts. Their advice and support over the years have been invaluable. I feel very privileged to have had the opportunity to draw on their vast knowledge and expertise. The work that follows would not have been possible were it not for their constant encouragement and direction and I am extremely grateful for the commitment they have shown to me and my work.

I am also very grateful to Daniel Williams and Dai Moon for always being on hand to provide helpful comments and suggestions while turning my thesis into a book, and for their guidance and support as I have developed my research and academic career. I would also like to thank James Phillips for his advice, feedback and enthusiasm towards this project over the past few years.

I would like to thank the staff at the National Library of Wales, the South Wales Miners' Library, the British Library and the Special Collections and Archives at Cardiff University for their help in collecting the articles and publications that are discussed in this research. I am also very grateful to Andrew Rosthorn for his help in sourcing the many issues of *Tribune* that were analysed in the current book.

Having already published with the University of Wales Press, I know how lucky I am to be supported by its great staff who have been on hand every step of the way. I would particularly like to thank Adam Burns,

Georgia Winstone, Dafydd Jones, Elin Williams and Llion Wigley for their support during the publication of both books.

Working at Cardiff University's School of Law and Politics and as a member of the Wales Governance Centre means that I work with immensely talented and supportive colleagues. I am particularly grateful to Rob Jones both for organising online writing retreats during the Covid pandemic and beyond, which allowed me to dedicate time to writing this book, and for his friendship, general enthusiasm and encouragement throughout. I am grateful to all my colleagues who provided regular support and encouragement over the past few years. Special thanks must go to Greg Davies, Adam Evans, Steffan Evans, Guto Ifan, Jac Larner, Thomas Leahy, Rachel Minto, Luke Nicholas, Hedydd Phylip, Ed Poole and Huw Pritchard. Their good humour, friendship and encouragement have been invaluable.

I owe a huge amount to my cariad Verity, whose love and kindness have been vital. Verity has had to endure listening to me ramble on for a whole *seven* years(!) about Aneurin Bevan, chapter structures and every other little detail about the PhD and then the book. I am extremely lucky to have met Verity within the first few months of starting my PhD and I owe her so much for the enthusiastic and passionate support that she has given me and for her unwavering patience.

Finally, I dedicate this book to my mum and dad. I will never be able to thank you enough for the encouragement you have given me, not just over the course of writing this book, but my entire life. You have always believed in me even when I have doubted myself. Your love and support have been a constant source of inspiration. This book would never have been possible if it wasn't for you and the sacrifices you have made for me.

INTRODUCTION

Aneurin Bevan's role in establishing the National Health Service (NHS) has secured his legacy. Today, more than sixty years after his death, Bevan is regularly invoked by politicians across the political spectrum, his values and principles being declared as a source of inspiration. If a politician is seen to be protecting Bevan's legacy or following his principles, then they can claim to be standing up for important values. Even in the Conservative Party, the party that Bevan declared as being 'lower than vermin', Bevan's name is invoked to defend preferred policies. In his battle with the British Medical Association (BMA) over a dispute with junior doctors, former Secretary of State for Health Jeremy Hunt compared his situation to that of Bevan, who faced serious opposition from the BMA when he was establishing the NHS.[1] Hunt attempted to defend his position by arguing that 'had Nye Bevan given way to the BMA there would be no NHS'.[2] In another instance, during a debate on creating a seven-day NHS, former Prime Minister David Cameron insisted that Bevan would have been in favour as 'he knew that the NHS was for patients up and down the country'. Former Labour leader Jeremy Corbyn responded by arguing that 'Nye Bevan would be turning in his grave if he could hear the Prime Minister's attitude towards the NHS. He was a man with vision who wanted a health service for the good of all'.[3] Bevan then is clearly a go-to figure in debates on health policy, no matter what side of the political divide someone may lie on. Hunt even once proclaimed: 'The vision of Nye Bevan before – the vision of a one-nation Conservative Party today.'[4] A comment that would of course be seen as sacrilege by Labour Party supporters.

However, as would be expected, appeals to Bevan are most commonplace within the Labour Party, to the extent that they have become almost obligatory references in speeches by its politicians. Bevan is held up as a hero of the labour movement, an autodidact who emerged out of poverty to take on the British ruling class and establish perhaps the most cherished institution in Britain. As a way of articulating the values that underpinned the Welsh Government's health policies since devolution, the late Welsh First Minister Rhodri Morgan referred to 'the traditions of Titmus, Tawney, Beveridge and Bevan' in his "Clear Red Water" speech[5] and the need to 'adhere to Nye Bevan's founding principles'.[6] Labour leaders from Neil Kinnock[7] to Gordon Brown[8] have praised Bevan's legacy, while former Chancellor Ed Balls declared that Bevan 'deserves the title of Labour's greatest hero'.[9] In Labour ranks it is clear that Bevan is considered as a symbol for principled politics. The importance of Bevan to the Labour Party is underlined by historian Kenneth O. Morgan, who wrote that 'Nye Bevan is firmly established in the socialist pantheon as a hero of Labour. This is not surprising. He was not only a prophet but also a great constructive pioneer'.[10]

Morgan also pointed to Bevan's having been adopted as a figurehead for the centre ground within the Labour Party, something that might seem surprising given Bevan's position as the figurehead for a left-wing faction. Bevan's parliamentarianism, Morgan suggested, has meant that he 'has been reinvented as a mainstream patriot ... The ultimate radical has been transplanted into the centre ground' (p. 182). Morgan also pointed to Tony Blair's foreword in *The State of the Nation: The Political Legacy of Aneurin Bevan* (1997), a book commemorating the centenary of Bevan's birth, as demonstrating how Bevan has become 'a pivot of the Progressive Alliance' (p. 181). That the legacy of Bevan can be claimed by the centre-ground in the Labour Party, and even by advocates of New Labour, demonstrates the extent to which, rhetorically at least, he has come to be regarded as a unifying figure across the different, disparate strands and factions of the Labour Party.

More recently Bevan has been weaponised against moves to shift the Labour Party in a more leftwards direction. During the 2016 Labour leadership election, Owen Smith regularly invoked Bevan throughout his campaign, claiming to be following in Bevan's footsteps and being inspired by his politics. Suggesting that Corbyn's politics were not vote-winning and that the Labour leader was unelectable, Smith stated: 'I want to be a force for good in the world. Therefore, you need to achieve power. Nye Bevan, my great hero, said it's all about achieving and exercising power. I've devoted my life to that.'[11] Smith even implied that Corbyn and his Shadow Chancellor John McDonnell were not interested in 'a Parliamentary route to socialism'.[12] Smith's appeals to Bevan emphasised the pragmatic nature of his politics and his focus on practicality. Bevan's biographer Nick Thomas-Symonds, in supporting Smith, argued that Bevan's 'application of socialist principles to government' and his belief in 'pursuing an ultimate goal and seeing the practical route towards it' had similarities with Smith's own ambitions and politics.[13]

All this was challenged by Matt Myers who maintained that Owen Smith is not a politician in the Bevanite mould. Myers claimed rather that the 'ideas, theories, and experiences that nourished [Bevan's] development, framed his worldview, and sustained his political activity could not be farther from Owen Smith's'. Myers underlined how, just like Corbyn more recently, Bevan and his followers were seen as a disruptive group within the Parliamentary Labour Party, aiming to shift its strategy leftwards. Myers concluded by arguing:

> Bevan is one of the great figures of British socialism. His career is marked by revolts against the established order, and defence of grassroots and socialist politics. He would have had little affinity with Owen Smith's campaign or his brand of 'Bevanism'. Smith's sudden and lackluster [*sic*] conversion to the Left cannot give him credibility. All it reveals is a desperation to garner legitimacy from someone else's radical past.[14]

The championing of Bevan by those who would wish to shift Labour to the centre-ground appears counterintuitive. As Morgan noted, when Bevan was an MP, he was a constant thorn in the side of the Labour Party leadership. He was expelled from the party in 1939, almost expelled again in 1944 and in 1955, and his group the Bevanites were 'accused by the party right of fomenting civil war'.[15] Barbara Castle, for instance, took issue with the idea that New Labour was continuing Bevan's legacy, arguing in *The State of the Nation* that 'if he were alive today, [Bevan] would be irritated by New Labour's claim to have a monopoly of ideas for bringing the party and the unions up to date'.[16] As Simon Hannah observed when studying the history of the left within the Labour Party, Bevan and his followers were considered by many as fighting against the orthodoxies of the leadership and of being a constant thorn in its side.[17]

Herein lies a major issue when considering Bevan's legacy. He is a hero for many different people within the Labour Party, no matter which side of the divide they sit on. He is often used as shorthand for Labour values, whether that be by figures on the left or the right.[18] However, many figures within the party would contest what those values are. Additionally, a commonality between many of these references to Bevan cited above is that they largely focus on his role in establishing the NHS. Thus, Bevan's values are equated with the values that underpinned the service.

It is perhaps inevitable that someone so revered in Labour Party history – and who is considered to be the founder of Britain's most cherished institution – would be invoked by different factions and groups across the political spectrum. But if Bevan's politics can be claimed by so many different people on so many different sides of the political debate, then the question arises as to what exactly Bevan's principles were? Beyond his status as 'founder of the NHS' and champion of the values apparently enshrined within it, what were his core political beliefs? This book aims to answer those questions.

Bevan Studies

In searching for answers to the above queries, a study of the extant literature on Bevan certainly helps to reveal important themes and concepts within Bevan's political thought. Broadly, there have been two methodological approaches to studying Bevan: the first is a biographical approach to his life and career, while the second involves analysing his place within the political thought of the Labour Party. An analysis of both categories of literature highlights common themes and issues in the interpretations of Bevan's thought. These include the importance of class conflict and Marxism, Bevan's advocacy of Parliament and public ownership, his views on international relations and his vision for a democratic socialist society.

BIOGRAPHY

Several biographies have been written about Bevan,[19] including more specific studies of Bevan's life in Tredegar.[20] The first significant biography of Bevan was published by his friend and political ally Michael Foot.[21] The first volume was originally published in 1962, covering 1897–1945, while the second volume was published in 1973, covering the remainder of Bevan's life up to his death in 1960. As a response to what he considered to be a work of hagiography by Foot, John Campbell's *Nye Bevan and the Mirage of British Socialism* (1987) offers a more critical perspective of Bevan.[22] Campbell raised questions about Bevan's legacy, particularly his status as a Labour Party icon. Campbell was more critical than Foot of many aspects of Bevan's career. More recently, Nick Thomas-Symonds's *Nye: The Political Life of Aneurin Bevan*[23] attempted to provide a balanced view of Bevan's life and career and to:

> move beyond the two views adopted by Foot and Campbell ... [as the] analytical space between the two biographies is vast. Foot may at times lapse into hagiography, but, equally, the life of the creator of the NHS should not be castigated as a failure on the Campbell thesis. (p. 12)

Resultantly, these three books are key in aiding our understanding of Bevan and the ways in which he has been interpreted. While other biographical sources are vital, and discussed throughout this book, the aforementioned studies represent a spectrum of interpretations. This spectrum, particularly the divide between the Foot and Campbell biographies, is highly indicative of some of the debates that have emerged about Bevan both in the literature and in political discourse.

LABOUR'S POLITICAL THOUGHT

In addition to biographical studies, there exists a substantial literature analysing the ideology and intellectual development of the Labour Party.[24] As expected, these studies also delve into Aneurin Bevan's political thought. The most detailed overview of Labour's ideological development is Geoffrey Foote's *The Labour Party's Political Thought: A History*

(1986).[25] Foote argued that up until the publication of his book, no comprehensive overview of Labour's political thought had been produced. Certainly, it is difficult to find a book as comprehensive as Foote's, which analyses the many different factions and theoretical positions throughout Labour's history.

Serious critiques of the Labour Party's political thought began to emerge during the 1960s via the work of the New Left. These studies tended to reflect on the record of the post-war Labour government and the party's subsequent period of opposition after its defeat in 1951. The critiques focus on 'labourism', a formulation that emphasises the non-revolutionary character of the party and its inherently moderate, rather than radical, nature. These critiques are commonly associated with thinkers such as Ralph Miliband, Tom Nairn and Perry Anderson. Some of their most prominent works include Miliband's 1961 book *Parliamentary Socialism*,[26] Nairn's two-part analysis 'The Nature of the Labour Party' in 1964,[27] and Anderson's 'Origins of the Present Crisis' in the *New Left Review*, also published in 1964.[28] These writers have influenced a number of subsequent studies of Labour and critiques of labourism.[29] Assessments of the Labour Party have, unsurprisingly, existed since the party's inception, but the work of the New Left is marked by its opposition to 'both the acceptance of capitalism implied by Gaitskell and Crosland, and the effective refusal by the Labour Left to accept that a new analysis was necessary for the post-war situation'.[30] This literature identifies Bevan as a participant in this perceived failure of the Labour left.

Beyond wider studies of Labour's thought, there exists a body of literature that analyses the Labour Party through particular conceptual lenses. These largely concern the issue of equality but have also encompassed: quality of mind, time, freedom and various other themes engaged with by the party. This includes studies of Labour policies – for example, Martin Francis's *Ideas and Policies Under Labour 1945–1951* (1997)[31] and Rhiannon Vickers' two volume account of Labour's foreign policy throughout its history.[32] Jeremy Nuttall has been the most prolific in analysing Labour through different lenses. He has written studies on the synthesis of ideas in the party, Anthony Crosland's politics, 'quality of mind and character', equality and freedom, and even 'time' in the thought of the British left.[33] Nicholas Ellison studied egalitarianism in Labour political thought,[34] as did Ben Jackson who has also analysed the concept of equality and egalitarianism in the British left more widely.[35] A common theme of these studies is the competing interpretations of the ideas that form the foundation of Labour's political thought.

Considering the prominence of the debate between the Bevanites and the revisionists in the literature, it is notable that there have been few studies dedicated to the study of the Bevanites beyond Mark Jenkins's historical account of the Bevanite movement (1979). There are a number of studies of the revisionists in the Labour Party,[36] yet a comparable body of work of similar weight that undertakes a theoretical analysis of the key ideas of Bevan and the Bevanites has not been produced. There are a few instances where Bevan has had works dedicated to his political thought. For instance, Foote's book includes a chapter on the Bevanites that features an account of Bevan's ideas,[37] while Roger Spalding's *Narratives of Delusion in the Political Practice of the Labour Left: 1931–1945* (2018), a generally critical account of the Labour left, explored the 'narratives, presented as analyses, which justified and rationalised [the Bevanites'] positions and arguments'.[38] Studies of the Bevanites include David Howell's pamphlet *The Rise and Fall of Bevanism* (1982),[39] Anthony Arblaster's chapter 'The Old Left' in *The Struggle for Labour's Soul* (2004), a collection of essays on the history of the Labour Party,[40] and John Callaghan's article, 'The Left and the 'Unfinished Revolution': Bevanites and Soviet Russia in the 1950s' (2001).[41] Foote's work remains the most detailed in outlining Bevan's political thought, while the other works provide an assessment of the Labour Party's political thought in broader terms. Crucially for the purposes of this book, they, alongside the biographies, reveal themes and questions that need to be kept in mind when assessing Bevan's thought.

THEMES AND DEBATES

A review of the the above literature on Bevan soon reveals that there are debates and, indeed, deep disagreements over a number of core elements of Bevan's politics. For example, there is significant controversy over the extent of Bevan's debt to Marxism and the extent to which he was able to reconcile his socio-economic radicalism with his respect for the British parliamentary tradition. While for some Bevan was undone by his apparently dogmatic Marxism, for others he was a pragmatic and principled politician. On the latter reading, Bevan's continuing veneration of Marx was little more than a legacy of his past life as a militant in the south Wales coalfield – or even, most damningly, an affectation.

A prominent theme in the biographies is the apparent dichotomy between Bevan as a pragmatic politician, willing to compromise on certain principles, and Bevan as a dogmatic politician who refused to budge from his ideological beliefs. While authors such as Foot and Thomas-Symonds claimed that Bevan was principled but never dogmatic, Campbell, on the other hand, argued that Bevan's career was a failure because he stuck too rigidly to dogma and did not understand the changes of history. Campbell claimed that there was a difference between Bevan the theorist and Bevan the robust practical politician, arguing that Bevan's socialism was characterised by its vagueness, which contrasted with the 'robust practical political Bevan' when he was not theorising.[42] Bevan, Campbell concluded, did not read correctly the lessons of the twentieth century (p. 368). Nuttall argued that Bevan's experience of being a minister led him to develop 'a greater sense of the multi-layered nature and constraints of politics'.[43] In Nuttall's view, this explained Bevan's eventual embrace of 'political pragmatism'. In considering the relationship between Bevan's apparent Marxism and his faith in Parliament, both David Marquand (1999) and Spalding (2018) argued that Bevan was not a Marxist, but rather a product of radical British political traditions.[44] This contrasts with Foote, who described Bevan's politics as 'Labour Marxism' presented in a way that appealed to labourism.[45]

The ideological debate between the left and the right of the party is prominent in defining Labour's history, particularly during the 1950s. Foot wrote of how debates within the party post-1945 initially centred on the differences between Bevan and Herbert Morrison, deputy prime minister during the 1945–51 Labour government and deputy leader of the party until 1956.[46] After Bevan's resignation from cabinet in 1951, the debate then centred on the differences between the Bevanites and the revisionists, who were led by Hugh Gaitskell, chancellor from 1950–1 and then Labour leader from 1955. Campbell argued that these debates practically destroyed the party, which became 'riven in two, doomed to waste itself in fractious opposition for half a generation, until both the principal protagonists were dead'.[47] This split certainly frames the literature's consideration of Bevan's role within the Labour Party during the 1950s.

This debate is particularly prominent in ideological studies of the Labour Party, with a general consensus emerging that the revisionists obtained ideological ascendancy within the party. Callaghan asserted that Bevan and the Left argued primarily from a defensive position and failed to develop a sufficient programme of action,[48] while Foote concluded that the 'revisionists seemed to have the edge in theoretical terms as well as in terms of political power during the decade'.[49] Bevan's real failure according to Marquand was that 'he never managed to hammer out a coherent alternative [to Gaitskell's revisionism]; that his tentative and uncertain gropings for a different kind of revisionism never got further than the occasional mordant insight'.[50] Jackson contended that the Bevanites 'composed fewer theoretical works than the revisionists', reiterating the dominant argument that Bevan (and the Bevanites) were limited theoretically.[51] Radhika Desai declared that in the ensuing ideological debate the Bevanites offered a 'stunted' ideological challenge to the revisionists,[52] while Arblaster concluded that the Labour left merely countered with 'erratic' responses on both domestic and international issues.[53] Bealey characterised Bevanism as a movement with clear socialist principles but one that offered little in terms of concrete solutions, having 'much to say about the fundamentals of socialism but little about the details of nationalisation'.[54] Desai described the Bevanites as 'a poor excuse' for a 'vigorous (and theoretical) working-class movement'.[55] The argument that Bevan failed to attain ascendancy for his politics in the Labour Party is prominent throughout the literature.

Despite disagreement over the precise nature of Bevan's thought, common themes emerge from a review of the literature. It emphasises the importance of Bevan's early industrial and political experiences in shaping his political outlook, particularly his analysis of class and capitalism, acknowledging the above debate concerning his Marxism. It details the strategies that Bevan advocated in order to achieve power for the working class, predominantly through Parliament and democracy, as well as the need to use the state to take control of the commanding heights of the economy and to change society. The literature also identifies Bevan's concern with the international environment. However, it is also evident that some tensions exist in Bevan's thought, particularly between its Marxist and parliamentarian aspects and over his pragmatism and his position in the Labour Party's ideological debates.

LIMITATIONS

Useful as these various sources are for those wishing to understand Bevan's political thought, they are not without their difficulties or pitfalls. Within the biographies, details of the political controversies that Bevan was embroiled in throughout his career – of which there were many – often serve to obscure a more complete understanding of his thought. Given the significance and inherent interest of these controversies – including his often turbulent relationship with the party leadership, as well as dramatic moments such as his denouncement of unilateral disarmament in 1957 at Labour Party Conference (for some Bevanite followers, the ultimate betrayal) – this is hardly surprising.[56] But from the perspective of interest in Bevan's political thought, focusing on his actions as a practical politician can serve to dilute the attention given to the relationship between his thoughts and actions, let alone the deeper foundations of his political philosophy and world view.

For different reasons, although there is now a significant body of literature that analyses the political thought of the Labour Party, considerations of the political thought of Bevan himself are often limited. In some cases, this is because studies focus on the Bevanites, the group of MPs for whom Bevan was the figurehead, rather than on Bevan himself. This is understandable given the tendency to focus on intellectual *movements* or *factions* within the party. However, Bevan's own politics can sometimes get lost. Other works focus on particular dimensions or issues in Labour's political philosophy and/or the process of policy development. While often touching on Bevan's ideas, naturally enough these works do not seek to do so in any detailed, let alone comprehensive, way.

Further, when we consider the ideological analysis of Bevan, it appears that he (and by extension his followers) struggled to offer a persuasive alternative to his ideological opponents. This is despite the reverence with which contemporary politicians, activists and the public have for Bevan. Why then are Bevan's 'principles' and 'values' considered so important today, and so inextricable from Labour Party values?

This impasse, and the nature of the debates regarding Bevan today, can be explained when we consider that none of the current treatments of Bevan approach his political thought in a systematic way. Although Bevan has been considered to have played an important part in the Labour Party's history, this has not resulted in a detailed analysis of his political thought. When this has been attempted, it has not provided a thorough critique of all the works written throughout his life. This literature focuses largely on *In Place of Fear* when analysing Bevan's thought, overlooking his voluminous writings in *Tribune* and other publications.[57] This could be due to the dominant feeling in the literature that the Bevanites were theoretically limited. Nonetheless, in order to develop a complete understanding of Bevan's thought, an engagement with his voluminous output is required. This will provide greater accuracy in detailing the key features of Bevan's political thought and provide a greater level of certainty to judgements about his ideas. This book demonstrates the benefits of doing this; namely, being able to identify continuity throughout Bevan's career, account for moments where he deviated from his broader analysis and recognise the connection between the various different elements of his political thought.

Bevan's Political Thought

In order to respond to the above challenges, this book offers a comprehensive analytical study of Bevan's political thought, taking the position that Bevan deserves to be treated as a political thinker, as well as a politician and institutional pioneer. Studying Bevan in this way provides for a better understanding of his ideas and also serves to shed light on the important debates about Bevan and the intellectual history of the Labour Party – debates that continue to this day. More formally, the book has two central aims: first, to investigate Aneurin Bevan through the prism of his political thought, reconstructing his political philosophy from his written works; and second, to use this reconstruction of Bevan's political thought to comment on the debates and disputes in the extant literature both on Bevan himself and on Bevan's place in the development of the political thought of the Labour Party.

BEVAN AS A POLITICAL THINKER

The first aim represents a new approach to studying Aneurin Bevan. While there are a number of works that cover his life and politics, it is my contention that studying Bevan as a political thinker offers a unique and valuable contribution to our understanding of him. The study of ideas has become increasingly important in the exploration of British politics. Dean Blackburn, for instance, has noted the need for historians to consider ideology as a 'ubiquitous feature of political life'.[58] Debates within the Labour Party cannot be reduced to personality alone, but can be studied to identify fundamental disagreements about concepts and ideas for change, focusing on the 'ideas, beliefs, practices and traditions' of politics.[59] While the biographies offer valuable insight into Bevan, studying him in a different way provides us with a new perspective on his disparate written work and his other publications. Michael Freeden, writing in 1990, argued that the role of ideas in the study of twentieth-century British politics had been overlooked, with less importance attached to it compared with other methodologies.[60] This is an oversight. The study of ideas and ideologies can prove valuable when trying to discern the nature of political life. As Freeden stated, the contest over the correct meaning of political language puts ideologies at the heart of the political process.[61] The way political actors think, the ideas behind policies and systems of thought are all fundamental to understanding politics.[62]

An argument is often presented that ideas and ideologies are somewhat harmful to politics, or even irrelevant. Certainly within the Labour Party itself, ideas have been seen as potentially harmful to the party's chances of obtaining power.[63] Ideas and ideologies are often seen as being insignificant, with a distinction made between 'practical' and 'ideological' modes of thought.[64] This problematic dismissal of ideology, Blackburn wrote, 'as an optional feature of politics' by historians fails to 'acknowledge that even the most non-doctrinaire statements were imbued with ideological assumptions and values' (p. 117). There is great value, therefore, in studying ideas. We can identify the ideological nature of different aspects of politics, while also being able to 'untangle the complex ideological contestation that informs the most ordinary political practices' (p. 120). Ultimately, '"pragmatic" politicians would become recognized as the producers of important ideas about appropriate political conduct' (p. 126).

While this development is welcome and necessary, there remains scope for the study of individual politicians and their political thought. Kari Palonen referenced Quentin Skinner's statement that 'political life itself sets the main problems for the political theorist',[65] a statement on the importance of theorists engaging with political debates. Palonen built on this to argue that the politician is vital in understanding the transmission of political ideas. Therefore, not only should we 'read theorists as politicians, but we should also consider the reverse side of the coin and read politicians as theorists' (p. 359). One of the difficulties faced when analysing a politician such as Bevan is that MPs are involved in the day-to-day activities of parliamentary life. Bevan was not writing political treatises and works of political theory, with his journalistic writing taking in a variety of topics. However, as Palonen made clear, political theorising should not focus only on 'that which is considered universal, timeless, invariant or law-like'. Instead, we must also focus on the contingent, the discussions that are 'singular, temporal, momentary, local and historical'. In this case, theorising among politicians is 'related to a political *reading of situations* that they encounter when acting politically':

> In other words, the politician is a person who has a keen sense with regard to the demands of the present situation, an ability to read the signs of the times, and who is, in keeping with this idea, even prepared to abandon long-term projects if they cannot be adapted to the singular requirements of the current situation. (p. 360)

This is not to suggest that when studying Bevan we should focus only on the contingent. As will be demonstrated throughout the course of this book, Bevan's discussions of the contingent were often underpinned by more fundamental ideas about society. Palonen emphasised that a politician is 'a person who always has to relate her judgement to that of her adversaries and competitors' due to the conflictual nature of political life (p. 360). Arguing for these values is therefore an essential part of politics. Palonen asserted the importance of political thinking in the life of a politician:

> My point is that one of the requirements of the politician may be to specify *how* political life can set the problems that are contemplated by political theorists, as well as *how* they can come to understand that politicians may, especially in crisis situations, be obliged to act as 'theorists' themselves in order to explain their

> position and, if possible, to create new *Spielräume* for their own actions. (p. 362)

Blackburn argued that many recent studies of Britain's political ideologies 'tend to privilege the thought and practices of those individuals who have been engaged in particular kinds of thinking'. Thinkers who produce 'elaborate and coherent statements of political thought are often conceived as the most influential producers of ideas'.[66] Yet, as Palonen demonstrated, the political actor, even if they do not produce coherent statements of political thought, is still important in the articulation of ideas and their operation in practice. Bevan is often dismissed as a thinker, namely because he did not produce a coherent body of work. However, by ruling out the role of ideas when studying Bevan, there is a risk that ideological contests within the Labour Party are ignored. In this book I want to re-evaluate claims to Bevan's intellectual legacy by studying Bevan as a political thinker. Even if the personal is understated as a result, studying Bevan's ideas illuminates key elements of both his and Labour's political thought.

Bevan wrote extensively throughout his career on domestic and international politics, ranging widely from considerations of the immediate political context to more reflective pieces on the nature of class and capitalist society. When it comes to reconstructing and outlining his political thought, Bevan's voluminous writings tend not to be extensively studied. To rectify this, *The Political Thought of Aneurin Bevan* attempts to pull together and draw on Bevan's disparate writings, not only to provide more detail than has been offered until now in the existing literature, but also to highlight areas of Bevan's political thought that tend to be neglected or overlooked. Studying Bevan as a political thinker can facilitate this process. A discussion of sources is included below.

BEVAN AND LABOUR'S POLITICAL THOUGHT

When it comes to the second aim of commenting on the debates and disputes regarding Bevan and his place in Labour's ideological traditions, the above reconstruction will prove extremely useful. As illustrated above, the disputes and divisions are deep and profound. But having reconstructed his thought, we will be able to consider what light the unique approach adopted in this book – that is, treating Bevan primarily as a political thinker – allows us to shine on its subject. As a result, not only will we be able to understand the nature of Bevan's thought more clearly, but we will also be able to understand the nature of the Labour Party and the debates within it. Throughout the book, Bevan's core ideas will be assessed in relation to the ideas of the Labour Party. Accordingly, we will be able to make broader assessments of their strengths and limitations.

To fully contribute to the debates regarding political thought within the Labour Party, a word is needed on the party's ideology and its intellectual development. Taking the time to explore this will allow for Bevan's ideas to be compared and contrasted with his contemporaries throughout the analysis. By the conclusion of this book, we will be in a better position to assess the claims that Bevan failed to offer a persuasive alternative to his political opponents.

When trying to describe the party's political thought in broad terms, scholars often deploy the term 'labourism' as a way to distinguish Labour socialism from other varieties. Foote presented the following as the characteristics of labourism: 'the theory that labour receives little of the wealth that it creates, redistributionism, hostility to capitalists and maintenance of capital, workers' self-reliance, and loyalty to the nation state.' He contended that these characteristics 'survived to become a set of assumptions in the labour movement ... flexible enough to accommodate many different political ideas – while distinct enough eventually to exclude the Liberal Party on the Right and various types of revolutionary on the Left'.[67] Leach echoed this analysis, arguing that the most important factor in the development of socialism in Britain has been the dialectic between evolutionary and revolutionary socialism, which eventually led to accommodation between different groups.[68] He defined labourism as:

> an ideology which articulates the felt interests of labour, or the working class, involving the protection of free collective bargaining, improvements in living standards and welfare benefits, such as cheap public housing and free health care, but accommodation with, rather than a fundamental challenge to, the dominant economic, social and political order. (p. 80)

This set of assumptions concerning the Labour Party has meant that a variety of different positions and theories of socialism have been encompassed within its political thought. These different positions have often competed for dominance within the party.

The arguments of New Left critics focus on the *limits* of labourism, the development of the labour movement in Britain and its relationship with the Labour Party. This critique is developed through a Marxist lens, focusing on 'the limitations placed upon the party by its particular history, ideology and structure' and its commitment to parliamentarianism.[69] Miliband defined labourism as:

> an ideology of social reform, within the framework of capitalism, with no serious ambition of transcending that framework whatever ritual obeisances to 'socialism' might be performed by party leaders on suitable occasions, such as Labour Party or trade-union conferences, to appease or defeat their activist critics. Labourism, in other words, is not, like Marxism, an ideology of rupture but an ideology of adaptation.[70]

Miliband also criticised the Labour Party for its heavy focus on parliamentarianism, arguing that:

> Of political parties claiming socialism to be their aim, the Labour Party has always been one of the most dogmatic – not about socialism, but about the parliamentary system ... [T]he leaders of the Labour Party have always rejected any kind of political action (such as industrial action for political purposes) which fell, or which appeared to them to fall, outside the framework and conventions of the parliamentary system. The Labour Party has not only been a parliamentary party; it has been a party deeply imbued by parliamentarianism.[71]

Nairn identified 'two basic conditions of Labourism as a system'. They are, first, 'the very defective ideological matrix behind British socialism, and secondly – and intimately related – the weakness of the entire left-wing political tradition incorporated into Labourism'. He described labourism as 'in part an organized contradiction between the two really vital sectors of the working-class movement, a system according to which they mutually inhibit one another instead of engaging in a genuine dialectic of growth towards socialism' (the two vital sectors appearing to be the unions and the party).[72] Labourism is therefore characterised as an ideology that fundamentally prevented the development of any sort of revolutionary character within the Labour Party. As Madeleine Davis summarises, the conclusion of these critiques is that the Labour Party has been defined and limited by four characteristics: the pre-eminence of the trade unions; the inherent weakness in indigenous British socialism and the Labour Left; the acceptance of parliamentarianism; and the failure of intellectuals to forge a counter-revolutionary hegemony.[73]

Critiques of labourism have also emerged from a diametrically opposed position to the New Left. David Marquand, as a social-democrat thinker, argued that the ideology of labourism has prevented the party from achieving a progressive alliance and securing the support of a larger proportion of society beyond the working class. Marquand maintained that the Labour Party has been too attached to the trade unions for it to appeal beyond the labour movement.[74] He argued that the party's commitment to a single class, the working class – the 'extraordinary, sometimes almost pathetic, loyalty' to its core constituency – inherent in the ideology of labourism, meant that the party was always a defensive party, and in government its instincts were 'cautious, even conservative, to a fault'.[75] Marquand's work is considered to be an exemplar of the 'social democratic' interpretation of the Labour Party.[76] His critique of labourism, therefore, does not reflect the same concerns as those of the New Left.

As we have seen, the ascendancy of the revisionists over the Bevanites within the party has led authors to conclude that Bevan and his allies failed to offer an intellectual strategy to win the party's ideological debates. The New Left's criticisms of Bevan relate to the argument that left-wing socialists were a failure within the party. Miliband argued that the Bevanites were unable 'to offer an alternative analysis of the narrow Fabian view' of public ownership, writing that 'many of the ambiguities of parliamentary Bevanism were but a reflection of its ideological ambiguities'.[77] The left of the party, Miliband argued, was unable 'to present either a clear diagnosis of the Party's troubles or a solidly-based argument for such policies as it wanted to see adopted' (p. 331). Bevan and his followers were unable to present themselves as a strong opposition to the party leadership and were also limited by following the principles of labourism. Nairn argued that the:

> only alternatives it [the left of the party] has ever had have been either to leave the Party, to resign, to threaten a split – or to submit, collaborate, make the best of a bad job within the rigid structures of Labourism, and tell itself that it may make things a little less bad than they would otherwise be and that in any case there is no 'practical' alternative.[78]

He concluded that this 'chronic and impossible choice' – to submit or to collaborate – was 'illustrated to perfection in the career of Aneurin Bevan'. He stated that this choice was imposed by 'the Left's lack of any real alternative, of a permanent point of view superior to the shabby middle-class limbo of Fabianism and containing in itself the source of a socialist hegemony over the movement, and ultimately over society' (p. 49).

Marquand described how Bevan was 'kicking against the pricks of Labourism', yet was never able to transcend it,[79] mourning what could have been if Bevan had lived up to what Marquand regarded as his undoubted potential and transcended labourism. He lamented the fact that Bevan's time in office was short relative to his time in opposition and that his practical abilities were not utilised to a great enough extent, the causes that he championed ultimately ending in defeat. For Marquand, Bevan's achievement in establishing the NHS demonstrated his potential.

When considering Bevan's political thought, it is imperative that he is not removed from this context. Throughout the chapters that follow, an attempt will be made to locate Bevan within Labour's intellectual traditions, helpfully summarised by considering the ideology of labourism (through both its explanatory and critical definitions). The analysis will consider many of the themes discussed here – the role of Parliament, revolution versus evolution, the role of the economy, disagreements over foreign policy, and disputes between Bevan and the revisionists. This way, the second aim of the book can be met. Debates regarding Bevan's legacy and his contribution to the development of Labour's political thought can more adequately be responded to, thus enhancing our understanding of both Bevan and the Labour Party's often fractious ideological conflict.

Structure and Approach

SOURCES

At this point, it is appropriate to make a few comments about sources. As has already been noted, *In Place of Fear* is the only book written by Bevan that can be conceivably considered as a concerted effort at systematising his ideas. As a result, it is the work most widely engaged with, particularly in studies of Labour Party political thought. This study goes beyond *In Place of Fear* to include Bevan's other writing. Most obviously, Bevan wrote more than 300 articles in his own name for *Tribune* between 1937 and 1960, as well as publishing additional articles under the pseudonym 'M.P.' during the early months of the magazine's existence. Moreover, during his time as the magazine's editor between 1942 and 1945, weekly editorials were produced, although it is not clear that all of them were written by Bevan, as some of them do not appear to be written in the same style (these are referenced as *Tribune*).[80]

His writings are, of course, not the only source we might use to try to reconstruct Bevan's thought. He also spoke frequently in the Commons as well as on innumerable public platforms, and records of these speeches provide a vivid insight into his ideas and his oratorical powers as well as his ability to dissect and eviscerate the arguments of his opponents. But given the sheer volume of Bevan's written output – as well as its unsystematic nature – the decision was taken to concentrate primarily on written sources (including, naturally, *In Place of Fear*) rather than try to collect and analyse all other potential sources of Bevan's political ideas. Although other sources will be drawn on throughout this book, this limitation was one necessitated by the challenges of the present task. I am confident that it does not detract from the validity of the analysis presented in the following chapters, and every effort has been made to ensure that I am presenting Bevan's work as fairly and systematically as possible.

A final note is required on how the sources will be analysed. Due to the unsystematic nature of Bevan's writing, treating him as a political thinker involves trawling through a very large body of writing, identifying and presenting the key ideas across it and making connections between them. In doing this, I have sought to adopt an approach characterised by philosopher John Rawls as 'interpretive charity'. The editor's foreword to Rawls' *Lectures on the History of Political Philosophy* (2007) includes an excerpt from an essay titled 'Some Remarks About My Teaching', written by Rawls in 1993 and left among his papers. In it, Rawls describes his approach to understanding and interpreting the work of others in the following terms:

> Another thing I tried to do was to present each writer's thought in what I took to be its strongest form ... I didn't say, not intentionally anyway, what to my mind they should have said, but what they did say, supported by what I viewed as the most reasonable interpretation of their text. The text had to be known and respected, and the doctrine presented in its best form.[81]

As Michael Freeden has noted, texts can be read in many different ways and can take on a life of their own away from the author.[82] By applying interpretive charity to my reading of Bevan, I have sought to present his ideas in their strongest form. I have endeavoured to make the most reasonable possible interpretations where there is ambiguity or uncertainty. This does not preclude criticism or pointing out weaknesses or contradictions where they exist. It does mean – perhaps hopefully – that such criticism is based on a fair assessment of what Bevan thought and might have been trying to say.

STRUCTURE: POWER AS A HEURISTIC DEVICE

Given the sheer range of written sources and their unsystematic nature, reconstructing Bevan's political thought presents challenges. The task is made all the more difficult by the very broad range of issues to which Bevan turned his attention. To facilitate the task of reconstruction, some method of organisation is clearly required. This book has therefore been organised around the concept of 'power'.

Power has been chosen as a lens through which to analyse Bevan's thought because of the importance he placed on achieving power for the working class. On the opening page of *In Place of Fear*, Bevan famously proclaimed:

> I started my political life with no clearly formed personal ambition as to what I wanted to be, or where I wanted to go. I leave that nonsense to the writers of romantic biographies. A young miner in a South Wales colliery, my concern was with the one practical

> question, where does power lie in this particular state of Great Britain, and how can it be attained by the workers? No doubt this is the same question as the one to which the savants of political theory are fond of addressing themselves, but there is a world of difference in the way it shaped itself for young workers like myself. It was no abstract question for us. The circumstances of our lives made it a burning luminous mark of interrogation. Where was power and which the road to it?[83]

Since then, Bevan's lifework has been portrayed as a search for power to allow the working class in Britain to improve its position. Foot, for example, stated that a moral 'deeply embedded' in Bevan's thinking was that '*politics was about power*' (Foot's emphasis),[84] while Thomas-Symonds painted Bevan's life as a continuous search for power, declaring that Bevan 'sought power with a purpose'.[85] We have already noted the way that Owen Smith also stressed the importance of power for Bevan's self-proclaimed followers. The significance that Bevan placed on power makes it extremely useful as a lens through which to analyse his political thought.

Power, of course, is an extremely broad concept. In political science, power is regarded as an 'essentially contested concept',[86] or 'what the philosopher Wittgenstein termed a "family resemblance" concept. This entails that when we use the concept in different contexts its meaning changes sufficiently so that there is no single definition of power which covers all usage'.[87] It should be stressed, therefore, that this study does not attempt to engage with the myriad understandings of power that exist, let alone contribute to that literature. Rather, it simply adopts (and slightly adapts) Michael Mann's now famous four sources of social power as a heuristic framework for its analysis.

Mann's model has been chosen because of the (broad) relevance of his categorisation to Bevan's political thought as well as its flexibility. Starting from Marxist-inspired beginnings,[88] Mann arrived at a broad (in his terms, non-reductionist) conceptualisation of power: the IEMP model of power, which encompasses ideological, economic, military and political forms of power. He regarded these four sources of power as being separate from each other but overlapping in different ways and in different societies. Using this framework, Mann wrote a hugely ambitious four-volume work that aimed to provide an historical analysis of power from Neolithic times through to the present. This is premised on his central claim that a:

> general account of societies, their structure, and their history can best be given in terms of the interrelations of what I will call the four sources of social power: ideological, economic, military and political (IEMP) relationships. These are (1) overlapping networks of social interaction, not dimensions, levels, or factors of a single social totality ... [and] (2) They are also organizations, institutional means of attaining human goals.[89]

Unsurprisingly, given his self-professed debt to Marxism, economic power was of central importance to Bevan, a politician who sought to develop strategies that would allow the working class to transform its position within society using political power, and in so doing transform society itself. Military power was also a key preoccupation of Bevan's as part of his wider, keen interest in international relations. Mann described ideological power as 'deriv[ing] from the human need to find ultimate meaning in life, to share norms and values, and to participate in aesthetic and ritual practices with others',[90] all themes with which Bevan was concerned. The Mannian framework is therefore broad enough for the breadth of Bevan's political thought to be captured.

It should perhaps be stressed again that Mann's framework is used here as no more and no less than an organising device. This study is not a Mannian reading of Bevan, nor, indeed, does it seek to establish a rival 'Bevanite' conceptualisation of power. Mann's framework is a heuristic device that has been used to organise Bevan's unsystematic and voluminous output. In structuring this book, Mann's original IEMP framework has been reorganised as an EPMI model, allowing us to better illustrate the determining role of the economic sphere in Bevan's thought. As such, the reconstruction of Bevan's ideas moves from the economic to the political and then to the military/international, before ending with a discussion of Bevan's political thought through the lens of ideological power.

Although this framework allows us to explore all the major themes in Bevan's work, it is important to recognise that not every issue with which Bevan dealt – or which might otherwise be thought to be relevant – can be neatly encompassed within it. For example, Bevan's attitudes towards

Wales are clearly of contemporary interest.[91] However, while they will be discussed, it would be hard to argue that they played a centrally important role in his political thought and they are therefore not given as much room as other key issues discussed in the following pages. In addition, following in this regard from Mann, it is clear that not every issue with which Bevan dealt can be confined under one heading or 'type' of power. For example, Bevan's analysis of economic power directly impacts on his consideration of other issues. Nonetheless, the Mannian framework adopted assists in the task of reconstructing the main themes in Bevan's political thought.

To summarise the approach of this book, three core interpretative decisions have been arrived at: first, to focus on Aneurin Bevan primarily as a political thinker rather than a politician or institution builder; second, in doing so, adopting power as a lens/framework through which to view and understand Bevan's political thought; and finally, in particular, adopting Mann's typology of power as a heuristic device that is particularly suitable for analysing Bevan's political thought. Overall, this is an approach that allows for a unique engagement with Bevan and his politics.

CHAPTER OVERVIEW

Following this introduction, the book is organised into five chapters. Chapters 1 to 4 attempt a comprehensive analysis and reconstruction of Bevan's thought within the EPMI framework. Chapter 1 analyses Bevan's writing on economics, exploring his analysis of capitalism, class conflict and the economic development of societies. It then proceeds to assess the strategies that Bevan contemplated to achieve economic power for the working class, including industrial action. This chapter identifies the influence of a Marxist understanding of the economy in Bevan's political thought, one that emphasised the material economic base and property relations in society. It also notes that Bevan's strategy to change these property relations was premised on the development and strength (as he saw it) of democracy in Britain. Although related to political power, Bevan's support for democracy is included in this section as it acts as a bridge between understanding his conception of class conflict and his strategy for obtaining power for the working class.

This discussion of Bevan's belief in British democracy as the strategy for working-class action leads directly into Chapter 2, which focuses on political power, including Bevan's analysis of Parliament and his vision for nationalisation and public ownership. This chapter details how Bevan envisioned the Labour Party taking control of Parliament and consequently the functions of the British state in order to manage key industries and to enact principles of economic planning. Although his reverence for liberal institutions represented a significant departure from Marxist political strategy, Bevan's analysis of the economy nonetheless remained central to his understanding of political power and the role of the state in changing property relations.

Chapter 3 analyses Bevan's attitude to international relations. Here we move beyond Mann's conceptualisation, focusing on Bevan's ideas about, and hopes for, international society rather than simply his views on military power – even if the latter also remains of central importance. Thus, the chapter ranges broadly, examining Bevan's analysis of the relationship between capitalism and war, his rejection of military power in international relations and power politics, his critique of the rise of nationalism throughout the world and his desire to see strong democratic international organisations. Through its analysis of Bevan's writings on developing nations and communist societies such as the Soviet Union, China and Yugoslavia, this chapter emphasises the centrality of Bevan's understanding of the relationship between the economic base and political superstructure.

Chapter 4, the last of the four chapters organised around conceptualisations of power, discusses the role that ideology plays in Bevan's analysis, his critiques of capitalism and communism and his vision for a democratic socialist society. It outlines the ideological battle that Bevan identified as taking place between the working class and the ruling class, his vision of how values of collective action could permeate society, his desire to see positive relations between individuals and the need for a greater understanding between society and the state. This chapter explores themes that are often overlooked in the literature, and again demonstrates the central importance of Bevan's analysis of the economy to his understanding of how ideas shape material conditions and *vice versa*.

In presenting Bevan's political thought these four chapters involve a substantive analysis of his work and reconstruction of his key ideas. Further, throughout these chapters, the political thought of the Labour Party will also be considered. This will allow for Bevan to be located within Labour's intellectual traditions and for the ideological debates within the party to be analysed. Chapter 5 then concludes by engaging in a critical and reflective analysis of Bevan's political thought. It engages with the key debates that emerge from the discussion of the literature and assesses the contribution of this ideational study, reflecting on the extent to which it contributes to the current knowledge of Bevan. It also offers its reflections on the coherence (or lack thereof) of Bevan's political thought, its relationship to Labour's intellectual traditions, and what this study has done to contribute to the literature on Labour thought.

The fundamental argument that emerges from this analysis is that Bevan's political thought is characterised by an understanding of economic development that emphasises the relationship between the material base of society and its political and ideological superstructure. As the four-chapter reconstruction of Bevan's thought shows, this understanding of base and superstructure permeates Bevan's writings on both domestic and international politics, and of both war and peace. The book emphasises the role that Bevan envisioned for the state in changing property relations, but ultimately demonstrates that these ideas were never properly developed, despite the fact that, pre-1945 at least, Bevan offered the outlines of more creative ideas around nationalisation and, relatedly, more critical analyses of the role of the state. Rather, Bevan's political thought appears to have become trapped between a rather orthodox (pre-New Left) understanding of economic development and a benign view of Parliament and related state-power that were limitations of his political outlook. While the analysis reveals instances of departure from this outlook, Bevan's thought, it is argued, failed to develop in ways that recognised the difficulties of using British Parliament as a means through which to transfer power to the masses. It is also argued that many of the core assumptions of Bevan's thought, rooted in the political traditions in which he was situated, fitted comfortably within the mainstream of Labour Party ideology, specifically the ideology of labourism. Yet, it also contained various elements that did not fit comfortably within this ideology and thus marked Bevan out as a unique political thinker within the party and on the British left.

Conclusion

Aneurin Bevan is a historical figure who has been subject to much debate, with no sign that discussion or interest are about to diminish. Regarded as one of the most controversial political figures of his day, he is also almost universally considered to be one of the most successful ministers that the Labour Party has ever produced. Disagreement over Bevan's legacy – and attempts to be regarded as its true inheritors – mean that he is likely to remain the subject of intense debate and disagreement for years to come.

Yet, just as ideology, as Freeden noted, cannot be reduced to *-isms* and 'to a simple list of characteristics',[92] neither can Bevan's politics. Bevan is not either/or – either a pragmatist or a radical. He is neither; he is Bevan. He described himself as a democratic socialist but also identified as a Marxist. He wanted to radically alter society yet believed in the parliamentary route to socialism. Reducing Bevan to personality and clashes between key individuals overlooks the complexities of his thought, its influences, its language and the (sometimes messy) interactions between ideas within it.

The study of Bevan as a political thinker is not an attempt to argue that this approach is necessarily better or more appropriate to studying such a figure. Instead, the study of ideas aims to provide unique insights into Bevan and Labour history. 'Methodological flexibility or pluralism', as Freeden asserted, 'is a *sine qua non* for illuminating the impact of ideologies and ought not to be confused with eclecticism'. Studying political beliefs 'will lead us to respect the important part played by values, purposes, prejudices, and misconceptions in the formation of both intended and unintended policies'.[93] In the case of Bevan, studying his ideas will lead us to respect and acknowledge the important part these beliefs played in shaping his political career, his relationship to the Labour Party, its traditions and its members, and his legacy.

The Political Thought of Aneurin Bevan is a study of Bevan as a political thinker. It seeks to reconstruct his political thought in order to offer an alternative perspective on this complex figure and provide new insight into his intellectual development and the ideas that drove his politics. In this way, the study seeks to make a significant contribution to the existing literature, enhancing our understanding of a key figure in British politics.

NOTES

1 'Watch: Jeremy Hunt compares himself to Nye Bevan', *The Spectator* (2016), *www.spectator.co.uk/article/watch-jeremy-hunt-compares-himself-to-nye-bevan/* (accessed 16 January 2023).

2 HC Deb, 25 April 2016, vol. 608, col. 1168.

3 HC Deb, 24 February 2016, vol. 606 col. 292.

4 Jeremy Hunt, 'Jeremy Hunt speech: Party of the NHS' (2015), *https://press.conservatives.com/post/130944862065/jeremy-hunt-speech-party-of-the-nhs* (accessed 5 January 2024).

5 Rhodri Morgan, 'Clear Red Water', *Socialist Health Association* (11 December 2002), *www.sochealth.co.uk/the-socialist-health-association/sha-country-and-branch-organisation/sha-wales/clear-red-water/* (accessed 5 January 2024).

6 'Bevan plaque for NHS anniversary', *BBC News* (5 July 2008), *http://news.bbc.co.uk/1/hi/wales/7490391.stm* (accessed 5 January 2024).

7 Kate Ferguson, 'Neil Kinnock praises his "political hero" Nye Bevan as he unveils plaque in his honour', *WalesOnline* (2015), *www.walesonline.co.uk/news/wales-news/neil-kinnock-praises-political-hero-10378669* (accessed 5 January 2024).

8 Gordon Brown, 'Power for a Purpose – Gordon Brown Speech: Sunday 16 August' (2015), *https://gordonandsarahbrown.com/2015/08/power-for-a-purpose-gordon-brown-speech-sunday-16-august/* (accessed 5 January 2024).

9 Ed Balls, 'Labour's greatest hero: Nye Bevan', *Guardian* (19 September 2008), *www.theguardian.com/commentisfree/2008/sep/19/labour.labourconference2* (accessed 5 January 2024).

10 Kenneth O. Morgan, 'Nye Bevan', in Wm. Roger Louis (ed.), *Resurgent Adventures with Britannia: Personalities, Politics and Culture in Britain* (London: I. B. Tauris, 2011), p. 180.

11 Rowena Mason, 'Owen Smith: who is the man challenging Corbyn as Labour leader?', *Guardian* (2016), *www.theguardian.com/politics/2016/jul/22/owen-smith-who-is-the-man-challenging-jeremy-corbyn-labour-leadership* (accessed 5 January 2024).

12 Paul Waugh, 'Owen Smith interview: on the "Likelihood" of a Labour split, politics of "The Street", and a "Real Living Wage"', *Huffington Post* (3 August 2016), *www.huffingtonpost.co.uk/entry/owen-smith-interview-on-the-likelihood-of-a-labour-split-politics-of-the-street-and-a-real-living_uk_57a1e26ce4b0f42daa4ba666* (accessed 5 January 2024).

13 Mason, 'Owen Smith: who is the man challenging Corbyn as Labour leader?'.

14 Matt Myers, 'More Blair than Bevan', *Jacobin* (19 September 2016), *www.jacobinmag.com/2016/09/aneurin-bevin-nhs-owen-smith-corbyn* (accessed 5 January 2024).

15 Morgan, 'Nye Bevan', p. 182.

16 Barbara Castle, 'A Passionate Defiance', in Geoffrey Goodman (ed.), *The State of the Nation: The Political Legacy of Aneurin Bevan* (London: Victor Gollancz, 1997), p. 66.

17 Simon Hannah, *A Party with Socialists in it: A History of the Labour Left* (London: Pluto Press, 2018), chapter 4.

18 Jeremy Corbyn, 'We must include everybody and exclude nobody. They were Nye Bevan's values, they are Labour's values. #NHS70', *Twitter* (3 July 2018).

19 Vincent Brome, *Aneurin Bevan: A Biography* (London: Longmans, Green and Co., 1953); Mark Krug, *Aneurin Bevan: Cautious Rebel* (New York: Thomas Yoseloff, 1961); Jennie Lee, *My Life with Nye* (Middlesex: Palgrave, 1981); Geoffrey Goodman (ed.), *The State of the Nation: The Political Legacy of Aneurin Bevan* (London: Victor Gollancz, 1997); Clare Beckett and Francis Beckett, *Bevan* (London: Haus Publishing, 2004).

20 Susan E. Demont, 'Tredegar and Aneurin Bevan: A Society and its Political Articulation 1890–1929' (PhD, University of Wales, College of Cardiff, 1990); Dai Smith, *Aneurin Bevan and the World of South Wales* (Cardiff: University of Wales Press, 1993).

21 Michael Foot, *Aneurin Bevan: 1897–1945*, vol. 1 (London: Granada Publishing, 1975); Michael Foot, *Aneurin Bevan: 1945–1960*, vol. 2 (London: Granada Publishing, 1975).

22 John Campbell, *Nye Bevan and the Mirage of British Socialism* (London: Weidenfeld & Nicolson, 1987).

23 Nicklaus Thomas-Symonds, *Nye: The Political Life of Aneurin Bevan* (London: I. B. Tauris, 2015).

24 Frank Bealey, *The Social and Political Thought of the British Labour Party* (London: Weidenfeld & Nicolson, 1970); Henry M. Drucker, *Doctrine and Ethos in the Labour Party* (London: Allen and Unwin, 1979); John Callaghan, 'The Left: The Ideology of the Labour Party', in Leonard Tivey and Anthony Wright (eds), *Party Ideology in Britain* (London: Routledge, 1989); Robert Leach, *Political Ideology in Britain*, 3rd edn (London: Palgrave, 2015).

25 Geoffrey Foote, *The Labour Party's Political Thought: A History* (London: Croom Helm, 1986).

26 Ralph Miliband, *Parliamentary Socialism* (Pontypool: Merlin Press, 2009).

27 Tom Nairn, 'The Nature of the Labour Party – 1', *New Left Review*, 1/27 (1964), *https://newleftreview.org/I/27/tom-nairn-the-nature-of-the-labour-party-part-i* (5 January 2024); Tom Nairn, 'The Nature of the Labour Party – 2',

New Left Review, 1/28 (1964), *https://newleftreview.org/I/28/tom-nairn-the-nature-of-the-labour-party-part-ii* (5 January 2024).

28 Perry Anderson, 'Origins of the Present Crisis', *New Left Review*, 1/23 (1964).

29 David Coates, *The Labour Party and the Struggle for Socialism* (Cambridge: Cambridge University Press, 1975); John Saville, 'The Ideology of Labourism', in Robert Benewick, R. N. Berki and Bhikhu Parekh (eds), *Knowledge and Belief in Politics: The Problem of Ideology* (London: George Allen & Unwin Ltd, 1975); Willie Thompson, *The Long Death of British Labourism: Interpreting a Political Culture* (London: Pluto Press, 1993); Gregory Elliot, *Labourism and the English Genius: The Strange Death of Labour England?* (London: Verso, 1993); David Coates and Leo Panitch, 'The Continuing Relevance of the Milibandian Perspective', in John Callaghan, Steven Fielding and Steve Ludlam (eds), *Interpreting the Labour Party: Approaches to Labour Politics and History* (Manchester: Manchester University Press, 2003).

30 Madeleine Davis, '"Labourism" and the New Left', in John Callaghan, Steven Fielding and Steve Ludlam (eds), *Interpreting the Labour Party: Approaches to Labour Politics and History* (Manchester: Manchester University Press, 2003), p. 41.

31 Martin Francis, *Ideas and Policies under Labour 1945–1951* (London: MacMillan, 1997).

32 Rhiannon Vickers, *The Labour Party and the World, Volume 1: The Evolution of Labour's Foreign Policy 1900–51* (Manchester: Manchester University Press, 2003); Rhiannon Vickers, *The Labour Party and the World, Volume 2: Labour's Foreign Policy Since 1951* (Manchester: Manchester University Press, 2011).

33 Jeremy Nuttall, '"Psychological Socialist"; "Militant Moderate": Evan Durbin and the Politics of Synthesis', *Labour History Review*, 68/2 (2003); Jeremy Nuttall, 'The Labour Party and the Improvement of Minds: The Case of Tony Crosland', *Historical Journal*, 46/1 (2003); Jeremy Nuttall, 'Tony Crosland and the Many Falls and Rises of British Social Democracy', *Contemporary British History*, 18/4 (2004); Jeremy Nuttall, 'Labour Revisionism and Qualities of Mind and Character, 1931–79', *English Historical Review*, 120/487 (2005); Jeremy Nuttall, *Psychological Socialism: The Labour Party and Qualities of Mind and Character* (Manchester: Manchester University Press, 2006); Jeremy Nuttall, 'Equality and Freedom: The Single, the Multiple and the Synthesis in Labour Party Thought Since the 1930s', *Journal of Political Ideologies*, 13/11

(2008); Jeremy Nuttall, 'Pluralism, the People, and Time in Labour Party History, 1931–1964', *Historical Journal*, 56/3 (2013).

34 Nicholas Ellison, *Egalitarian Thought and Labour Politics: Retreating Visions* (London: Routledge, 1994).

35 Ben Jackson, *Equality and the British Left: A Study in Progressive Political Thought, 1900–64* (Manchester: Manchester University Press, 2007); Ben Jackson, 'Revisionism Reconsidered: "Property-Owning Democracy" and Egalitarian Strategy in Post-war Britain', *Twentieth Century British History*, 16 (2005).

36 Stephen Haseler, *The Gaitskellites: Revisionism in the British Labour Party 1951–64* (London: MacMillan, 1969); Radhika Desai, *Intellectuals and Socialism: 'Social Democrats' and the Labour Party* (London: Lawrence & Wishart, 1994); Ilaria Favretto, '"Wilsonism" Reconsidered: Labour Party Revisionism 1952–64', *Contemporary British History*, 14/4 (2000); Patrick Diamond (ed.), *New Labour's Old Roots: Revisionist Thinkers in Labour's History 1931–1997* (Exeter: Imprint Academic, 2004); Kevin Jeffries, 'The Old Right', in Raymond Plant, Matt Beech and Kevin Hickson (eds), *The Struggle for Labour's Soul: Understanding Labour's Political Thought Since 1945* (London: Routledge, 2004), pp. 68–85; Nuttall, 'Labour Revisionism and Qualities of Mind and Character, 1931–79'.

37 Foote, *The Labour Party's Political Thought*, chapter 12.

38 Roger Spalding, *Narratives of Delusion in the Political Practice of the Labour Left: 1931–1945* (Cambridge: Cambridge Scholars Publishing, 2018), p. 12.

39 David Howell, *The Rise and Fall of Bevanism*, Labour Party Discussion Series 5, (Leeds: Independent Labour Party, 1982).

40 Anthony Arblaster, 'The Old Left', in Raymond Plant, Matt Beech and Kevin Hickson (eds), *The Struggle for Labour's Soul: Understanding Labour's Political Thought Since 1945* (London: Routledge, 2004), pp. 7–23.

41 John Callaghan, 'The Left and the "Unfinished Revolution": Bevanites and Soviet Russia in the 1950s', *Contemporary British History*, 15/3 (2001), 63–82.

42 Campbell, *Nye Bevan and the Mirage of British Socialism*, p. 213.

43 Nuttall, 'Equality and Freedom', p. 25.

44 David Marquand, *The Progressive Dilemma: From Lloyd George to Tony Blair*, 2nd edn (London: Phoenix, 1999); Spalding, *Narratives of Delusion in the Political Practice of the Labour Left*.

45 Foote, *The Labour Party's Political Thought*, p. 273.

46 Foot, *Aneurin Bevan: 1945–1960*, pp. 254–5.

47 Campbell, *Nye Bevan and the Mirage of British Socialism*, p. 245.
48 Callaghan, 'The Left'.
49 Foote, *The Labour Party's Political Thought*, p. 281.
50 Marquand, *The Progressive Dilemma*, p. 122.
51 Jackson, *Equality and the British Left*, p. 159.
52 Desai, *Intellectuals and Socialism*, p. 101.
53 Arblaster, 'The Old Left', p. 21.
54 Bealey, *The Social and Political Thought of the British Labour Party*, p. 40.
55 Desai, *Intellectuals and Socialism*, p. 102.
56 Hannah, *A Party with Socialists in it*, pp. 108–9.
57 Nye Davies (ed.), *This is My Truth: Aneurin Bevan in Tribune* (Cardiff: University of Wales Press, 2023).
58 Dean Blackburn, 'Still the Stranger at the Feast? Ideology and the Study of Twentieth-Century British Politics', *Journal of Political Ideologies*, 22/2 (2017), 125.
59 Marc Geddes and R. A. W. Rhodes, 'Towards an Interpretive Parliamentary Studies', in Jenni Brichzin et al. (eds), *Soziologie der Parlamente: Neue Wege der politischen Institutionenforschung* (Wiesbaden: Springer VS, 2018).
60 Michael Freeden, 'The Stranger at the Feast: Ideology and Public Policy in Twentieth Century Britain', *Twentieth Century British History*, 1/1 (1990), 9–34.
61 Michael Freeden, *Ideology: A Very Short Introduction* (Oxford: Oxford University Press, 2003), p. 55.
62 Freeden, *Ideology*, p. 123.
63 Diamond, *New Labour's Old Roots*.
64 Blackburn, 'Still the stranger at the feast?', p. 116.
65 Kari Palonen, 'Political Theorizing as a Dimension of Political Life', *European Journal of Political Theory*, 4/4 (2005), 351.
66 Blackburn, 'Still the stranger at the feast?', p. 119.
67 Foote, *The Labour Party's Political Thought*, p. 11.
68 Leach, *Political Ideology in Britain*, pp. 70–3.
69 Davis, 'Labourism', p. 42.
70 Ralph Miliband, 'Socialist Advance in Britain', in *Class War Conservatism and Other Essays* (London: Verso, 1983), p. 293.
71 Miliband, *Parliamentary Socialism*, p. 13.
72 Nairn, 'The Nature of the Labour Party – 1', 65.
73 Davis, 'Labourism', p. 44.

74 Steven Fielding and Declan McHugh, 'The Progressive Dilemma and the Social Democratic Perspective', in John Callaghan, Steven Fielding and Steve Ludlam (eds), *Interpreting the Labour Party: Approaches to Labour Politics and History* (Manchester: Manchester University Press, 2003), pp. 134–5.
75 Marquand, *The Progressive Dilemma*, pp. 21–2.
76 Fielding and McHugh, 'The Progressive Dilemma', pp. 134–5.
77 Miliband, *Parliamentary Socialism*, p. 327.
78 Nairn, 'The Nature of the Labour Party – 2', p. 49.
79 Marquand, *The Progressive Dilemma*, p. xi.
80 In an Appendix this book lists the *Tribune* articles published under Bevan's name as well as under his pseudonym of 'M.P.' with the hope that this will prove valuable to future researchers. The usefulness of this resource is enhanced by the fact that it is organised in such a way that researchers can identify specific articles that relate to core themes in Bevan's political thought.
81 John Rawls, *Lectures on the History of Political Philosophy* (Cambridge MA: Harvard University Press, 2007), pp. xiii–xiv.
82 Freeden, *Ideology*, p. 49.
83 Aneurin Bevan, *In Place of Fear* (London: William Heinemann, 1952), p. 1.
84 Foot, *Aneurin Bevan: 1897–1945*, p. 27.
85 Thomas-Symonds, *Nye*, p. 5.
86 Walter Bryce Gallie, 'Essentially Contested Concepts', *Proceedings of the Aristotelian Society*, 56 (1956).
87 Mark Haugaard (ed.), *Power: A Reader* (Manchester: Manchester University Press, 2002), p. 1.
88 George Lawson, 'A Conversation with Michael Mann', *Millennium: Journal of International Studies*, 34/2 (2006), 3.
89 Michael Mann, *The Sources of Social Power, Volume 1: A History of Power from the Beginning to A.D. 1760* (Cambridge: Cambridge University Press, 1986), p. 2.
90 Michael Mann, *The Sources of Social Power, Volume 3: Global Empires and Revolution, 1890–1945* (Cambridge: Cambridge University Press, 2012), p. 6.
91 Dai Smith, 'Ashes to the wind', in Geoffrey Goodman (ed.) *The State of the Nation: The Political Legacy of Aneurin Bevan* (London: Victor Gollancz, 1997); Daniel G Williams, *Wales Unchained* (Cardiff: University of Wales Press, 2015); Ben Gwalchmai, 'Aneurin Bevan Killed my Sheep: Labour and Welsh Independence', *New Socialist* (2019), *https://newsocialist.org.uk/labour-and-welsh-independence/* (accessed 5 January 2024).
92 Freeden, 'The Stranger at the Feast', p. 11.
93 Freeden, 'The Stranger at the Feast', p. 34.

1

CLASS, CAPITALISM, POWER

> Then again, we had a long tradition of class action behind us stretching back to the Chartists. So for us power meant the use of collective action designed to transform society and so lift all of us together. To us the doctrine of laissez-faire conveyed no inspiration, because the hope of individual emancipation was crushed by the weight of accomplished power. We were the products of an industrial civilisation and our psychology corresponded to that fact. Individual ambition was overlaid by the social imperative. The streams of individual initiative therefore flowed along collective channels already formed for us by our environment.[1]

Bevan's analysis of capitalism and the resulting class conflict was fundamental to his political thought. It stemmed from his experience in industrial south Wales, and was supplemented by his reading of political theory, particularly Marxism.[2] Bevan was happy to boast in the House of Commons that he saw himself as 'a considerable student of Marx'.[3] He insisted, however, that it was important to reassess Marxist theory. He wrote that a 'sympathetic understanding of what Marxists are trying to say to the world is a prerequisite to learning where the Marxist practitioners are liable to go wrong'.[4] As this chapter demonstrates, Bevan's engagement with Marxism informed his analysis of society.

The first section of this chapter examines Bevan's reflections on capitalism, its essential features and its effects on society. Further, it considers his conception of class conflict, which he saw as a central feature of capitalism. The second section traces Bevan's analysis of the historical development of society and begins to identify the relationship between base and superstructure in Bevan's thought. The third section details the role of working-class action in Bevan's thought, while the final section emphasises the importance that Bevan placed on the development of democracy in changing people's circumstances. These four sections highlight the economic foundations of Bevan's political thought and his analysis of power relations under capitalism.

As we saw in the Introduction, the Labour Party emerged out of the trade union movement, with its ideology being shaped by the tenets of labourism. The result of this was the creation of a party that, as John Saville wrote, was both for 'the encouragement of social change and the preservation of the basic structures of society'.[5] It is within this context that Labour's approach to the economy developed. While Bevan fitted within many of Labour's intellectual traditions, his discussion of the economy, property and social change was quite different from the prevailing economic thought within the party. Appreciating that there were a diversity of voices within it, the chapter also compares Bevan's analysis to that of his colleagues and the Labour Party more broadly.

Capitalism and Class

CAPITALISM

Central to Bevan's political thought was his analysis of the development of private property and private enterprise. He argued that the 'chief characteristic of the modern competitive society is the feverish accumulation of property in private hands'.[6] Alongside the development of private property was the important role that 'private economic adventure has played in bringing modern industrial techniques into existence. The stimulus of competition, the appetite for profits, and the urge for wealth and power and status – all these played their part in the making of modern society'

(p. 37). The development of private property therefore became the central feature of capitalist society.

Bevan argued that the preservation of private property informed the dynamics of capitalism. Any ideas of public spending or public involvement in the economy were disregarded by the British ruling class, as it was generally 'seen as an interference, not only with the rights of the individual, but as an enemy of the process of capital accumulation' (p. 52). The capitalists were able to make sure that public spending was kept off the agenda and that capital accumulation was the primary concern. For example, during the Second World War Bevan argued that the government did not look at the possibility of a large-scale public housing initiative because this would 'deprive private enterprise of a most juicy bit of profit-making'.[7] Bevan disputed the priority given to private enterprise, believing that capitalism's foundation was deeply flawed.

According to Bevan, capitalism and the privileging of private enterprise was sustained by an incoherent logic. In 1937, he wrote of the government's attitude towards a potential oncoming depression. Rather than the onset of the depression being responsible for the fear of it, the government believed that it was 'the fear of it that *causes* the depression' (emphasis added). Bevan mocked the attitude of the government, presenting their logic as: 'If by some means we could create a more optimistic state of mind in those responsible for the conduct of our industrial life depression of trade need never come ... What we need apparently is not statesmen but hypnotists.' He described this as 'the kind of mystic Mumbo-Jumbo to which capitalism is driven when austere reason pronounces sentence of death upon it'.[8] This 'mystic Mumbo-jumbo' could not be relied on to create a desirable society for the masses.

Although Bevan admitted that capitalism achieved great technological advances, he argued that it also created a life of poverty for the masses. Bevan was moved by witnessing these damaging effects. Thomas-Symonds argued that Bevan's rage was against 'a *political and economic system* that could organise the country's resources in such a way to cause this misery'.[9] Bevan was a keen reader of Jack London, the American author whose novel *The Iron Heel* told the story of a dystopian future and detailed the struggle of the working class and the mismanagement of society by capitalists.[10] As the novel's main protagonist Ernest Everhard asserted:

> In face of the facts that modern man lives more wretchedly than the cave-man, and that his producing power is a thousand times greater than that of the cave-man, no other conclusion is possible than the capitalist class has mismanaged, that you have mismanaged, my masters, that you have criminally and selfishly mismanaged.[11]

This sentiment that would have resonated with Bevan.

Bevan's critique of capitalism's effects encompassed a variety of issues. For instance, he believed that it turned people into prisoners:

> Actually, nothing short of the abolition of capitalism can give us a civilised penal code. Capitalism, through unemployment and insecurity, turns people into criminals, and then prohibits them when in prison from undertaking any creative work which might redeem them into good citizenship.[12]

He even argued that capitalism created a situation where women did not want to have children:

> The fact is that the women of Britain in refusing to bear as many children as formerly are exercising a silent vote against the sort of world capitalism is creating for the reception of their children ... In denying the progress of mankind capitalism denies the existence of mankind. Judged from this angle capitalism is a vast contraceptive condemning the old world to death by refusing the birth of the new. (p. 7)

Further, Bevan argued that the worker was oppressed in this society and was simply seen as a thermostat for when capitalism wasn't working:

> Remember you are not only a man and a citizen. You are also a potential 'thermostat' on tap to adjust the fluctuations of private investment. So that every now and then you may be thrown out of work, and then pounced upon and converted into a labourer, engaged on building the 'permanent equipment of society', probably away from your family and friends. You will work at that until the

> public expenditure has pumped enough oxygen into the system of private investment to start it off again. Then you will go back to your work as a mechanic and continue at that until the machinery of private enterprise breaks down again, and then once more you will be converted into a 'thermostat'.[13]

The effects of capitalism on economic, political, international and ideological issues are considered in further detail throughout the following chapters. It is worth highlighting here, however, that this analysis was a cornerstone of Bevan's political thought.

Bevan maintained his critique of private enterprise throughout his career. For instance, in 1958 he highlighted a debate in Parliament concerning the economy as evidence of how capitalism was deeply flawed. He reflected that 'Private economic adventure – miscalled "private enterprise" – insists upon mystery. If the behaviour of market forces could be predicted, capitalism could not survive'. He asserted that capitalism was 'wholly opposed to the scientific spirit of the age, which strives to understand and to control what is happening around us'. He questioned the wisdom of economists, insisting that a debate on economics:

> among Western economists is rather like a peculiar kind of crystal gazing. They anxiously read the portents, trying to perceive the significance of almost wholly unknown phenomena. It is impossible to reconcile a belief in economic mystery with the search for predictability.[14]

Bevan argued that if economists succeeded in predicting the future, they would 'destroy that gambling and speculation upon the future which is the essence of an economy based on private economic adventure. You cannot gamble on the temperature of the water if the thermometer is always to hand' (p. 1).

Bevan's analysis of capitalism appears to echo a Marxist understanding of property relations. In *The Communist Manifesto*, Marx and Engels asserted that modern 'bourgeois private property is the final and most complete expression of the system of producing and appropriating products, that is based on class antagonisms, on the exploitation of the many by the few'.[15] Bevan's thought reflected this view, and he explained the development of private property in similar terms. While Bevan's understanding of Marxism cannot be considered as total, we can see that it influenced his thinking in many important ways. As Palonen noted, the:

> heuristic use of analogies, the transfer of metaphors, tropes and figures, the recourse to thought experiments and the construction of ideal-typical alternatives are just some examples of styles of thinking in the humanities which may also inspire reflections on principles, policies and practices for acting politicians. It is the political agents who decide whether or not to use such figures and, if so, how and to what extent. The situational character of the politician's insight can concern occasions of inventing or revising both the projects and their legitimation.[16]

The metaphors and tropes of Bevan's Marxist education and his belief in some of its core principles, helped to shape his politics. As the next section considers, his close connection to Marxism is further exemplified by his views on the consequences of this property relation: the formation of classes and the existence of class conflict in capitalist society.

CLASS

Biographers are generally in agreement regarding the influence of Marxism on Bevan.[17] However, there is disagreement as to whether it was a strength or a weakness in Bevan's thought.[18] Foot contended that the Marxist theory of class struggle never left Bevan:

> His Socialism was rooted in Marxism; whatever modifications he had made in the doctrine, a belief in the class struggle stayed unshaken. Marxism taught him that society must be changed swiftly, intrepidly, fundamentally, if the transformation was not to be overturned by counter-revolution.[19]

Several Marxist writers are identified as having influenced Bevan. We have already seen that Bevan admired Jack London, who was joined by American socialists Eugene V. Debs and Daniel de Leon as well as south Wales socialists such as Sydney Jones, Walter Conway and Noah Ablett. These figures instilled in Bevan a belief in collective action.[20] Further, Dai Smith emphasised the influence of German Marxist Joseph Dietzgen's materialist conception of history on the development of Bevan's political thought. Dietzgen's work was taught at the Central Labour College in London when Bevan was a student, where, as Stuart Macintyre explained, he 'served as an introduction to the philosophical foundations of Marxism for many young working-class autodidacts'.[21] Smith contended that 'Dietzgen's "monism" (everything in the world is interconnected and interdependent) appealed greatly to Labour College students ... because it provided a readily comprehensible philosophical analysis of thought and matter that emphasized their real unity'. Central Labour College students were able to see that 'Ideas could interact with material existence to cause further change',[22] which, as we will see, is evident in Bevan's writings.

Early evidence of Bevan's engagement with the nature of class conflict can be found in his 1921 review of *The Communist Manifesto*. Bevan wrote that the book's 'treating of the development of the modern capitalist class and its counterpart the proletariat' was the 'best and most convincing exposition of the Marxian point of view'.[23] When Bevan asked, 'Where was power and which the road to it?', the question for him and those suffering under capitalism was 'shaped into a class form, not an individual form'.[24] Bevan's analysis of the dynamics of capitalism reflected this conflict between the proletariat and the bourgeoisie.

Bevan emphasised the importance of collective action to the working class, writing that 'power meant the use of collective action designed to transform society and so lift all of us together'. Instead of viewing society as individual self-interest, the working class, Bevan argued, saw it as the collective striving of classes. Society 'presented itself ... as an arena of conflicting social forces and not as a plexus of individual striving'. He saw these three forces as poverty, property and democracy – 'They are forces in the strict sense of the term, for they are active and positive. Among them no rest is possible' (p. 2). Bevan had previously outlined this formulation in the House of Commons in 1933[25] and in *Why Not Trust the Tories?* in 1944.[26] Poverty, property and democracy are central elements to Bevan's understanding of society. It was in *In Place of Fear* where he elaborated on them in further detail.

Bevan offered quite broad definitions of these three forces. He defined poverty as 'the normal state of millions of people in modern industrial society, accompanied by a deep sense of frustration and dissatisfaction with the existing state of social affairs'. Property in this tripartite schema was wealth, and those 'who, by possession of wealth, have a dominating influence on the policy of the nation'.[27] He described democracy as putting 'a new power in the possession of ordinary men and women'. Further, he wrote that the 'conflict between the forces, always implicit, breaks out into open struggle during periods of exceptional difficulty'. In a capitalist society, the conflict between the three forces 'resolves itself into this: either poverty will use democracy to win the struggle against property, or property, in fear of poverty, will destroy democracy' (p. 3). Bevan concluded that from '1929 onwards in Great Britain the stage was set and all the actors assembled in the great drama which is the essence of politics in modern advanced industrial democracies'. The actors in this great drama corresponded to the three forces in society:

> Firstly, there was wealth, great wealth, concentrated in comparatively few hands although cushioned by a considerably developed middle class. Second, there was a working class forming the vast majority of the nation and living under conditions which made it deeply conscious of inequality and preventable poverty. Third, there was fully developed political liberty, expressing itself through constitutional forms which had matured for many centuries and had as their central point an elected assembly commanding the respect of the community. (p. 11)

Wealth concentrated in relatively few hands, and a working class that formed the majority of the nation, demonstrates Bevan's interpretation of the class conflict inherent in society. The clash between poverty and property also represents Bevan's formulation of this conflict.

Two of these forces can be assigned to traditional class distinctions: property with the bourgeoisie and the ruling class; poverty with the proletariat or the working class. Democracy, however, does not align with a certain class in society. Gerry Healy, reviewing *In Place of Fear* on its release in 1952 for the Trotskyist publication *Labour Review*, pointed out that 'social forces in the scientific sense are classes of people having definite relations to existing types of property and specific functions in the processes of production', these being 'capitalists, wage-workers, and a varied range of groupings which are a buffer between them'. In contrast, he wrote, 'democracy is not a social force', but is a '*political* form, an institution of government arising out of and based upon the relations and struggles of the diverse classes within a country'.[28] Democracy is a significant element of Bevan's political thought that is analysed further in the final section of this chapter and in Chapter 2, particularly in relation to this class conflict. Healy was correct to identify this formulation as an expression of class conflict: the clash between poverty and property is reminiscent of class conflict as traditionally described by Marx and Engels.

Michael Foot certainly saw this tripartite as Bevan's 'individual elaboration of Marxist prophecy'.[29] Although Marx did not offer a systematic analysis of the concept of class,[30] the *Communist Manifesto* saw Marx and Engels posit the formulation of two classes in society:

> the epoch of the bourgeoisie, possesses, however, this distinct feature: it has simplified class antagonisms. Society as a whole is more and more splitting up into two great hostile camps, into two great classes directly facing each other – Bourgeoisie and Proletariat.[31]

While Marx did write of other classes,[32] Bevan's own formulation follows the *Communist Manifesto* in identifying two social classes. Bevan's 1921 review of the *Manifesto* and his agreement with the classification of society into two classes support this claim. The review is also one of the very few texts where Bevan directly interrogates and analyses Marx's work.

Bevan recognised that in capitalist society, economic power resided with the owners of property. He asserted that the discontent of the working class needed to be aimed at wealth as those who possessed it had 'a dominating influence on the policy of the nation'.[33] Bevan viewed the power of the ruling class as a wholly negative form as it derived 'from the power to exploit the exertion of others. This is a predatory power made possible by carrying over into modern society the concepts of barbarism, when theft, raid and pillage were accepted ways of acquiring property' (p. 64). Bevan argued that the 'merciless exploitation which formed the basis of the unprecedented accumulation of capital equipment in Britain, was made possibly [*sic*] only by a class dictatorship' (p. 39). This predatory power and exploitation was the foundation of Bevan's critique of contemporary society and the relations between poverty (the proletariat) and property (the bourgeoisie).

A class analysis informed Bevan's thought on most issues – a theme that runs through all the chapters in this book. From his understanding of war to his views on the values of society, the way struggles shape themselves into a class form were at the heart of Bevan's politics. Campbell noted that, on paper, the south Wales coalfield represented 'an almost perfect Marxist situation, ripe for class conflict', even though he argued that the Marxist struggle did not take place there, no matter how conducive the conditions were to it.[34] He presented Bevan's conception of class conflict as deriving from the most 'deeply held tenet' of his socialism, namely that it was based 'not on Marx but on the social experiences of the industrial masses'. He continued that 'Marx explained that social experience, but doctrine came second to class; his fundamental doctrine was still the class struggle' (p. 257).

While the lived experience of Bevan and his class were vital,[35] theory and practice cannot be separated when explaining Bevan's intellectual development. Bevan appreciated the importance of Marx in informing and explaining working-class experience:

> Marx, and the school of thought which he founded, put into the hands of the working-class movement of the late nineteenth and the first part of the twentieth centuries the most complete blueprints for political action the world has ever seen ... No serious student who studies the history of the last half century can deny the ferment of ideas associated with the names of Marx, Engels and Lenin. Their effectiveness in arming the minds of working-class leaders all over the world with intellectual weapons showed that their teaching had an organic relationship with the political and social realities of their time.[36]

Bevan stressed the importance of working-class self-education in providing him with the theory to explain and make clear his experiences. He wrote that:

> In so far as I can be said to have had a political training at all, it has been in Marxism. As I was reaching adolescence, towards the

> end of the First World War, I became acquainted with the works of Eugene V. Debs and Daniel de Leon of the U.S.A. At that time I was reading everything I could lay my hands on. Tredegar Workmen's Library was unusually well stocked with books of all kinds. (p. 17)

Bevan reflected that he was not alone in this experience. He declared that the 'self-educating naturally seize on the knowledge which makes their own experience intelligible'. He wrote of how the 'self-educating cling to what they learn with more tenacity than the university product ... As a general rule he learns only what has a significance in his own life'. Bevan proclaimed that the 'abstract ideas which ignite his mind are those to which his own experience provides a reference'. Therefore:

> action and thought go hand-in-hand in reciprocal revelation. The world of concrete activity renovates, refreshes and winnows the ideas he gets in books. The world of abstract thought rises from strong foundations of realised fact, like a great tree, whose topmost leaves move in obeisance to the lightest zephyr, yet the great trunk itself issues the final command. (p. 18)

It is therefore wrong for Campbell to dismiss the ideas that were at the heart of Bevan's socialism. As S. O. Davies, a contemporary of Bevan's in both the South Wales Miners' Federation and in Parliament explained, the conditions that Bevan experienced instilled in him his 'torrential vituperation, his deadly ridicule and acid wit'[37] – but it was also underpinned by an analysis of society. Bevan's analysis of capitalism and class demonstrates the combination between theory and social experience in his political thought.

Despite Bevan's appreciation of Marxism and his conception of class struggle, this was a theory that did not fit comfortably within Labour's intellectual traditions. For instance, Labour's economics was not based on Marx, but rather on the work of thinkers such as Thomas Hodgskin and J. A. Hobson. Geoffrey Foote noted that *Labour Defended Against the Claims of Capital*, written by Hodgskin in 1825, influenced the theory of labourism (Foote, 1986, p. 8). Hodgskin argued for the redistribution of wealth and the necessity of trade unions to fight for rightful wages. However, he did not believe in the abolition of the economic and social system, instead advocating for negotiation within it.[38] Similarly, Hobson challenged the arguments of supply and demand in *The Physiology of Industry*, written in 1889, but believed in regulated capitalism and insisted on an underlying harmony between the interests of capital and labour, with trade unions being vital to improve collective bargaining (pp. 128–32). Rather than Marx then, it was economic thinkers who broadly accepted the economic structure of society who influenced the economic thought of the Labour Party.

The place of intellectuals within the Labour Party has always been a matter of debate. New Left writers such as Nairn, for instance, have considered intellectuals to have no substantive role within the party.[39] However, it was not the case that intellectuals were not given a platform in the party; rather, the party tended to eschew Marxist and similarly radical intellectuals. The Marxist Social Democratic Federation had left the Labour Party in 1901, with the Fabians becoming its dominant intellectual group, profoundly shaping the party's ideological development. Perry Anderson argued that a socialist party that wanted to create a working-class hegemony needed a theoretical underpinning and an understanding of social transformation.[40] Yet, the form of socialism that became dominant in the party was not the Marxism that Bevan was influenced by. Further, rather than basing policies and positions on political thought, emphasis was placed on 'labour interest'.[41] The economic, social and political theory of the Fabians was seen as the most appropriate while the working class were beginning to have a voice.[42] This rejected Marxism and more radical interpretations of economic power. Marx saw wage-labour as a disease that needed to be cured, whereas labourism saw greed of the capitalists (the symptom of the system according to Marx) as the problem.[43]

Nevertheless, despite tensions within labourism, the dominance of private enterprise and the struggles of the working class were central to Bevan's political thought. As long as the power relation between the two classes meant that property was dominant, poverty would not triumph. This led Bevan to the conclusion that in order to change society and for the working class to prosper, there was a need to agitate for the reversal of this relationship and for poverty to triumph over property. This resulted in Bevan's viewing society as a process of historical development where the relationship between the economic base and the superstructure was important.

Historical Development

BASE AND SUPERSTRUCTURE

Bevan saw the development of society as taking place through stages with the political and ideological superstructure adapting to changes in the economic base. He wrote that the *Communist Manifesto* was 'the first time the world learned of that conception of history by which the study of social development matured into a definite science'. He declared that the 'Materialist Conception of History runs through the historical part of the *Manifesto* like a golden thread'.[44] This materialist conception of history and the relationship between the economic base and the political-ideological superstructure appears to be implicit in Bevan's analysis of the historical development of societies. As discussed earlier in this chapter, authors such as Smith identified it as influencing Bevan's intellectual development (specifically the work of German philosopher Joseph Dietzgen). The study of historical materialism was included as part of the 'Lectures on Method' provided by the Central Labour College.[45] To begin with, it is worth noting Bevan's interpretation of society before the onset of industrialisation:

> Before the rise of modern industrialism it could be said that the main task of man was to build a home for himself in nature. Since then the outstanding task for the individual man is to build a home for himself in society. I do not pretend that this definition has any sociological validity. I do claim that it is useful in enabling us to study widely differing experiences in the history of mankind.[46]

Before industrial society, there were few man-made items, agriculture was dominant, and the immediate struggle was with the forces of nature. Social relations were personal relations and social institutions were also immediate and personal. In this situation, 'physical nature ruled over all' and the:

> physical elements were the main source of [someone's] sorrows as of his joys ... Floods, famines, fires, crop failures, earthquakes, the majestic immensity of the heavens and the overpowering violence of storms, all drove home the lesson that by comparison, he was a

> pigmy grudgingly permitted a brief life, a fleeting smile and then oblivion. (p. 35)

Therefore, in these circumstances, 'the social organism was an instrument forged by man to hold in check the forces of nature'. The individual and society became inseparable from each other and it never occurred to the individual to be outside that society, as in exile there was only 'death, physical and spiritual. Between him and the terrors of nature stood only his tribe, his clan, his small society. Inside it he was warm, comforted, and to some extent safe. Outside he was nothing'. The difference between that society and the society of the 1950s was, Bevan believed, that the 'individual today in the industrial nations is essentially an urban product. He is first a creature of his society and only secondarily of nature' (p. 35). This description of the move from pre-industrial to industrial society sets out Bevan's argument on historical development and the influence of material conditions on social life.

Bevan detailed how the individual had overcome the threats of nature as a result of the advancement of technological science. 'In short', he concluded, 'man in making society has brought nature under control'. Bevan warned, however, that 'in doing so society itself has got out of the control of man'. The problems that individuals now faced 'have their source in society. Personal relations', Bevan wrote, had 'given way to impersonal ones. The Great Society has arrived and the task of our generation is to bring it under control. The study of how it is to be done is the function of politics' (p. 36). Changes in the material conditions of society had altered it significantly, moving beyond the control of personal relations between people.

To bring society under control, Bevan's focus on the importance of class relations reveals an emphasis on changes to the economic base, specifically property relations. Bevan's initial view, expressed in his review of the *Manifesto*, was that property had become so concentrated in private hands that the conditions were now in place for the 'Social Revolution' to occur, leading to the destruction of '*all* private property relations' (emphasis added).[47] Bevan saw this need to reverse property relations clearly in the coal industry where 'the relations between employers and workers have reached a state of chronic maladjustment, resulting in a failure to produce what the nation needs for its life'. He insisted that socialists always recognised this situation as 'the classic prelude to a revolutionary solution. That solution is to re-unite the forces of production by changing the property forms. The only change now possible in our society is the abolition of private property in the coal mines'.[48] This, written in 1944, demonstrates the continuing relevance of Bevan's analysis of property relations.

The complete abolition of private property is not, however, something Bevan proposed in his later writing. Bevan altered his opinion and did not see the abolition of *all* private property as attainable. While acknowledging the economic power that capitalism possessed to create a modern and technologically advanced society,[49] Bevan insisted that in the future 'power relations of public and private property must be drastically altered' in developing a better society. Bevan instead argued for a mixed economy: 'It is clear to the serious student of modern politics that a mixed economy is what most people of the West would prefer' (p. 118). This idea in Bevan's thought is explored in greater detail in Chapter 2 when considering Bevan's vision of the relationship between public enterprises and private property. For now, it is important to note that Bevan maintained that a fundamental change in property relations needed to be carried out. While this may confirm Campbell's argument that Bevan's belief in the march of socialism was questioned later in life when reality made him doubt what Campbell described as 'deterministic Marxism',[50] a belief in historical development, based on Bevan's understanding of property relations, is evident in his later writings, as will be seen in subsequent chapters.

FUTURE SOCIETY

Bevan described the changing social and economic power relations in terms of moving from capitalism to a new order of society. The concentration of private property led to societal development being halted. Therefore, the relations between private and public property needed to be drastically altered to bring about change. Marx and Engels emphasised that 'All property relations in the past have continually been subject to historical change consequent upon the change in historical conditions'.[51] Bevan supported this interpretation, stating:

> Before we can dream of consolidation, the power relations of public and private property must be drastically altered. The solution of the problems I have been discussing cannot be approached until it

> becomes possible to create a purposive and intelligible design for society. That cannot be done until effective social and economic power passes from one order of society to another.[52]

Bevan's view on the development of society can be seen clearly in his analysis of countries such as Russia. Praising the seven-year plan conducted by the Soviet Union, Bevan argued in 1959 that the 'old Marxist argument that the relations of private property and the social stratifications that come within them tend to stultify and even inhibit technical progress and maximum production of wealth, is receiving fresh reinforcement'.[53] Bevan was here reaffirming a Marxist position that the dominance of private property stifled the economic development of society. Note too that Bevan was reaffirming this view in 1959, one year before his death, demonstrating the endurance of this position.

Writing a year earlier in 1958, Bevan concluded that the changes in property relations had not occurred in Britain. He argued that the nature of private enterprise and capitalism prevented further economic development, writing that 'increases in national wealth, made possible by new scientific and industrial techniques, have been blocked by the social and political peculiarities of capitalist society'. He reflected on the 'old Marxist thesis [that] stated that a time would be reached in the development of capitalist society when property relations would limit the expansion of the productive forces'. He admitted that this analysis 'was too austere', instead suggesting that the 'position today is not that capitalist society is plunged into an epic economic crisis. Instead, the economy functions but in an enfeebled condition, like a patient with a persistent low fever'. He concluded that, 'We are not in the old phase of boom and bust. There is never a real boom and never a real bust. There is only a persistent sabotage of productive potentialities'.[54]

In 1959, Bevan wrote that private enterprise was still attempting to maintain its dominance but was still ineffective. Economists were trying to rely on outdated theories, but they no longer worked. Instead, he stated that 'the more economists are attempting to establish the validity of capitalism, the more clearly they disclose its uncertain and declining state of health'.[55] Although the inevitable destruction of the capitalist system had not occurred, Bevan still maintained that capitalism was not conducive to the development of the economy.

In contrast to Bevan's prescriptions for the economy, Labour's approach to reform did not envisage a similar transformation of economic relations. As David Howell wrote, 'From the beginning a major strain in Labour's socialism was in sympathy with the existing order'.[56] This derived from the assumptions on class that had been established within the Labour Party. Labour was to be a national rather than a class party.[57] When it got into government, Labour was concerned with becoming acceptable to the establishment. In David Coates' view, this meant class collaboration. Throughout the 1920s, Labour leader Ramsay Macdonald criticised strike action, while the Labour government of 1929 did not challenge capitalism. Rather, the party was criticised by the left for its reactionary approach to the economy, instead of trying to radically change its underlying foundations.[58] In 1929, Labour accepted the orthodoxy of the bankers and private financiers, although Coates argued that Macdonald's 'betrayal' was a myth; rather, it was a consequence of Labour's collaboration and accommodation with capital and private interest, that had been a feature of the party's policies throughout the 1920s (p. 31). This was also ultimately the result of the labour movement's defensive positioning. Willie Thompson wrote that Chartism was replaced in the nineteenth century by a 'more loosely articulated, much less politically ambitious network of organisations and agencies, willing to pursue their objectives within the framework of established political and social institutions under the mixed aristocratic/bourgeois hegemony which commanded the British state and social order'.[59]

There were some challenges to this thinking within the Labour Party. For years, a number of ideas had been articulated by its members, including Marxism, syndicalism and guild socialism.[60] While some of these ideas were held by future leaders – for example, Clement Attlee was influenced by the principles of guild socialism (p. 107) – they were ultimately subsumed by the principles of labourism. Throughout the 1920s and 1930s, extra-parliamentary efforts emerged, which questioned the efficacy of using Parliament to achieve power for the working class, such as the Triple Alliance in 1919, the General Strike of 1926 and the Popular Front movement in the 1930s. Throughout the early to mid-twentieth century, there was plenty of socialist rhetoric, but commitment to economic orthodoxy meant that Labour did not seek to challenge property relations in the same way that Bevan argued for.

In the following chapters, Bevan's views on the relationship between historical development and democracy, war and ideas are explored in greater detail together with the relationship between the economic base and the political-ideological superstructure. A study of Bevan's writing on the nature of capitalist development and property relations reveals an understanding of class conflict and the development of society that closely relates to a materialist conception of history. The next line of enquiry is to study *how* Bevan envisioned changing the economic base and the relationship between poverty and property.

Working-Class Strategy

PRAXIS

To change property relations, the working class needed to engage in conscious activity. In *Theses on Feuerbach* Marx wrote his famous phrase, 'The philosophers have only *interpreted* the world in various ways; the point is, to *change* it'.[61] This phrase explained the importance of seeking to change society rather than just explain its features. This has often been described as praxis, referring to 'the free, universal, creative and self-creative activity through which man creates (makes, produces) and changes (shapes) his historical, human world and himself'.[62] Bevan also believed in the need for human activity to change society. His political thought cannot be seen simply as a *theory* of society; it must also be seen as a call to action to the working class. It was a call for an active engagement in changing the circumstances of their lives. Bevan saw capitalism as ultimately being transcended by a new order of society conforming to the principles of democratic socialism, an idea that is 'based on the conviction that free men can use free institutions to solve the social and economic problems of the day, if they are given the chance to do so'.[63]

Bevan's early engagement with Marxism made clear this need for action. He stated in his 1921 review that the *Communist Manifesto* taught the working class that 'want and misery' alone would not lead to revolution; the means to make one needed to be available. The *Manifesto* had detailed how modern industry had provided those means. Bevan wrote that 'Marx points out that the means to end capitalism have been supplied by modern industrial development, and that this development has been the historic purpose of the capitalist epoch'. Previous revolutions had failed because there did not exist a 'permanent identity of interests'. Once a dominant class was overthrown, the 'class distinctions within the revolting elements came to the surface, thrusting the lowlier classes into what was revealed to be simply another form of economic servitude'.[64] Bevan detailed how this could not be otherwise, as during previous revolutions property had been widely distributed: 'A successful revolution directed against private property is only possible where property is so centralised that the subject class is able to see in the ruling class simply a personification of private property.' Capitalism had accomplished this, denying property from nine-tenths of the population. Bevan then referred to the next revolution as having 'for its main object the destruction of "all private property relations" and with this, the "division of society into classes will come to an end"' (p. 20). Although, as we have seen, Bevan reverted from calling for *all* private property to be destroyed. A reading of his work suggests that he initially envisioned that this revolutionary activity would take the form of industrial action.

INDUSTRIAL ACTION

Bevan was heavily engaged in the trade union movement in south Wales. How the workers could organise to effect social change and to win a conflict for power was Bevan's main concern, as he explained in his account of the inter-war period in *In Place of Fear*. As previously noted, Bevan acknowledged the influence of syndicalist thinkers in south Wales such as Noah Ablett, one of the principle authors of *The Miners' Next Step* in 1912, a syndicalist pamphlet that called for the miners to 'build up an organization, that will ultimately take over the mining industry, and carry it out in the interests of the workers'.[65] For syndicalists such as Ablett, economic power was at the point of production. Bevan quoted Ablett as asking, 'why cross the river to fill the pail?' – why seek political means of achieving power when power was available for the workers at the point of production?[66] This interpretation of Marxism viewed 'Parliamentary action ... as an auxiliary of direct action by the industrial organisations of the workers'. Bevan and his comrades were taught that power 'was at the point of production ... Going to Parliament seemed a roundabout and tedious way of realising what seemed already within our grasp by more direct means' (p. 19).

Bevan's education would suggest that he initially supported industrial action first and foremost. This belief in direct action throughout the 1920s is noted by writers detailing his early political development. W. W. Craik, writing on the Central Labour College where he was vice president and a teacher during Bevan's time there, noted that Bevan was known to debate with his fellow students 'into the small hours of the morning, the merits of direct action and the demerits of parliamentary action'.[67] Bevan's belief in the merits of industrial action is not surprising considering the type of Marxism that he would have been exposed to in Tredegar and in the Central Labour College. Although syndicalism did not triumph over other forms of action in south Wales, it would have appealed to many workers active in these industrial struggles.[68]

However, although collective power was important, it was meaningless if the will to wield it did not exist. This became perfectly clear to Bevan during periods of industrial unrest in the inter-war period. Bevan claimed that during the 1919–21 Triple Alliance and the 1926 General Strike, the labour leaders had not grasped the implications of mass industrial action and those that did were not prepared to accept them.[69] The leaders did not take advantage when their coercive power was greater than that of the state (p. 21). The collective power of the working class may have enabled it to take control of the means of production and emancipate themselves. Nevertheless, Bevan suspected that the will to seize this power was not apparent in the industrial leaders of this period.

The popular representation of this period paints Bevan as being attached to the industrial and syndicalist outlook of miners such as Ablett.[70] Perhaps the most significant example of Bevan's belief in collective action is demonstrated through his role in organising the Tredegar Iron and Coal Company colliery lodges into the Tredegar Combine Lodge. Susan Demont presented the motivations behind the establishment of the lodge: one large single organisation 'could wield more bargaining power than a series of small, semi-autonomous branches' and it could 'exercise a bigger influence over District affairs'.[71] The Combine Lodge can be seen as demonstrating Bevan's 'belief that collective strength was crucial'.[72] Bevan, Demont argued, 'played an influential role in the movement to establish the Combine'.[73] He was also 'deeply involved in the day to day running of the [Tredegar Combine] strike' of 1918 and 'he no doubt gained valuable experience as a result'. Demont emphasised the importance of this strike as it was a 'practical demonstration of the power of the industrial workers, proving at the very least that by withdrawing their labour at a time when demand for it was great they could win important concessions' (p. 214).

According to Bevan's own reflections on events, it was after the failure of the 1926 General Strike that he realised the industrial weapon was not strong enough by itself to win power for the working class. Instead, the parliamentary route was needed. This representation of his political development is easy to accept as it fits with Bevan's own reflection on this period in *In Place of Fear*.[74] Nevertheless, it has been disputed, most notably by Demont who argued that too much attention has been paid to Bevan's recollections and not to his actions during this period. Instead, Demont insisted that Bevan's views on industrial action should be seen within the context of a wider political strategy. Demont contended that the interpretation of Bevan as someone who converted from a belief in industrial action to a belief in parliamentary action:

> is only viable if one subscribes to the view that the pre-1926 Bevan was an anti-parliamentarian syndicalist for whom the only arena for the conduct of the class struggle was the industrial front – a view borne out neither by his speeches nor his actions from the age of nineteen onwards.[75]

During the 1920s, Bevan was a councillor in addition to being an official of the South Wales Miners Federation. He held posts on a variety of local groups and institutions, his aim being 'to involve the [Labour] Party in every committee, organisation and interest group within the town with a view to influencing the course of events from a socialist stand-point' (p. 355).

Demont also pointed out that the confusion over Bevan's beliefs 'derives in part from the equation of "syndicalism" with "direct action" followed by the conclusion that advocates of the latter by definition spurn all forms of orthodox political action'. Direct action, Demont argued, 'in the form of marches, demonstrations or strikes for a political purpose does not preclude adherence to the labour movement's political wing'. The combination of Bevan's political and industrial actions during the 1920s demonstrates that 'though not a syndicalist', Bevan was:

> a supporter of direct action in those instances where there seemed little prospect of his class's needs being met by any other means. This in no sense contradicts his fundamental belief in the political road, however critical he was of some of those who espoused it. (p. 243)

Thomas-Symonds arrived at a similar conclusion, highlighting Bevan's time on the Tredegar District Council and the Monmouthshire County Council as a significant period in Bevan's political development, particularly his analysis of democracy and representative institutions.[76] For Demont, Bevan's activities in the Labour Party during this period demonstrated his belief 'in a synthesis of industrial and political action rather than the supremacy of one over the other',[77] while Smith asserted that Bevan's apparent move from syndicalism to parliamentary action should not be identified as a break in his political education. Instead, he wrote that it was an acknowledgement by Bevan of the need to adapt strategy to changing events and circumstance, quoting Bevan as arguing that as truth changes, ideas need to be regularly revitalised.[78]

The importance of working-class organisation through trade unions is still evident in Bevan's political thought, although it must be noted that Bevan had a difficult relationship with strikes, particularly during his time Minister of Labour in 1951. Geoff Ellen actually argued that Bevan increasingly showed an antipathy towards strikes against a Labour government.[79] When Labour was in opposition, however, Bevan saw the potential in industrial action.[80]

Bevan's rejection of direct industrial action along the lines of syndicalism is an indication of how he began to fit more comfortably within labourism. It also signifies Bevan's view of Parliament as the ultimate source of power in Britain. The defensive positioning of the working class and the commitment to gradual, constitutional reform within the Labour Party meant that industrial action was seen as an adjunct of the parliamentary struggle. It was more important when Labour was in opposition than when it was in government. The industrial struggles of the nineteenth century and early twentieth century had led to vital reforms and gains for the labour movement. Yet, the more gains the working class made, the more embedded it became within the *status quo*, acting as E. P. Thompson described it as 'partners' in the 'running of the machine'.[81] The labour movement was not just about the industrial wing – Bevan saw the parliamentary route as paramount in his quest for power. The interactions and tensions between the different sections of the labour movement would later lead to frustration on Bevan's part, but it was an important fact of Labour's economic and political strategy.

Foot suggested that Bevan stumbled on becoming a member of parliament (MP) in 1929 and that he could have easily attempted to rise through the ranks of the South Wales Miners' Federation.[82] Trade unions were a central part of Bevan's political life, and it is in the trade union movement that he first attempted to put theory into practice and obtain power for the working class through practical means. Even when Bevan had become an MP in 1929, he continued to argue for the importance of trade unions, although he felt that they should not get involved in politics and should supplement, not replace, political action,[83] even arguing that once capitalism was abolished 'trade unions would lose practically all their value ... Are we then to preserve capitalism in order to maintain the trade unions? Trade unions are weapons the worker forged in his war against an unjust society'.[84] The combination of the industrial and the political wings of the labour movement, and the tensions arising from this relationship, become clearer when Bevan's analysis of democracy is considered.

Democracy

POLITICAL LIBERTY

Bevan's advocacy for democracy is documented in this chapter because, although it lends itself to an analysis of political power, the third force – democracy – was fundamental to Bevan's vision of working-class strategy. Considering democracy in relation to working-class action provides a bridge between Bevan's economic analysis and his view of political power. Bevan's assessment of democracy's development in Britain demonstrated why he rejected the thesis that power resided at the point of production and was a significant deviation from orthodox Marxism. In the conflict between poverty and property, Bevan included democracy as an important force that could be used or destroyed. It can also be interpreted in the context of his understanding of the historical development of societies. As material forces developed in Britain, the masses agitated for reform, eventually leading to the enactment of universal franchise in 1929. In Bevan's analysis, the development of political liberty went hand in hand with the emancipation of the working class. As economic conditions changed, political freedom was won by the people:

> Freedom is the by-product of economic surplus. I speak here not of national independence, freedom to use one's own language, and religious liberty, although even these have often been involved in the economic struggles. I am speaking of the full panoply of political democracy which includes these liberties and others besides. It is wholly unhistorical to talk as though political liberty had no secular roots. Political liberty is the highest condition to which mankind has yet aspired, but it is a condition to which he has climbed from lowlier forms of society. It did not come because some great minds thought about it. It came because it was thought about at the time it was realisable.[85]

The development of political freedom was an important aspect of Bevan's analysis. It is not surprising that Bevan had great reverence for democracy, considering his activities in Tredegar and his understanding of British history. The syllabus for the Central Labour College included a 'Course of Lectures on the History of Socialism in England' as well as other courses on British (or 'English') history.[86]

Bevan's reflections on the strikes that took place during the inter-war years are useful in explaining his understanding of democracy. He attributed the failure of the 1919 Triple Alliance and the 1926 General Strike to the reverence towards democracy existing in Britain:

> It was not so much the coercive power of the state that restrained the full use of the workers' industrial power. That is a typical error of the undeveloped Marxist school. The incident I have described illustrates that. The workers and their leaders paused even when their coercive power was greater than that of the state. *The explanation must be sought in the subjective attitude of the people to the existence of the franchise and all that flows from it. The opportunity for power is not enough if the will to seize it is absent, and that will is attendant upon the traditional attitude of the people towards*

> *the political institutions that form part of their historical heritage.*[87] (emphasis added)

Bevan wrote that 'Even as a very young man, when I was studying Marxism, I was deeply conscious of the failure to take account of what, for want of a better phrase, I call the subjective attitude of the people' (p. 21). The 'subjective attitude of the people' towards Parliament was a central component of the psyche of British citizens and was a cause of industrial action's failure. Bevan's statement that the miners' leaders paused when they sought to obtain power was an acknowledgement of the importance of democracy in understanding the development of British society.

Bevan proclaimed that 'Political democracy brings the welfare of ordinary men and women on to the agenda of political discussion and demands its consideration' (p. 5). Democracy could give people a voice and provide the liberty to live life in the knowledge that political representatives were listening to the demands of the people. Bevan wrote that 'Political liberty is the highest condition to which mankind has yet aspired' (p. 40). He stated that political democracy 'in a society based on private property, is an instrument which exposes the rich to the attack of the poor'.[88] By utilising political liberty, the people had the opportunity to challenge the ruling class.

Bevan saw the development of democracy as being in direct conflict with the interests of the ruling class and of private enterprise. In response to democracy's attack on the rich, the rich reply 'by depriving the poor of their democratic rights'.[89] As democracy involved 'the assertion of the common against the special interest',[90] it posed a threat to the ruling class. Bevan wrote that the Conservatives 'have doubts about the virtues of democracy. Their conception of a sound democracy is one which is prepared to make whatever sacrifices are necessary for the preservation of the institution of private property'. He even suspected during the 1930s that the Conservatives began to 'look longingly at Fascist States, which do not have to bother about what the people think or want'.[91] Bevan warned that the ruling class would attempt to restrict democracy as much as possible.

MARXIST REVISIONISM

Bevan's conception of democracy represented a deviation from the Marxism that he had studied during his time at the Central Labour College.

Although Craik, as noted above, maintained that Bevan argued for the merits of direct over parliamentary action during his time there, Bevan's analysis of the *Communist Manifesto* also included an insistence that the manifesto's tactics needed to be adapted to contemporary conditions. Bevan maintained that the *Communist Manifesto* was tactically valueless as 'tactics must always be sought in the conditions immediately at hand',[92] insisting that 'we should be misunderstanding the spirit of its authors if we attempted for one moment to give its findings the rigidity of a dogma or to make it anything like a touchstone for all time' (p. 21). He assessed the *Manifesto* in the light of events that had transpired since it was written and argued that 'time has ... rendered obsolete the tactical proposals' that appear at the end of section two (p. 20). Although Bevan did not specifically refer to democracy in the review, it hints at an early acknowledgement of the need to adapt political tactics to contemporary conditions.

Those contemporary conditions also meant appreciating social and political context. Bevan claimed that traditional Marxist theory had not fully appreciated the importance of political democracy in achieving change for the working class. He wrote that:

> Quite early in my studies it seemed to me that classic Marxism consistently understated the role of a political democracy with a fully developed franchise. This is the case, both subjectively, as it affects the attitude of the worker to his political responsibilities; and objectively, as it affects the possibilities of his attaining power by using the franchise and parliamentary methods ... This is especially the case in a country with a fully matured parliamentary democracy like Great Britain.[93]

Bevan recognised that the likes of Marx, Engels and Lenin had analysed parliamentary democracy to some degree, but he argued that they 'never developed this feature of their philosophy to anything like the extent of the rest [of their philosophy]' (p. 19). This understanding of democracy echoes that of Eduard Bernstein, the German philosopher who engaged in a substantial revision of Marxism. Bernstein rejected the theory of the inevitable collapse of capitalism and the materialist conception of history.[94] Instead, Bernstein stressed the importance and potential of democracy. According to Christopher Pierson, Bernstein 'insisted that the expansion of democracy and the broadening of political rights, through both their concession and their subsequent usage, made possible, and were indeed effecting, a gradual alteration in the nature of society' (p. 33). Bevan certainly shared this outlook on the potential of democracy, if not the rejection of the materialist conception of history.

Bevan saw democracy as a relatively new phenomenon as it was 'only with the beginning of the 20th century that ordinary folk emerged from the darkness of despotism into the light of freedom, and began to consciously shape the governments of the world'. In that short time, mankind had:

> made more progress in the sciences, in the arts, in literature, than was made in the ten thousand years that preceded it. So far from democracy having failed mankind, it lifted man higher and quicker than any other lever which has suggested itself to the brain of man.[95]

Bevan maintained that political democracy was a direct consequence of the build-up of economic surplus, an interpretation of democracy that is described further when Bevan's attitude towards the developing world is considered in Chapter 3.

Bevan pointed to the Soviet Union as an example of how political liberty would develop as a result of technological and industrial advances. For example, he contended that the Soviet worker supported the regime due to the 'knowledge that all around him the framework of a modern industrial community is being built, that he is helping to build it, and that in the meantime his life is substantially, if slowly, improving'.[96] Nevertheless, in a House of Commons debate in 1951, Bevan argued that the Soviet Union was slow to recognise the revolutionary power of democracy:

> Soviet thinking has not adjusted itself to the fact that the most revolutionary power in the world is political democracy. She has not adjusted herself to the fact that progress can only be made in modern complicated industrial civilisation on the basis of peace ... It has always been assumed that Soviet Marxism would gain its first and easiest victories in the heavily industrialised nations. That was always the assumption. It was because the theory of Marxism was born in Brussels, London, Paris, and New York and not in the agrarian areas. As a consequence of that, she expected to find

> easy allies. But I am convinced, as I have said before, that the only kind of political system which is consistent with a modern artisan population is political representative democracy.[97]

The aims of achieving class empowerment and the transcendence of socialism over capitalism required the development of political liberty.

DEMOCRACY AND THE RULING CLASS

Bevan insisted that major concessions were yielded by the ruling class only after popular agitation against it. He argued that the institutions of property had always tried to fight back against agitation from the labour movement, but slowly had to concede to public opinion. Bevan interpreted the art of democracy in Britain as the ruling class making concessions but being clever about how much it gave:

> The political representatives of property were always engaged in nicely balanced calculations as to how far they dare resist the pressure of public opinion and as to how little they need to give in order to buy it off. This delicate and complicated task is the art of ruling-class government in a political democracy. The British ruling class have always won the admiration of their fellows throughout the world by the skill with which they do it.[98]

Bevan warned, however, that the ruling class would reverse these concessions if it was threatened by democracy. He predicted that in such a situation, the 'historical process is reversed. Instead of the people improving their position at the expense of property, property takes the offensive and improves its position at the expense of the people and of the democratic tradition' (p. 11).

Bevan recognised that the development of democracy had not been a peaceful process. He wrote that the 'record of the Industrial Revolution in Britain ... is a record of bloodshed, misery, oppression, accompanied by a century and a half of social dislocation'. He argued that if 'liberty was the foundation of society and not its highest expression, it would be as old as the human race', but this had not been the case. 'Poverty and liberty', Bevan wrote in 1955, 'have always been uneasy bedfellows. It is not a coincidence that the history of mankind, for thousands of years, was the story of poverty joined to tyranny'.[99] The development of democracy, therefore, was not a natural condition, but one that had to be fought for in the face of the ruling class. When reflecting on the development of democracy in Britain, Bevan's elaboration on the material conception of history can again be identified.

Bevan saw that the onset of democracy in Britain carried great potential for changing society. Whereas previously the workers had few means of articulating their grievances beyond strikes and demonstrations, Bevan argued that democracy put 'a new power in the possession of ordinary men and women'.[100] Through the Labour Party the masses in society could have their voices heard and be represented by a party fighting for their interests against the ruling class. Although not completely rejecting the role of trade union activity, Bevan's political thought emphasised the importance of political power and democracy. In Britain, Parliament was the institution that could express the concerns of the working class and Bevan saw it as an important location of class struggle. The role of Parliament is analysed in the next chapter.

Conclusion

Bevan's analysis of society was inspired by a Marxist understanding of the nature of capitalism and class conflict. For him, society was an arena of conflicting social forces, and these were organised around the forces of poverty and property, roughly representing the proletariat and the bourgeoisie respectively. Class and property relations were central to understanding the dynamics of capitalism and the domination of wealth over the vast majority of society. Bevan's analysis of class conflict and the concentration of property did not differ significantly from his reading of the *Communist Manifesto*; Bevan owed a large debt to it. His engagement with Marxism informed and made clear his experiences of south Wales in the inter-war years.

Bevan's analysis of the historical development of society explained to him how it had reached the position where private property and private enterprise were dominant. Bevan argued that as society developed, property became more and more concentrated in the hands of a wealthy few, leading to the accumulation of capital and the development of productive forces. This does not depart from Marx and Engels' elaboration of class conflict outlined in the *Communist Manifesto*. It also does not depart from the materialist conception of history, which Bevan praised. The next step in this development, however, represented a deviation from this theory. Rather than arguing for the complete abolition of private property, Bevan argued instead for a reversal in property relations. He argued for public property to be dominant and for the economy to be run in the interests of the masses in society, allowing, however, for private property to still exist.

Bevan's strategy to achieve power, his praxis, also represented a significant revision to orthodox Marxism. Rejecting the thesis that power was at the point of production, Bevan saw the development of democracy in Britain as a significant factor in shaping the strategy of the working class. Political institutions existed in Britain through which the working class could have their voices heard. The political wing of the labour movement, the Labour Party, was an important vehicle in achieving power for the working class. Thus, political power, as we will see in the next chapter, could be used to alter the economic base.

It was established in the Introduction that Bevan's Marxism is the subject of discussion in the biographies and in the literature on Labour Party political thought. Foot, Campbell, Foote and others emphasised the centrality of Marxism to Bevan's politics, while Marquand and Spalding disagreed, claiming that to understand Bevan he must be seen as a parliamentarian. The analysis in this chapter supports the arguments of the former. Although it included revisions and deviations, as we will explore further in the next chapter, Bevan's analysis of economic power reveals an approach that is heavily influenced, particularly in the language deployed, by a Marxist analysis of capitalism and class. It is also evident, despite contrary claims in the literature, that Bevan's emphasis on property relations remained consistent throughout his career. Further, the analysis has highlighted Bevan's interpretation of the materialist conception of history and its importance to his political thought. Nonetheless, before firm conclusions can be arrived at, further analysis of the many features in Bevan's thought must be undertaken.

We have also seen the tensions that existed between Bevan's analysis and the ideology of labourism. Labour's economic thought owed more to theorists such as Hodgskin and Hobson rather than Marx, while Labour intellectuals were not as radical as Bevan in calling for the serious upheaval of property relations. More radical interpretations of economic power were rejected within the Labour Party, the dominant approach being to work within the existing economic and political system.

Andrew Thorpe asserted that socialism was ultimately not a priority for the Labour Party, that it had never been concerned with how to fundamentally create a socialist society in a utopian sense. He wrote that it was mainly revisionist throughout its history and that the Left have never been able to fully convince the leadership, or the public, of their arguments. Socialism though has been used as a 'unifying myth' that has helped the party sustain a unified sense of purpose in its strategy. In government, Thorpe wrote, the record of the Labour Party had been mixed, concerning itself more with economic management, although he did reserve special praise for the NHS. Thorpe argued that as the Labour Party was founded by the trade unions, it was initially set-up as a defensive party to protect the workers, not to seize power. Although this limited the scope for radical change, it helped foster a sense of solidarity within the party. It also helped Labour embody values of community and comradeship.[101] While this comradery would become important to the Labour movement, critics of the party have insisted that its defensive attitude – to protect and preserve the interests of organised labour rather than to seek radical change – was a debilitating element of it.

Bevan's economic theory was not defensive; it emphasised the importance of radically shifting economic power. This is demonstrated by Bevan's writing that trade unions would not be necessary in a socialist society, as they served to preserve existing economic relations. While taking into account Bevan's championing of parliamentary institutions, detailed further in the next chapter, Labour's lack of revolutionary spirit was opposed to Bevan's more radical perspective when it came to the economy and society.

Still, Bevan's championing of British liberal democratic institutions allowed him to comfortably adapt his economic thought to labourist traditions. Bevan made significant revisions to his understanding of Marxism, most notably his conception of democracy and parliamentary politics. The third force, 'democracy', is an important addition to Bevan's analysis of the social forces in conflict with each other in society. There were others who shared similar a similar vision, but Bevan's Marxism appeared as distinctive among labourist thinkers. As Foote noted, for an ideological faction to have any success within the Labour Party, it needed to adapt itself to the principles of labourism.[102] However, while intellectual tension still remained, Bevan did attempt this reconciliation, as the next chapter demonstrates. To understand Bevan's views on the relationship between politics and class conflict, capitalism and the ruling class, trade union politics and his arguments to reverse the dominance of property over poverty, his conception of political power needs to be analysed. The following chapter highlights the continuing relevance of Bevan's economic analysis to the role of democracy and Parliament in his political thought, as well as the tensions within it.

NOTES

1 Bevan, *In Place of Fear*, p. 2.
2 Campbell, *Nye Bevan and the Mirage of British Socialism*, pp. 264–5; Demont, 'Tredegar and Aneurin Bevan', p. 182; Foot, *Aneurin Bevan: 1897–1945*, p. 82; Smith, *Aneurin Bevan and the World of South Wales*, p. 192; Thomas-Symonds, *Nye*, p. 20.
3 HC Deb, 15 February 1951, vol. 484, col. 733.
4 Bevan, *In Place of Fear*, p. 17.
5 John Saville, *The Labour Movement in Britain: A Commentary* (London: Faber and Faber, 1988), p. 6.
6 Bevan, *In Place of Fear*, p. 76.
7 Aneurin Bevan, *Why Not Trust the Tories?* (London: Victor Gollancz, 1944), p. 76.
8 M.P., 'Why Mr Ernest Brown infuriates opposition and Tory members alike', *Tribune* (9 April 1937), p. 5.
9 Thomas-Symonds, *Nye*, p. 250.
10 Bevan, *In Place of Fear*, p. 17–18.
11 Jack London, *The Iron Heel* (Marston Gate: Amazon, 1908), pp. 41–2.
12 M.P., 'Softening soap for workers and convicts', *Tribune* (18 June 1937), p. 6.
13 Bevan, *Why Not Trust the Tories?*, p. 56.
14 Aneurin Bevan, 'Tory gamblers pour £1,500 million down the drain', *Tribune* (7 November 1958), p. 1.
15 Karl Marx and Frederick Engels, 'Manifesto of the Communist Party', in *Marx/Engels Selected Works* (Moscow: Progress Publishers, 1969), p. 22.
16 Palonen, 'Political Theorizing as a Dimension of Political Life', p. 359.
17 Smith, *Aneurin Bevan and the World of South Wales*, p. 203; Thomas-Symonds, *Nye*, p. 33.

18 Campbell, *Nye Bevan and the Mirage of British Socialism*, p. xiii.

19 Foot, *Aneurin Bevan: 1945–1960*, p. 17.

20 Thomas-Symonds, *Nye*, pp. 24–6.

21 Stuart Macintyre, *A Proletarian Science: Marxism in Britain, 1917–1933* (London: Lawrence and Wishart, 1986), p. 130.

22 Smith, *Aneurin Bevan and the World of South Wales*, p. 203.

23 Aneurin Bevan, 'Socialist Classics: The Communist Manifesto', *The Plebs*, 13/1 (1921), 20.

24 Bevan, *In Place of Fear*, p. 1.

25 HC Deb, 4 December 1933, vol. 283, col. 1318–1319.

26 Bevan, *Why Not Trust the Tories?*, pp. 88–9.

27 Bevan, *In Place of Fear*, p. 2.

28 Gerry Healy, 'The Way to Socialism: A Full Analysis of Bevan's New Book', *Labour Review*, 1/2 (1952), 2, *www.marxists.org/history/etol/newspape/lr/vol01/v01n02-may-aug-1952-lr.pdf* (accessed 5 January 2024).

29 Foot, *Aneurin Bevan: 1945–1960*, p. 20.

30 David McLellan, *The Thought of Karl Marx: An Introduction* (London: Macmillan, 1971), p. 151.

31 Marx and Engels, 'Manifesto of the Communist Party', p. 15.

32 McLellan, *The Thought of Karl Marx*, p. 152; Karl Marx, *Capital: A Critique of Political Economy*, vol. 3 (New York: International Publishers, 1959), p. 633, *www.marxists.org/archive/marx/works/download/pdf/Capital-Volume-III.pdf* (accessed 5 January 2024).

33 Bevan, *In Place of Fear*, p. 3.

34 Campbell, *Nye Bevan and the Mirage of British Socialism*, pp. 4–5.

35 Demont, 'Tredegar and Aneurin Bevan'.

36 Bevan, *In Place of Fear*, p. 17.

37 S. O. Davies cited in Robert Griffiths, *S. O. Davies: A Socialist Faith* (Llandysul, Dyfed: Gomer Press, 1983), p. 51.

38 Foote, *The Labour Party's Political Thought*, p. 9.

39 Mark Wickham-Jones, 'An Exceptional Comrade? The Nairn-Anderson Interpretation', in John Callaghan, Steven Fielding and Steve Ludlam (eds), *Interpreting the Labour Party: Approaches to Labour Politics and History* (Manchester: Manchester University Press, 2003), p. 88.

40 Wickham-Jones, 'An Exceptional Comrade?', p. 90–1.

41 Alastair J. Reid, 'Class and Politics in the Work of Henry Pelling', in John Callaghan, Steven Fielding and Steve Ludlam (eds), *Interpreting the Labour Party:*

Approaches to Labour Politics and History (Manchester: Manchester University Press, 2003), pp. 102–3.

42 Reid, 'Class and Politics in the Work of Henry Pelling', p. 105.

43 Foote, *The Labour Party's Political Thought*, p. 20.

44 Bevan, 'Socialist Classics', p. 20.

45 William W. Craik, *The Central Labour College: A Chapter in the History of Adult Working-Class Education 1909–29* (London: Lawrence & Wishart, 1964), p. 169.

46 Bevan, *In Place of Fear*, p. 34.

47 Bevan, 'Socialist Classics', p. 20.

48 Aneurin Bevan, 'Are miners different?', *Tribune* (17 March 1944), p. 7.

49 Bevan, *In Place of Fear*, p. 37.

50 Campbell, *Nye Bevan and the Mirage of British Socialism*, p. 346.

51 Marx and Engels, 'Manifesto of the Communist Party', p. 23.

52 Bevan, *In Place of Fear*, p. 118.

53 Aneurin Bevan, 'Private enterprise vs public ownership: the moon and the £', *Tribune* (9 January 1959), p. 5.

54 Bevan, 'Tory gamblers pour £1,500 million down the drain', p. 1.

55 Aneurin Bevan, 'The decline of capitalism', *Tribune* (30 January 1959), p. 9.

56 David Howell, *British Social Democracy: A Study in Development and Decay* (London: Croom Helm, 1976), p. 27.

57 David Edgerton, *The Rise and Fall of the British Nation: A Twentieth-Century History* (Milton Keynes: Penguin Books, 2019), p. 9.

58 Coates, *The Labour Party and the Struggle for Socialism*, pp. 20–1.

59 Thompson, *The Long Death of British Labourism*, p. 7.

60 Foote, *The Labour Party's Political Thought*.

61 Karl Marx, 'Theses on Feuerbach', in David Wootton (ed.), *Modern Political Thought: Readings from Machiavelli to Nietzsche* (Indianapolis IN: Hackett Publishing, 1996), p. 15.

62 Gajo Petrović, 'Praxis', in Tom Bottomore (ed.), *A Dictionary of Marxist Thought* (Oxford: Blackwell, 1983), p. 384.

63 Bevan, *In Place of Fear*, p. 96.

64 Bevan, 'Socialist Classics', p. 20.

65 Unofficial Reform Committee, *The Miners' Next Step*, (1991), p. 28.

66 Bevan, *In Place of Fear*, p. 19.

67 Craik, *The Central Labour College*, p. 124.

68 Hywel Francis and Dai Smith, *The Fed: A History of the South Wales Miners in the Twentieth Century* (London: Lawrence and Wishart, 1980), p. 14.
69 Bevan, *In Place of Fear*, p. 19–20.
70 Campbell, *Nye Bevan and the Mirage of British Socialism*, p. 18; Thomas-Symonds, *Nye*, p. 23.
71 Demont, 'Tredegar and Aneurin Bevan', p. 193.
72 Thomas-Symonds, *Nye*, p. 25.
73 Demont, 'Tredegar and Aneurin Bevan', p. 197–8.
74 Bevan, *In Place of Fear*, p. 21.
75 Demont, 'Tredegar and Aneurin Bevan', p. 330.
76 Thomas-Symonds, *Nye*, chapters 3 and 4.
77 Demont, 'Tredegar and Aneurin Bevan', p. 249.
78 Smith, *Aneurin Bevan and the World of South Wales*, pp. 201–2.
79 Geoff Allen, 'Labour and Strike-Breaking 1945–1951', *International Socialism*, 2/24 (1984), *www.marxists.org/history/etol/newspape/isj2/1984/isj2-024/ellen.html* (accessed 5 January 2024).
80 Aneurin Bevan, 'A declaration of class war', *Tribune* (22 March 1957), p. 4.
81 E. P. Thompson cited in Coates, *The Labour Party and the Struggle for Socialism*, p. 7.
82 Foot, *Aneurin Bevan: 1897–1945*, p. 95.
83 Aneurin Bevan, 'Big Wage Problem Faces the T.U.C', *Tribune* (12 August 1938), p. 3.
84 Editorial, 'The people versus the prudential', *Tribune* (30 October 1942), p. 2.
85 Bevan, *In Place of Fear*, pp. 39–40.
86 Craik, *The Central Labour College*, pp. 169–71.
87 Bevan, *In Place of Fear*, p. 21.
88 Aneurin Bevan, 'Rubber stamp M.P.'s', *Tribune* (20 August 1943), p. 11.
89 M.P., 'Storm meets Baldwin's efforts to save democracy for the rich', *Tribune* (12 March 1937), p. 7.
90 Aneurin Bevan, 'How the landworker pays for the experts', *Tribune* (13 May 1938), p. 7.
91 Aneurin Bevan, 'Premier's future depends on Rome', *Tribune* (16 December 1938), p. 4.
92 Bevan, 'Socialist Classics', p. 20.
93 Bevan, *In Place of Fear*, p. 19.

94 Christopher Pierson, *Marxist Theory and Democratic Politics* (Oxford: Polity Press, 1986), p. 32.
95 Aneurin Bevan, 'Hope and new strength', *Tribune* (2 May 1941), p. 12.
96 Bevan, *In Place of Fear*, p. 139.
97 HC Deb, 15 February 1951.
98 Aneurin Bevan, 'Make the government act!', *Tribune* (17 March 1939), pp. 10–11.
99 Aneurin Bevan, 'Give China the help she needs', *Tribune* (26 August 1955), p. 4.
100 Bevan, *In Place of Fear*, p. 3.
101 Andrew Thorpe, *A History of the British Labour Party* (Basingstoke: Macmillan, 1997), p. 234.
102 Foote, *The Labour Party's Political Thought*, p. 12.

2

PARLIAMENT, THE STATE, PUBLIC OWNERSHIP

We weren't born with liberty, we had to win it![1]

Bevan's entire parliamentary career was geared towards obtaining political power through the Labour Party. The failure of the trade union movement during the industrial conflicts of the inter-war years led him to develop a theory of political power that, he argued, had historically been ignored by Marxists. He understood that the political power of capitalism was so strong that it was an impediment to the workers. The ruling class were not only in possession of private property and the wealth that stemmed from it, but also controlled Britain's political institutions. Therefore, Bevan stressed the importance of the political road to power.

This chapter highlights the significance of democratic institutions in Bevan's political thought. It begins by analysing his stress on the role of Parliament as the instrument through which democracy is given form. It then outlines how Bevan envisioned the use of political power to transform the economic base of society through nationalisation. Finally, the chapter explores Bevan's vision for a mixed economy as a result of the changing relationship between private and public property. This chapter continues to further explore Bevan's deviations from Marxism to document his reverence for liberal democratic political institutions, although it is demonstrated that his economic analysis was central to his conception of political power. At the same time, it considers the prevailing attitude within the Labour Party towards the use of parliamentary institutions. Following from the discussion in Chapter 1 on Labour's approach to the economy, the present analysis demonstrates that Bevan's political thought shares many assumptions of labourist ideology, but diverged in his consideration of the power and purpose of public ownership in changing the economic conditions of society.

Parliament

PARLIAMENT AS A WEAPON

The Labour Party has always been committed to electoral politics, a commitment that was critical to the social democratic perspective of the party.[2] Labour intellectuals and politicians emphasised the uniqueness of the British socialist project, transforming society on socialist lines but through traditional British institutions.[3] Labour's 'dogmatic' commitment to parliamentarianism forms the main thrust of the New Left critique, as it incorporated the party firmly within the British parliamentary system.[4] While these writers have criticised a commitment to parliamentarianism as abandoning the class struggle, the Labour Party's advocacy of gradual reform has been consistent and unwavering.

Bevan argued that Parliament could be used as a weapon in the struggle against capitalism. Reflecting on his early engagement with Marxism, Bevan concluded that orthodox Marxist theory misunderstood the contemporary importance of the state in the development of society. He wrote that the 'classic principles of Marxism were developed when political democracy was as yet in its infancy. The State was a naked instrument of coercion'. Widespread mass inequality may have existed previously, but progress was won by the masses due to sympathy, fear of unrest and the need to educate people in 'the techniques of modern production methods'. Bevan noted that before the onset of mass democracy, the initiative for change always came from the top because the lower stratum of society was politically inarticulate: 'Progress lacked the thrust which comes from the people when they are furnished with all the institutions of a fully developed political democracy.' The only inevitable outcome of such a situation was the 'theory of the class struggle and the conception of the State, as the executive instrument of the ruling class'. Bevan argued that in such a situation, where 'political freedom' did not exist, the only change would come from social revolution and civil war.[5] Bevan did not agree, however, that the state was inevitably an instrument of the ruling class. The extension of the franchise gave it a potentially powerful character. As noted in Chapter 1, the primacy of democracy in Bevan's thought was an important deviation from the classical Marxist analysis of historical development.

Bevan conceived of Parliament as being 'a weapon, and the most formidable weapon of all, in the struggle'. In Parliament, 'from the outset [the Socialist] asserts the efficacy of State action and of collective policies ... The Socialist dare not invoke the authority of Parliament in meeting economic difficulties unless he is prepared to exhaust its possibilities' (p. 32). Bevan believed that the British Parliament's unwritten constitution meant that it possessed a 'revolutionary quality, and enables us to entertain the hope of bringing about social transformations, without the agony and prolonged crises experienced by less fortunate nations' (p. 100). If socialists were willing to use Parliament effectively then it had the potential to transform society.

We saw in Chapter 1 how, according to Bevan, the ruling class was frightened of democracy and its consequences. Therefore, while Parliament was a weapon for the working class, it was also a weapon for the bourgeoisie. Bevan did not see British Parliament as an inherently benevolent system for changing people's lives, particularly during periods when it was dominated by the Conservative Party. He agitated regularly against what he saw as the class privilege historically emanating from the institution. In 1944 when the expectations of the people were being built up for 'a fundamental and equitable reconstruction of society' after the Second World War, Bevan suspected that the Conservatives were wondering 'how to ride the crisis, how to lie, deceive, cajole and buy time so as once more to snatch a reprieve for wealth and privilege'.[6] Bevan's 1944 book *Why Not Trust the Tories?* clearly demonstrated his view that the Conservative Party's role in Parliament was to keep the ruling class in power. He wrote at length on the ways in which the Conservatives delayed and prevented policies for post-war reconstruction and attempted to preserve the old way of life.

Bevan interpreted the function of the Conservatives in Parliament as being to preserve the institution of private property and 'to protect the profit maker' (p. 51) as the party was 'the politically organised body of the most powerful vested interests in the British Empire'.[7] A *Tribune* editorial in 1943 declared that the aim of the 1922 Committee, the Conservative parliamentary group, was the defence of private property. The Committee would look upon a bill and declare, 'What has been gained if we win the whole world and lose our profits?'[8] Bevan argued that whenever the budget was formulated by the Conservatives, because it affected the 'financial well-being of the richer members of the community, and as they are the most articulate and influential class in society, the things that concern them are regarded as of vital importance'.[9] Parliament was certainly not immune from vested interest.

Particularly during the Second World War and during the period of the National Government, Bevan argued that 'The resistance of vested interests appears to be stronger than the voice of the people. There is a conflict between what the people desire and what the Government is doing'.[10] Whereas Labour regarded 'the House of Commons as a lever to improve the condition of the people', the Conservative Party saw it as 'a means to safeguard the welfare of capital'.[11] Conservatives would 'fight to the bitter end for the right of property to exploit the needs of the people'.[12] Bevan saw Parliament as 'a conflict between power groups'[13] and a 'conflict of interest'.[14] He suggested that the dominance of the capitalist class in Parliament reflected the dominance of private property in capitalist property relations. The economic base was informing the political superstructure.

Years after the reforms of the 1945–51 Labour government, Bevan accused the Conservatives of attempting to remove the benefits achieved. He accused the Conservative Party of launching 'a carefully prepared attack on the structure of the Welfare State, and upon those principles which Labour fondly imagined had been irresistibly built into the fabric of British society'.[15] He still suspected the ruling class of using the Conservative Party as a vehicle to preserve its own interests: 'In a political democracy, theirs [the Tories'] is the task of holding on to power and to privilege with the consent of popular opinion.'[16] He argued that the ruling class would not be satisfied with retaining post-war changes.

Bevan insisted that the struggle between poverty and property could be waged by the Labour Party using Parliament as a weapon. He argued that 'The British constitution, with its adult suffrage, exposes all rights and privileges, properties and powers, to the popular will'. As well as setting out his analysis in terms of poverty, property and democracy, he also wrote of 'two sets of forces' striving for ascendancy in human affairs: 'There is the collective will as expressed in representative institutions ... [and] the will of authority expressed through a variety of other organised groups.'[17] This phrase refers to the battle taking place between poverty and property in capitalist society. Bevan argued that representative institutions should express the collective will of the people and challenge property. He wrote that the 'first function of representative government is advocacy. The people must know that their representatives are alive to their needs and are pressing them on the attention of the State. To suffer is bad. To suffer in loneliness is death'. He asserted that 'Discussion of vital questions in Parliament breaks through the loneliness which always threatens to engulf the individual in modern great communities'.[18] Although he looked upon a Parliament dominated by the Conservative Party as a means for the preservation of private property, Bevan stated that the Labour Party had the ability to change the way Parliament operated so that it represented the people. The link between Parliament and the people can be summed up in the following quote from *Tribune* in 1937: 'It is almost impossible for a party to be a good fighting opposition in Parliament unless it is constantly stimulated and egged on by a roused and keen electorate. Members reflect in the Commons the mood they find in their constituencies.'[19] Parliament could act as a voice for the masses.

Parliament was a central forum for the struggle between poverty, property and democracy. In a 1938 article titled 'People versus Property', Bevan wrote of how 'the will of the people' would come up against the 'will of property' in Parliament. The role of Parliament was not that of a 'court of appeal in the struggle between the sectional and the general interest or between Property and the People, which is endemic in capitalist society'; rather it is 'one of the weapons of the general interest – the people'. Bevan argued that the 'more effectively Parliament asserts the general against the sectional interest the more bitter grows the conflict between the People and Property'. This conflict would continue 'until the climax is reached' when 'either Parliament destroys the sectional interest, which is Socialism, or the sectional interest destroys Parliament, which is Fascism'. Bevan surmised that in a capitalist democracy political peace 'is therefore a time in which the forces of the sectional interests, of Property in short, are universally triumphant'. He continued that a 'Tory Government could not be expected to stand up to a vested interest because it is itself a weapon of the vested interest'. A Parliament dominated by the Conservatives was for Bevan:

> a Parliament dominated by property, and such a Parliament, so far from mobilising the forces of the people, disperses those forces and renders them impotent. For a Tory majority puts a megaphone in the mouth of Property and a gag in the mouth of the People.[20]

Therefore, to challenge the sectional interests of property, Parliament needed to be controlled by the 'democratic forces of the people':

> This, of course, can easily become an empty phrase. The test of its value is the right of the people to organise for political and industrial action, and the percolating of democracy and progress into all functions performed by the State: education, social services, health and the wider cultural and social problems.[21]

Ultimately, the only fundamental answer to the problems facing the country was that 'the power of the State to own and control must at all cost and with a completeness hitherto undreamt of be brought under the progressive control of the Labour Movement' (p. 2). Bevan granted the Labour Party a major role in Parliament. A role, as we shall see in later chapters, that he did not always find it to be performing.

Although some have questioned whether Bevan had always advocated political action, his faith in Parliament remained with him throughout his career. Successive election defeats from 1951 onwards did not shake his belief that the working class needed to strive for parliamentary power. He continued to defend Parliament as an institution even when it was under attack. For instance, in 1959 Bevan highlighted criticisms that had been levelled at Parliament. He took these criticisms seriously, as he maintained that Parliament was vital to the nation. He argued that the institution had the support of the nation, but the particular Parliament in 1959 did not. He reiterated his long-held belief that whenever Conservatives were in power, they simply adopted acceptable elements of their opponent's policies and gave the impression that they supported them. He contrasted this Parliament to the Parliament of 1945–51, a Parliament he claimed had engaged with the issues that affected the nation and inspired the people:

> Can anyone seriously say that the Parliament after the war was listless, uninspired and unfruitful? Of course not. The Parliament concerned itself with almost every aspect of national life. However controversial its measures, they ignited the imagination of the country, aroused and held political interest, and by so doing, grounded Parliament in the esteem of the British people.[22]

Any problems with the 1959 Parliament were the problems of the Conservative Party: 'In the last analysis – and this is no extenuation of the Opposition – the vitality or lack of vitality of Parliament is an expression of the vitality of the ruling party. Stabbing water is an unrewarding exercise' (p. 12). Bevan dismissed criticism of Parliament as an institution, instead laying any criticism of poor performance at the door of the government and the opposition.

Bevan insisted that to maintain a link to the people, Parliament needed to be continually refreshed as 'social institutions, like muscles, depend upon their use. If they are not used they become atrophied'.[23] He certainly did not look romantically on Parliament and did not appreciate the reverence for it as an historical institution: 'The future would probably be better and certainly easier to make if the past did not press so closely in upon us, and Parliament would be a more efficient workshop if it were not at the same time a great museum.'[24] Rather than preserving Parliament as it was, it needed to be adapted so that it could be used effectively and respond to the needs of society.

PARLIAMENT AND THE STATE

At first glance, it appears that Bevan's strategy for winning power was simply to obtain a Labour Party majority in Parliament and then use that majority to form a government and enact changes. A majority would give the Labour Party control of the state apparatus. Campbell certainly presented Bevan's strategy in this way, summarising his attitude as:

> All the Labour Party had to do – descending from theory to practice – was, first, to unite the working class so as to be able

> to translate the majority of the population in the country into a majority in the House of Commons; and, secondly, having once won a majority, to use it resolutely.[25]

The preceding discussion would also seem to point to this conclusion as Bevan emphasised the changes that could be enacted by a Labour majority. Labour Party politicians and intellectuals also seemed wedded to this notion of state power. Intellectuals from the Independent Labour Party to the Fabians saw the state as a neutral entity: all that was needed was for Labour to achieve a majority in Parliament and it could then use the state to enact its legislation in the interests of society.[26] The election of twenty-nine Labour MPs in 1900, followed by significant legislation such as the revoking of the Taff Vale judgement, gave justification to this strategy. This attitude of the state's neutrality became rooted in the Labour Party and among both the left and the right.[27]

However, there are signs that Bevan understood the limitations of this strategy. One article suggests that Bevan was not entirely confident that this approach would easily lead to obtaining power. In an extensive article in *Tribune* in 1938, Bevan critiqued what he argued was the prevailing socialist view of the role of state power:

> We have but to achieve a majority in Parliament, so the argument goes, in order to have at our disposal the whole machinery of the capitalist State, to use against our enemies as they have used it against us. From this standpoint the State looks very much like a gun which can be made to point in any direction at the will of the one who, at the moment, is in command of it ... If the courts are biased against the workers, if the police serve property, if the Civil Service is saturated by Conservative thought, if the armed forces of the Crown are officered by neo-fascists, if the Crown itself fertilises, by insidious channels, all the reactionary growths in society; all this, we are assured, will be transformed when the supreme centre of power the House of Commons is in the hands of representatives of the workers.[28]

Bevan argued that while this 'current coinage of Socialist thought in Britain' was naive, it had become so predominant that it was 'considered unwise to cast even a shadow of doubt upon it'. Nevertheless, he warned, 'doubt it we must, because I believe this point of view is a dangerous delusion'. Bevan did not view the state as an autonomous institution, separate from the class conflict in society or simply as an instrument that could be utilised by the majority in Parliament. He wrote that the state 'and the assumption of the supremacy of the "will of the people", upon which it rests, are not immune from the issues of the economic and political struggles of the day'. In fact, he argued that the state was heavily involved in these struggles. He prophesised that 'as the struggle grows keener, crevices appear in the formerly solid facade of the State structure, until it breaks and finally melts away in the heat generated by contending social forces'. Bevan predicted that 'One of the ways in which the cleavage in the structure of the British capitalist State may show itself is in the antagonism between the House of Lords and the Commons, which is latent in the relations between the two institutions' (p. 7). Bevan argued that the existence of the House of Lords challenged 'the fundamental assumption upon which certain people approach the possibility of a steady and even Socialist progress', the fundamental assumption being that 'the will of the people is supreme in the British Constitution'. Bevan understood that the common justification for the Lords was that the immunity from being voted in by the people was its 'chief virtue'. He gave the example of the Amendments to the Coal Bill, which the Commons had been discussing in 1938, as evidence of the Lords' true function. He claimed that the 'vulgar self-interest' of the Lords meant that its members carried amendments 'which were designed to better themselves. They behaved more like highwaymen than legislaters [*sic*]'. Discussing the opposition between the Commons and the Lords, Bevan wrote that the 'principle of election in the Commons protects the people from pillage by the aristocratic Lords'. He maintained that the 'rapacity of property must always disguise itself before it can win the support of the people'. However, when the 'mask wears thin ... then the authoritarian principle, which is latent in the British Constitution and enshrined in the Lords, will be invoked to set aside the people's will as expressed in the vote'. 'Thus', Bevan concluded, 'the Constitution itself becomes an issue in the struggle for the control of the Constitution' (p. 7).

This article is an interesting instance of Bevan considering the role of the state as being part of the economic struggle of society, foreshadowing debates on the 'relative autonomy' of the state that were a feature of the writings of theorists such as Ralph Miliband and Nicos Poulantzas.[29] In the article, Bevan concluded that the state's autonomy was limited by the class struggle that was being waged in society. He did not view the state simply as an autonomous institution but as an institution with a more complicated relationship with the economic base. Ultimately though, Bevan's analysis did not go into significant detail on the role of the different elements of the state. Instead, it focused primarily on differences between the House of Commons and the House of Lords. Bevan did not go into further detail about the role of the civil service, the police or other institutions, for example. As with the Labour Party more broadly, a serious critique of the civil service and its role was not undertaken by Bevan.[30] Nevertheless, this article still demonstrates the importance Bevan placed on the economic conditions of society in shaping the role of the state.

There is further evidence of Bevan's more critical analysis of state power and its relationship with private enterprise six years later in 1944. Discussing the Trades Union Congress' (TUC) report on post-war reconstruction, Bevan criticised its recommendation to create industrial boards for industries left in private hands, which would include collaboration between trade unions and the employers' federations of the relevant industry. He argued that the unions would be forced to accept decisions arrived at by the board at the expense of their members, leading to the creation of a 'Fascist Labour Front'. Bevan predicted that collective organisation of private industry would lead to the development of fascism. He wrote:

> When private interests organise themselves in the fashion recommended by the T.U.C. Report they take over the apparatus of the State itself. The result is not control of industry by the State. It is the control and domination of the State by private interests, disciplined and organised by the necessities and technical requirements of modern industrial society.[31]

Bevan argued that when the economy consisted of competition between small-scale enterprises, the 'conflicting interests of different groups of capitalists left a considerable degree of freedom of action by the Government'. He wrote that the state 'could be, and was, manipulated by the capitalist class as a whole where and when its general interest was involved as in conflicts with the working class and in waging war'. Nonetheless, he continued, 'a particular section of capitalists found it difficult to use the State apparatus in its own narrow interests without coming into conflict with other sections of capitalists'. This situation, he argued, 'led many people to the superficial conclusion that the State was above the battle, and able to intervene without regard to what the Americans describe as pressure-groups' (p. 7). He pronounced this view of the state, however, as a 'delusion', criticising the report for making a fundamental error:

> Indeed, its error is even more crass. It appears to think it can facilitate the creation of collective capitalist industrial organisations and yet preserve the power of the State machine to impose concern for the public welfare upon them. In addition to that it imagines it can identify the workers' organisations with this new capitalist collectivity without affecting the 'purity' of the State machine. Where, in these circumstances, do they think the Government is going to derive its power and authority to impose the public will – assuming one can be created in such circumstances? (p. 7)

Bevan criticised what he saw as 'the theory of the immaculate conception of the State'. When private enterprise was effectively organised, the state could not play the role of a neutral arbiter. The result, Bevan concluded:

> is democratic indigestion, which becomes chronic at a time of economic difficulty – as in Germany – and it finds the institutions of democracy too debilitated to put up an effective defence of itself when Fascist elements carry the logic of the situation to the point of liquidating the then moribund State apparatus. (p. 7)

Bevan argued that the conclusion the report should have reached was this:

> When collective industrial organisation is the only means by which the technical resources of industry can be properly utilised then the point has come for the socialisation of the industries concerned. It is not the democratic State apparatus which becomes redundant in those circumstances, but rather the private ownership of industry. The T.U.C. proposals attempt to place the benefits of collective

> organisation at the disposal of discredited private ownership. That is the very essence of the Corporate State. (p. 7)

This reiterated Bevan's argument from 1938 that the state was not a neutral arbiter and reinforced his belief that the state needed to directly change property relations.

Although he saw challenges to the effectiveness of the state, Bevan was still insisting in the 1950s that there were no constitutional limits to socialism in Britain. He declared that 'the will of the House of Commons is supreme'. He again reiterated that the House of Lords was a potential barrier to implementing socialism, writing that there was no need to seek 'second thoughts' when enacting policy as this 'usually conceals a wish for a second wind for the vested interests opposed to the legislation in question'. Nonetheless, he determined that the unwritten nature of the British constitution was favourable to the development of socialism. He concluded that: 'we cannot say that we have inherited a constitution that bars the approach to Socialism. But, of course, this is assuming that Socialists do not raise barriers in their own spirit, that we pursue our policies with sufficient dedication and robustness.'[32] The tools to change society were available to socialists in Britain if they were willing to use them.

Throughout his career Bevan maintained that Parliament and the state had transformative roles to play in shaping society. For example, in 1957 he stated that the British people had 'come to look upon the House of Commons as being not only their court of appeal but also the most potent instrument in their struggles'.[33] The unique nature of British parliamentary democracy made Parliament a formidable weapon in reversing property relations. It is important to keep in mind, however, that, as demonstrated in Bevan's analysis of the state, it was tied up with the economic realities of society: it was not enough to simply take control of Parliament and other state institutions to enact radical change. They needed to be used to transform the economy. This more critical understanding of Parliament and the state, however, was not followed through in Bevan's later writings. The 1938 and 1944 *Tribune* articles discussed above are rare instances of Bevan outlining a more critical view of the state's relationship with economic forces. Post-1945, Bevan returned to extoling the power of Parliament, perhaps reflecting his experience of establishing the NHS. Nonetheless, Bevan continued to argue passionately that to change property relations, socialists needed to use the power of Parliament and the state for the establishment of public ownership.

Public Ownership

ECONOMIC PLANNING

Bevan's views on public ownership, and the debates within the party concerning its establishment, feature heavily in the literature and in histories of the party. Clause IV of the Labour Party constitution, committing the party to nationalisation, has been a central focus of attempts at changing the party's core principles, with Hugh Gaitskell (unsuccessfully) and Tony Blair (successfully) attempting to revise the clause.[34] Bevan, however, stressed that it 'must never be forgotten that the heart and centre of Socialism is public ownership'.[35] Public ownership was certainly central to his understanding of the relationship between politics and the economy. In his analysis, Ben Jackson emphasised the importance of state ownership to the Bevanites, identifying it as the fundamental difference between the Bevanites and the revisionists. Pointing to the revisionists' focus on equality, Jackson wrote that 'In so far as there was a distinctive Labour Left position on this issue it was that while equality, understood in a quantitative, distributive sense, was an important goal for socialists, it should not be seen as exhaustive of socialism'.[36]

Despite Labour's symbolic commitment to public ownership, the zeal for its implementation was somewhat limited within the party. Coates noted that rather than being discussed within the party as a transfer of power, public ownership focused largely on economic efficiency.[37] In the 1930s, the commitment to public ownership was ambiguous (pp. 38–9), while the party's proposals post-1945 were not particularly radical, exciting limited opposition (apart from the nationalisation of steel).[38]

At the heart of Bevan's advocacy for public ownership was the question of power. Bevan argued that leaving economic power in the hands of private enterprise would render Parliament helpless. For example, in 1937 he claimed that Parliament was only able to 'offer capitalists a number of bribes to establish industries in the distressed areas', which meant that 'Parliament is made responsible for the results, but is forbidden to deal directly with the provision of work, because this is reserved for private enterprise.

Parliament is charged with the responsibility but is denied the power'. He argued that 'it is the denial of effective economic power to the representative assembly which is responsible for the decline of political democracy'. Further, he wrote that:

> For those who believe in private enterprise government is a regrettable nuisance useful mainly for imposing discipline on restless workers. For the Socialist, government is an instrument with which to attain the more intelligent organisation of men's economic activities.[39]

Bevan maintained that denying the representative Parliament responsibility would limit its effectiveness, therefore it needed to capture economic power.

Early in his parliamentary career, Bevan urged the Labour Party to be forceful in its commitment to challenging the interests of property. Writing in John Strachey's *The Coming Struggle for Power* (1932),[40] Bevan asserted that Labour needed to abandon a 'gradualist' approach to changing society.[41] Instead, he argued for a dedicated commitment to socialism. He disparaged the argument that the 1931 Labour government was brought down by a bankers' plot, arguing that if a gradualist, 'weak and comparatively innocuous Minority Government can be broken by a conspiracy of finance capitalists, what hope is there for a Majority Government, which really threatens the bankers' privileges?' Bevan reflected that if 'capitalism is in such a state of self-consciousness that it can conspire against a Government and bring it down by moving its international financial forces against it, what hope is there for a gradual and peaceful expropriation of the bankers?'[42] If the capitalists were so well organised, then gradualism as a policy needed to be abandoned by the Labour Party.

Bevan presented two options available to the Labour Party for its approach: it could either drop 'its gradualism and tackle the emergency on socialist lines', or it could 'drop its socialism in the hope of reassuring private enterprise in order to get a breathing-space'. The gradualist policy of the Labour Party needed to be 'drastically overhauled' (p. 319). Bevan argued that gradualism involved 'the assumption that capitalism can be carried on more efficiently by socialists than by capitalists: that the sacrifices demanded of the workers are the result, not of the needs of private enterprise, but of its stupidity'. This, Bevan argued, was consistent with gradualism, which required that 'private enterprise shall continue reasonably successfully whilst it is being slowly and painlessly eliminated' (p. 320). The interests of property could not be placated if a new society was to be established.

Bevan insisted that the Labour Party needed to 'offend' the interests of the individual investor and fight the class struggle. He demanded that a party:

> climbing to power by articulating the demands of the dispossessed must always wear a predatory visage to the property-owning class ... Thus in a society involved in the throes of an ever more heavily waged class struggle, the Labour Party must wear the face of the implacable revolutionary. (p. 320)

He insisted that the Labour Party needed to 'fulfil the threat of its face, and so destroy the political conditions necessary to economic gradualism. To calm the fears of private enterprise, it must betray its promise to the workers, and so lose their support' (pp. 320–1). The only way to truly wage class struggle effectively was to use Parliament and the state as forcefully as possible.

Bevan insisted that the economic life of the country needed to be planned. He framed the discussion as a decision between 'private or collective spending'.[43] A question of central importance in his thought was, 'What is most essential and who is to decide it?' (p. 59). Or, as he set out in one of his most widely quoted and misappropriated phrases, 'the language of priorities is the religion of socialism'.[44] This was an issue that went to the heart of the relationship between economic power and the state's role in possessing it. State power needed to be wielded to prevent the damage that economic power, left in private hands, could inflict. 'If economic power is left in private hands', Bevan wrote, 'and a distressed people ask Parliament in vain for help, its authority is undermined'. Bevan maintained that:

> If confidence in political democracy is to be sustained, political freedom must arm itself with economic power. Private property in the main sources of production and distribution endangers

> political liberty, for it leaves parliament with responsibility and property with power.[45]

By nationalising key industries, the Labour Party could reverse the relationship between public and private property. Private enterprise could not be directed. Therefore, the only way that Bevan envisioned creating a new society along socialist lines was for Parliament to arm itself with economic power and direct the economy in the interests of society. Bevan maintained that 'the area of private property must be drastically restricted, because power over property is the instrument of economic planning'.[46] In Parliament, the Conservative's remedy would be to allow private enterprise to 'suck at the teats of the state',[47] but Bevan asserted that competitive industry could never solve the problems of the nation. Creating a new design for society could not be done 'until effective social and economic power passes from one order of society to another'.[48] The people would not possess 'economic responsibility ... until the main streams of economic activity are publicly canalised'.[49] Bevan stressed that 'Socialist planning demands plannable instruments and these are not present if industry is the domain of private, economic adventure'.[50] Because Bevan saw the state as being part of the class struggle, it therefore had the potential to initiate significant changes to the economic conditions of this struggle.

Nationalisation needed to be enacted in such a way that control over certain industries was entirely in the hands of the government. Bevan insisted that if 'we are to surmount our economic difficulties it can only be at the expense of industrial and financial interests'.[51] For example, if nationalisation of the coal industry left economic power in private hands, then industry would still be run in the interests of the coal owners. So, when problems occurred it would be state direction that received the blame: 'The State steps in not in substitution of private interests but as its guardian.'[52] In criticising the nationalisation carried out by the 1945–51 Labour government, Bevan believed that the party bowed to pressure from the press who feared having civil servants in charge. The result was that nationalised industries were in the hands of management boards. This, Bevan argued, reflected the old belief in private enterprise. As an alternative, Bevan argued for ministerial control of nationalised industries, rather than power over these industries being in the hands of unelected boards.[53] The boards of nationalised industries, he argued, were a 'constitutional outrage' (p. 98). He insisted that an important part of public ownership was accountability through Parliament:

> Part of the modern case for public ownership is therefore the need to establish some form of communal accountability for these industrial operations on which so many people depend for a livelihood. Some of the criticisms of nationalisation arise from the fact that this principle of accountability has been lost sight of by not bringing the central boards of the nationalised industries under direct parliamentary control.[54]

Bevan was proud of the achievements of the Labour government but argued that Parliament needed to possess greater responsibility for controlling major economic industries.

Bevan maintained that the only way in which resources could be distributed for the benefit of society was for the principles of economic planning to be followed. He contended that public ownership was not argued for by the Labour Party for its own sake. The party, he wrote, 'did not come into existence demanding Socialism, demanding the State ownership of property, simply because there was some special merit in it'. Rather, the Labour Party believed in nationalisation because 'only in that way can society be intelligently and progressively organised. If private enterprise can deliver all these goods, there will not be any argument for Socialism and no reason for it'.[55] Throughout his career Bevan stressed that governments needed to challenge private enterprise. For example, in 1954 he wrote that governments:

> dare not, indeed cannot, disinterest themselves in the economic activities of their countries after the fashion of early twentieth century statesmen. They cannot today leave questions of employment and investment to the automatism of a free market and plead the 'laws of supply and demand'.[56]

People were not prepared 'to believe that their livelihood and their expectations from life must be left to the mercy of blind forces however impressively these may be garbed in the jargon of the economists' (p. 1). Nationalisation was not an end but a means to an end, a means to establishing a democratic socialist society.

BEVAN'S PLAN FOR PUBLIC OWNERSHIP

At various stages of his career, Bevan set out what a planned economy might look like. For example, he detailed his vision in an essay for the Fabian Society titled 'Plan for Work' in 1943, based largely on an article he wrote for *Tribune* in 1940.[57] In this essay Bevan argued that a plan for action was needed to shape society immediately after the Second World War had concluded:

> The kind of industrial controls, the forms of political organisation, the relationship between different classes in the community, the texture of all these is being determined by how we are conducting the war and the means with which we are doing it.[58]

Bevan then outlined his vision of how a planned economy could create a new society. He stressed two principles that needed to be adhered to in any plan argued for by socialists: 'We seek to obtain the advantages of economic planning in society, and at the same time to retain the benefits of individual liberty and representative democracy' (p. 35). Bevan worried that corporations were being progressively enfranchised, but individuals were not. He warned that:

> if those who exercise power in the State are not continually subject to the checks and restraints of popular opinion and of organised representative institutions, nothing can prevent the State from becoming tyrannical; because it is the right of the ordinary man or woman to pull at the coat-tails of those in power to exert their influence over them. (p. 36)

Any changes to the economic responsibilities of the state needed to ensure that principles of democracy remained.

Bevan argued for a revolutionary transformation of the economy by the state. He stressed, however, that 'if the economic activities of society change, if alterations occur in the relationships between classes in the community, if economic functions undergo revolutionary transformations, then there must be constitutional adaptations to those conditions' (pp. 36–7). He also warned that attitudes towards public ownership would not be positive if the proposals meant handing over power to the bureaucracy of the civil service. He insisted that socialists 'have for over a hundred years stood for the nationalisation of the means of production, distribution and exchange; but, we may as well confess it, those ancient slogans no longer ring a bell'. Although the civil service was 'an estimable organisation' in Bevan's eyes, he thought that 'no one can suggest that the slogan of handing over great industries to the Civil Service of this country would fill anybody with revolutionary zeal'. Nevertheless, he insisted that nationalisation was important because it was impossible to 'have control without ownership'. To plan economic life, ownership of key industries was vital (p. 38). Any alteration in the material conditions of society needed to preserve the principles of political liberty and democracy while keeping pace with economic change.

Bevan outlined a list of industries that he wanted to see nationalised. They were light, power, production of steel, shipbuilding, coalmining and transport. He proclaimed that 'all those economic instruments must become national property ... fairly quickly'. He predicted that if they were not made national property during the war they would 'not be made national property after the war without a bloody revolution' (pp. 38–9) (Bevan at this stage must have not envisioned a Labour government being swept to power two years later). He concluded that 'the main economic instruments must be taken out of private hands' (p. 39). Bevan did not want private enterprise to be in control of industries vital to the country.

After explaining the importance of nationalisation, Bevan then outlined a potential design for society. He set out five organs of the state: first, a 'Supreme Economic Council'; second, a representative assembly; third, a planning commission; fourth, an auditing commission; and finally, a judiciary. The Supreme Economic Council (SEC) would be formed to take control of the day-to-day running of the newly nationalised industries. Bevan envisioned that it would be formed of a number of 'able men', responsible to the government and with the 'right of employment and discharge over their own personnel' (pp. 39–40). Further, the SEC should not be subject to 'day-to-day questioning and interrogation in the House of Commons', instead being allowed to operate without parliamentary interference (pp. 40–1).

This appears to reduce the role of Parliament in the planning of the economy. However, Bevan argued that the role of the House of Commons, 'or whatever institution we decide to have', should exercise 'supreme control over the general plans and designs of the Supreme Economic Council'. Plans would periodically have to be submitted to the government, who would also produce its own plans laying down what the SEC was to do. Here, the SEC and the representative assembly would work in harmony with each other (p. 41). Bevan argued for the separation of economic and political functions between the SEC and the government, believing that the representative assembly should retain control over 'all the social agencies of coercion and of education' (p. 42). He declared that with the:

> division of function, economic technical administration by the Supreme Economic Council and Parliamentary control over the armed forces of the State, then you have the central design of a society which is coherent, which is self-contained, and yet based upon functionalist principles. (pp. 42–3)

But socialists, Bevan warned, needed to keep in mind that 'they cannot permit the economic changes, now taking place, to continue unless they try to bring their constitutional machinery into line with it, because if they allow that situation to continue, then you are bound to have disorder' (pp. 42–3). This essay is the most detailed plan produced by Bevan outlining a vision of public ownership and emphasising the importance of adapting parliamentary institutions to economic changes.

In the essay, Bevan attempted to explain the relationship between economic and political power, insisting that the necessary changes in the economic base needed to be driven by a faith in democracy and representative institutions. It highlighted the importance of the base-superstructure relationship in his thought. Whereas classical Marxist thought, Bevan concluded, did not appreciate the positive potential of the state, he argued that it was a central tool to change the material conditions of society. This is a fundamental aspect of Bevan's praxis that representative institutions played a crucial role in the development of society. It demonstrates the reciprocal relationship between the economic base and the political superstructure. This essay, however, is largely overlooked in the literature. Yet, a reading of it emphasises a crucial aspect of Bevan's political thought.

WORKERS' CONTROL

It has been suggested by some authors that Bevan sought the establishment of workers' control in industry. Thomas-Symonds, for example, believed that Bevan regretted later in life not arguing for workers' control,[59] while Campbell suggested that *In Place of Fear* contained an argument for its implementation.[60] Mark Krug quoted Bevan as stating to the *New York Times*: 'Nationalisation is the transfer of property from the individual to the state. Socialism is the full participation of the people in the administration and operation of that property.'[61] Ultimately, however, according to Thomas-Symonds Bevan did not develop a coherent plan for workers democracy.[62] Demont also argued that Bevan was 'never an advocate of workers' control of industry'.[63] Nevertheless, there is evidence in Bevan's writing that he envisioned control being handed to the workers in nationalised industries, although these ideas were not fully developed.

Workers' control has been much debated within the Labour Party throughout its history, but it has never been adopted as a proposal and policy position. There have been periods where the rank and file have been frustrated by the parliamentary leadership, such as in the early 1900s when Labour was in opposition and the rank and file considered themselves to be making more gains through strikes than through Parliament.[64] Yet, this has not led to the advocacy of workers' control. Various intellectuals, such as R. H. Tawney, G. D. H. Cole and Harold Laski sought to include an element of industrial democracy to Labour Party strategy,[65] but they were unsuccessful. Nationalisation measures from the 1945 government did not introduce an element of workers' control, instead putting power in the hands of national boards.[66]

Bevan did emphasise on numerous occasions the importance of workers involvement in industries. In 1944, for example, he wrote: 'At the workshop level the participation of the worker in the administration of the industry is an essential condition of industrial democracy, and a direct contribution to increased efficiency and smooth working.'[67] In *In Place of Fear*, Bevan discussed the 'advance from State ownership to full socialism' being 'in direct proportion to the extent the workers in the nationalised sector are made aware of a changed relationship between themselves and the management'. He continued that the 'persistence of a sense of dualism in a publicly owned industry is evidence of an immature industrial democracy. It means that emotionally the "management" is still associated with the conception of alien ownership, and the "workers" are still "hands"':

> Until we make the cross-over to a spirit of co-operation, the latent energies of democratic participation cannot be fully released; nor

> shall we witness that spiritual homogeneity which comes when the workman is united once more with the tools of his craft, a unity which was ruptured by the rise of economic classes. The individual citizen will still feel that society is on top of him until he is enfranchised in the workshop as well as at the ballot box.[68]

This is the strongest evidence of Bevan discussing anything like workers' democracy in industries. He went on to write that, because the division of labour made the worker 'a cog in the machine', it was 'more essential ... to refresh his mind and spirit by the utmost discussion and consultation in policy and administration' (p. 104). Bevan stressed freedom in industry, writing that:

> In the societies of the West, industrial democracy is the counterpart of political freedom. Liberty and responsibility march together. They must be joined together in the workshop as in the legislative Assembly. Only when this is accomplished shall we have the foundations of a buoyant and stable civilisation. (p. 105)

It must be kept in mind, however, that Bevan discussed this in relation to the worker carrying out executive action, therefore following a 'general scheme' (p. 104). Although he called for a new attitude on the part of managers that would see them value the worker as integral to the productive process (p. 105), Bevan did not call for workers to take complete control of industry and was vague about the way that workers' control would be organised.

Bevan's comments on the role of doctors within the NHS highlight the same reservations about workers' self-management:

> I have never believed that the demands of a democracy are necessarily satisfied merely by the opportunity of putting a cross against someone's name every four or five years. I believe that democracy exists in the active participation in administration and policy. Therefore, I believe that it is a wise thing to give the doctors full participation in the administration of their own profession. They must, of course, necessarily be subordinated to lay control – we do not want the opposite danger of syndicalism. Therefore, the

> communal interests must always be safeguarded in this administration.[69]

It is true that Bevan wanted workers to play a more involved and important role in the running of key industries, but he did not develop this aspect of his views on nationalisation to any great extent. His insistence on the importance of parliamentary responsibility remained central.

There is evidence that Bevan critically assessed the assumption that Parliament and the state could transform society, as well as evidence that he considered the form that public ownership needed to take. These aspects of his thought, however, were not developed significantly and he returned to an emphasis on Parliament as a radical vehicle for social change, thus fitting more comfortably within labourism. The following section now considers Bevan's vision of the continuing relationship between public and private property that would result from the state's involvement in the economy.

The Mixed Economy

MIXED ECONOMY

It was demonstrated in the previous chapter that Bevan's initial view, expressed in his 1921 review of the *Communist Manifesto*, was that private property should be completely abolished. This view did not last however, as this chapter has also highlighted Bevan's changing belief that not all forms of private property were bad. Writing in *Why Not Trust the Tories?* in 1944, Bevan expressed the view that the dominant role in the economy should be played by public ownership. He argued that 'A political democracy, based on private ownership of industry, finance and commerce, is an essentially unstable society'. He hinted that there was merit in certain industries being kept in the hands of private enterprise, but that public ownership should be the dominant form of property: 'Whatever merits there may be in leaving certain segments of industry to private enterprise is beside the point of this book. The first consideration is to see to it that the dominant role in society is played by public ownership.' Only 'once you break the back of the big Tories', Bevan wrote, might it 'be safe to allow a few of the small ones to crawl around'.[70]

Again, on the surface, this approach does not appear as fundamentally different from Labour's continual commitment to the mixed economy. While the party contained within it a multitude of attitudes, positions and visions of the future,[71] they appeared to agree on an approach to the economy that meant there would be a variety of both public and private property.

Bevan's vision of society was one of a mixed economy where key industries would be planned in the interests of society, but which also allowed for a measure of competitive business, thus maintaining choice for the individual. In 1940, he envisioned society's economic life compromising of 'three main streams'. These three streams of economic life[72] were:

1. Industries the products of which are distributed (i.e., they have no price because they are provided for free).
2. 'Industries the products of which are sold at an artificially fixed price in order to secure the agreed standard of consumption.' Some would be publicly owned, some in a 'quasi-private relationship' (e.g., milk production).
3. Private economic adventure.

Bevan predicted that society would move from the third stage to the second then to the first, a kind of law of development:

> Society will then be provided with a measure of progress – the extent to which products pass from the third to the second and thence to the first category. The conscious application of this idea will give the economic life of the nation a sort of concrete raft, a kind of economic back-bone, fixed and stable, around which the activities of privately owned industry will group themselves, supplying the infinite diversification of products which the caprice of private choice may determine, without at any time threatening economic chaos. (p. 7)

In this view, the stages of development of a society and the taming of economic chaos would be determined by changes in the condition of the products of society.

Bevan reiterated these views in his 1943 Fabian Society essay discussed earlier. After setting out his vision for nationalisation and the relationship between the economic and political arms of the state, Bevan outlined these three categories of products existing after this new society had been established. Bevan insisted that:

> a Socialist society must always consider how to create mass consumption for the mass production of the modern machine. Therefore, the price of certain categories of products must be designed in order to secure their consumption at the level society thinks to be necessary.[73]

The products of these industries could no longer conform to capitalist price competition (the fixing of prices remained important for Bevan's plan for public ownership in later years).[74]

Free-market pricing would then be allowed in some sectors of the economy. This element of free-market competition would form part of Bevan's vision of a society in which there would be 'privately owned industry on a very, very considerable scale, because the purpose of a Socialist economy is to secure enough of those instruments of economic activity through which the central designs of society can be regulated'. The society that Bevan envisioned would be a 'complex society'. The purpose of socialists was to ensure 'throughout that complex community there runs all the while the dominating principle of Socialist design and sense of direction'. Bevan insisted that no socialist had ever 'claimed that there is anything wrong with the profit-making motive, if the motive is harnessed to social welfare'.[75] The constitutional changes outlined by Bevan in his Fabian Society essay on the SEC would be sufficient in reflecting the dominance of public property. Despite Bevan's engagement with Marxism and his political thought being influenced by some key tenets of Marxist economics, he moved quite far away from this position by insisting that the profit motive could be allowed in some industries.

Bevan maintained this position on the mixed economy throughout his career. He saw the balance being too heavily weighted towards private property, but this did not mean that he envisioned its complete aboltion as he did in 1921. He would allow for competition to exist in a number of business enterprises, but only as long as the principle activities of society were publicly owned: 'We shall be able to afford the light cavalry of private enterprise and competition in a number of business enterprises if the principal economic activities of society are articulated by means of a sector of publicly owned industries.'[76] He set out his views of the mixed economy in *In Place of Fear*:

> It is clear to the serious student of modern politics that a mixed economy is what most people of the West would prefer. The victory of Socialism need not be universal to be decisive. I have no patience with those Socialists, so-called, who in practice would socialise nothing, whilst in theory they threaten the whole of private property. They are purists and therefore barren. It is neither prudent, nor does it accord with our conception of the future, that all forms of private property should live under perpetual threat. In almost all types of human society different forms of property have lived side by side without fatal consequences either for society or for one of them. But it is a requisite of social stability that one type of property ownership should dominate. In the society of the future it should be public property. Private property should yield to the point where social purposes and a decent order of priorities form an easily discernible pattern of life. Only when this is accomplished will a tranquil and serene attitude take the place of the all-pervading restlessness that is the normal climate of competitive society.[77]

This represents a significant deviation from orthodox Marxism. Instead of arguing for the abolition of private property, Bevan's vision for society was based on a combination of both public and private property. A summary of Bevan's discussions of state ownership and the changes in society can be found in an article he wrote for *Tribune* at the end of 1944.[78]

PUBLIC OWNERSHIP AND SOCIETY

The consequences of nationalisation were central to Bevan's political outlook. He asserted that nationalisation could create new conditions for society, implanting values of co-operation and leading to a higher quality of life for the masses. The entire purpose of nationalisation was to create a better society based on socialist principles. Economic planning could lead to 'the fullest efflorescence of personal liberty ... Without personal liberty an ordered economic life is like a plant that never flowers'.[79] Once the economic power of the nation was in the hands of the people through Parliament, policy could be shaped to their needs. Collective action could help to cultivate individual life:

> There is no test for progress other than its impact on the individual. If the policies of statesmen, the enactments of legislatures, the impulses of group activity, do not have for their object the enlargement and cultivation of the individual life, they do not deserve to be called civilised.[80]

The purpose of capturing economic power through the state was to change society so that the life of the individual could be made better, a theme that is explored further in Chapter Four.

Public ownership was central to Bevan's vision of what the 1945–51 Labour government needed to work towards. Where once private enterprise was the basis of society, Bevan saw an opportunity for the Labour government to reverse this dominance. Reflecting in 1955 on Labour's record in government, Bevan wrote that 'If public enterprise had not come to the rescue, employment in the basic industries, including agriculture, would now be drastically reduced with disastrous consequences'.[81] The transformation of society that Parliament could enact was to be carried out through these nationalisation measures.

Bevan warned that the relationship between the state and the people needed to be constantly renewed throughout the 1950s to build on existing achievements. In 1956, he wrote that the 'character of the state has changed in a revolutionary manner'. He stated that it 'impinges on the lives of ordinary men and women to a far greater extent than did the personal rule of kings'. This could not be attributed to the inevitability of 'the complexity of modern society and of the need to maintain a huge apparatus of government administration'. However, it was vital to consider how the state 'affects the modern citizen – especially in the capitalist democracies'. Bevan was concerned about the financing of the Welfare State through taxation, for 'if welfare is to be financed solely by taxes taken from the incomes of private citizens, then a conflict is inevitable'. He understood that people would not want to see their money taken away to finance publicly owned institutions and services. Even so, he argued that a key issue was that businesses and people were not treated as equals when it came to collecting taxes. Businesses could get away with avoiding tax by setting up trusts, Bevan claimed. He suspected that this was happening more and more. The only way, he argued, for communal activities to be extended was by limiting the amount of the national income distributed to private citizens. This is evidence of Bevan's reflecting on the changing nature of the state in society during the 1950s; however, Bevan went no further than reasserting that this could be achieved only by 'an extension of public ownership which gives the state direct control over the revenues of industry'.[82]

Bevan was proud of the achievements of the Labour government between 1945 and 1951, even if his praise was caveated with criticisms. He reflected that the Labour government had made advances on three fronts: higher wages and salaries, nationalisation and redistribution. Bevan stated that each advance had been 'based upon a philosophical appreciation of the relationship of the working-class in the modern world towards modern society'. Nationalisation was a 'fundamental change, because it [represented] a transference of power'. The redistributive element was 'the one which has its roots more deeply in Socialist philosophy than any other'. Bevan claimed that it represented 'the slow destruction of the inequalities and disadvantages arising from the unequal possession of property and the unequal possession of individual strengths and opportunities'.[83] Reflecting in 1958 on the development of public ownership, Bevan asserted that in Britain, 'the public sector consists in the main of coal, electricity, roads, railways, airways and, to a partial extent only, steel; and, of course, the National Health Service and schools'. He wrote that there was 'no mystery about what to do with these. In them, the levers are to our hand. They can be expanded or contracted at the public will and in the service of national objectives. They constitute the rational element in an otherwise irrational society.'[84] While Bevan argued that in the 'ethos of capitalism, mystery is equated with liberty', in the public sector 'conscious intention can be an instrument of economic activity that the British people are free to bring about an oasis of progress amidst the surrounding chaos' (p. 3). Bevan certainly believed that the relationship between property and the State had altered substantially since the reforms of the Labour government.

Despite significant achievements, Bevan warned that more was needed to change the British economy on a permanent basis. For example, he was wary of the dangers posed by the Conservatives once they achieved power in 1951. He pointed to attempts by the Tories to privatise steel in 1953 in the name of creating a 'property owning democracy'. Bevan even insisted that the type of public ownership arrived at for steel had allowed the Conservatives to put the industry back into private hands.[85] A year earlier, Bevan had warned against 'Fresh Thinkers' and 'Socialist Revisionists' in the Labour Party who he accused of attempting to stultify Labour's drive for public ownership by seeking 'novel remedies' instead of 'the struggle for power in the state', and who suggested that public ownership was outdated. Bevan urged socialists to be clear that 'one of the central principles of Socialism is the substitution of public for private ownership'. He insisted that the success of 1945–51 was because the Labour government stuck to its mandate. He admitted that there were administrative difficulties involved with nationalisation and the attempt to carry out 'a revolution by consent' but maintained that the remedy was 'a greater ruthlessness ... and a wider application of the principle of industrial democracy'.[86] Bevan, however, did not sufficiently elaborate on what this would entail.

BEVAN AND THE LABOUR PARTY

Bevan's attempts to ensure that Labour continued with public ownership met fierce resistance within a party that was increasingly becoming influenced by the thinking of leaders such as Hugh Gaitskell who did not see further public ownership as necessary due to the changes brought about by the post-war Labour government. In light of the election defeats throughout the 1950s, Bevan had to consistently urge for further public ownership and defend against those who wanted to 'blunt the edge of the socialist case'[87] and those who argued that Labour needed to be more 'pragmatic' or 'practical'.[88] He insisted that one of the major premises of the labour movement was the transformation of societies based on private ownership to ones of public ownership. He argued that he did not want to be part of the movement if it did not have that as its aim.[89]

The debate between the Bevanites and the revisionists came to define Labour in the 1950s. Thomas-Symonds identified the debate as 'consolidation versus advance'. Advocates of consolidation argued that the role of government was to manage capitalism after Labour's nationalisation measures between 1945–51, while the advocates of advance argued that public ownership needed to be extended.[90] In support of consolidation, figures such as Anthony Crosland began to provide a detailed analysis of the post-war economic situation, arguing that the reforms brought about by the Labour government had fundamentally changed the economic structure of British society. In his most famous work *The Future of Socialism* (1956), Crosland stated that equality should be the most important aim of socialists as public ownership was unlikely to lead to the attainment of social goals. He argued that after the policies enacted by the 1945–51 Labour government, society was no longer capitalist.[91] A commonality between Bevan's work and Eduard Bernstein's revisionism was referenced earlier, yet it was Crosland who specifically acknowledged Bernstein's work. He saw himself as following in the philosopher's footsteps, writing that he was 'engaged on a great revision of Marxism, and will certainly emerge as the modern Bernstein'.[92] Bevan's theories in the 1950s were still rooted in the ideas of property relations and the need to move beyond capitalist society, while Crosland was a theorist engaged in a profound revision of Marxism and socialist principles in Britain. It is evidently true that Crosland's *The Future of Socialism*, together with his other writing, represented a more systematic attempt at studying society than Bevan ever managed to achieve. Even still, *The Future of Socialism* and *In Place of Fear* defined the theoretical debate within the Labour Party.[93]

Consolidation became the dominant trend within the Labour Party after 1948. Gaitskell, Douglas Jay and Evan Durbin saw the bureaucracy of nationalisation as becoming an electoral liability for Labour, while Crosland considered state intervention to have exposed capitalism, meaning that socialism could be achieved through Keynesian means.[94] Income had been redistributed successfully, and capitalism was becoming manageable and tamed, with Labour intellectuals arguing that social revolution had taken place, even when the basic structure of society had largely remained intact.[95]

As Saville and others have argued, the 1945–51 government represented significant achievements for the advancement of socialism in Britain, with its programme being more radical than previous Labour administrations. The Labour government had achieved many reforms, such as improving welfare and taming private enterprise to a certain extent,[96] but it was not necessarily a step towards the socialist commonwealth that Bevan had envisioned. The distribution of power, so vital to Bevan's politics, had only been slightly altered. Saville argued that capitalism, rather than eliminating inequality, had simply bred new types of inequality,[97] while private enterprise was still dominant, comprising 80 per cent of this new 'mixed' economy (p. 85). Public ownership never changed the structure of society, Saville bemoaned, and reflected the reformist nature of the Labour Party as it did not look deeply into the structure of industries, instead relying on piecemeal reforms. Labour middle-class intellectuals created a reformist, moderate and empiricist movement, which was anti-capitalist but also very traditional (pp. 111–12).

Foote recognised that Bevan's support for a mixed economy was 'in perfect accord with the main traditions of the Labour Party's political thought'. The mixed economy was 'one of the characteristics which excluded a full-blooded Marxism from ever being accepted, and belief in it was one of the unifying factors between Right and Left in the party'.[98] While both Bevan and the right of the party agreed in principle to nationalisation, Foote identified a major difference between them; namely, the importance that Bevan placed on power 'as the main instrument which could secure welfare and equality'. He argued that Bevan saw the need for the planned sector to be dominant in the economy. Foote stated that 'Where the revisionists believed that the old arguments about capitalism were outdated, Bevan held that the domination of the economy by capitalists or by the State was still the crucial element determining all other socialist aims' (p 276). A thesis supported by the analysis in this chapter.

Several industries were nationalised by the 1945–51 Labour government without much opposition or controversy. The system of nationalisation set up was modelled on the London Transport Board: 'Each [publicly owned industry] was to be run by a board; however, rather than have workers as members of these committees, the government appointed members.' The government nationalised the Bank of England, coal, Cable and Wireless Ltd, civil aviation, electricity, gas, rail and eventually steel.[99] It has been claimed that by 1957 Bevan had acquiesced by letting through policies in Labour manifestos that prevented the extension of nationalisation as a result of his becoming closer politically to Labour leader Hugh Gaitskell.[100] Krug argued that Bevan had become cautious in his approach to nationalisation and claimed that in 1957 Bevan did not oppose proposals by Gaitskell to sell shares in nationalised industries.[101] Further, Thomas-Symonds claimed that, contrary to the view of much of the literature, Bevan was more in favour of consolidation than it at first seems, arguing that the debate over nationalisation in the party 'was to prove more theoretical than practical'.[102] Thomas-Symonds believed that the deeper divisions within the party concerned foreign policy, claiming that there was not much difference in the domestic positions of Bevan and Gaitskell (p. 207).

Campbell argued that Bevan was unable to develop a theory of nationalisation that matched the theoretical strength of the revisionists. He contended that Bevan's *In Place of Fear* failed to become the bible that Crosland's *The Future of Socialism* was to become.[103] He asserted that the left did not offer a 'coherent analysis of what was wrong with welfare capitalism and a clear programme to set Labour back on the road to socialism' (p. 375). Thomas-Symonds appears to agree, arguing that the issue of nationalisation highlighted the lack of coherent thinking from the Bevanites. He stated that a belief:

> in public ownership was an abstract principle without practical proposals for implementation. Thus, it was the revisionists who provided a practical policy to show that public ownership should be seen as a means with which to achieve greater equality, rather than an end in itself.[104]

Yet, Bevan had outlined a plan for public ownership as described above. His 1943 Fabian Society essay was a concerted attempt to develop a plan for the nationalisation of industries. Further, as we have seen, Bevan's plans for public ownership were not merely based on vague, abstract principles. Public ownership was a fundamental element of Bevan's understanding of property relations. It was, as we saw noted by Foote above, a central part of capturing power. It is therefore both theoretically and practically opposed to the view of the revisionists who sought consolidation.

The evidence also suggests that while Bevan may have compromised by not opposing watered-down nationalisation plans, he was determined in his argument for public ownership. Right until the end of his life, Bevan maintained a firm belief in economic planning. After Labour's election defeat in 1959, he reaffirmed this commitment:

> To what extent are hon. members opposite prepared to interfere with private enterprise in order to plan the location of industries?

> Are they prepared to stand up against private vested interests to secure the intelligent ground plan for the economy of the nation as a whole? If they are not, then we shall have an aggravation of the problems, with all the social and economic consequences involved.
>
> Unless we plan our resources purposefully, unless we are prepared to accept the disciplines that are necessary, we shall not be able to meet the challenge of the Communist world. As the years go by, and the people see us languishing behind, trying to prevent the evils of inflation by industrial stagnation, trying all the time to catch up with things because we have not acted soon enough – when they see the Communist world, planned, organised, publicly-owned and flaunting its achievements to the rest of the world – they will come to be educated by what they will experience. They will realise that Western democracy is falling behind in the race because it is not prepared to read intelligently the lessons of the twentieth century.[105]

Despite claims that Bevan had become more pragmatic in his later career, a study of his political thought reveals that principles of economic planning and public ownership remained central to his beliefs.

Conclusion

Bevan's analysis of democracy is a fundamental part of his political thought. He deviated from classical Marxism to champion British representative institutions. Although his analysis was sometimes limited, he did highlight the importance of Parliament and the state to the class struggle. While emphasising the role of the economic base in determining the political superstructure, Bevan also underlined the importance of this political superstructure in shaping the economic base. He believed that political institutions, when used effectively, could represent the masses and be used to transform society. Public ownership was central to this vision. Bevan argued that key economic industries needed to be taken over by the state and the economy planned in the interests of all. Although he described how the state could be influenced by the representatives of private property, and criticised the effects of private enterprise, Bevan still envisioned a mixed economy that would allow private enterprise to exist and the profit motive to continue. The more critical analysis of the state that Bevan put forward in the 1940s was not developed upon into the 1950s. Instead, he reverted to simply insisting on the need for further public ownership and reform through Parliament, rather than developing his proposals for the reform of institutions and nationalised industries.

Bevan's understanding of Parliament and the state represents a significant deviation from the Marxism that he identified as being important to his political education. Many authors have identified the relationship between the two strands of Bevan's thought, with Marquand (1997) and Spalding (2018) arguing that Bevan should be understood within the British radical tradition rather than the Marxist tradition. It is true that although he agreed with the analysis of class conflict contained in *The Communist Manifesto*, Bevan believed that Marxist thinkers had underestimated the potential of democracy and representative institutions. While this represented a deviation from orthodox Marxist theory, this chapter has nevertheless highlighted that Bevan still saw the establishment of democracy as part of the process of society's historical development. The establishment of representative institutions such as Parliament was a stage in this process, and Bevan insisted that this was relevant not just to Britain but to other nations such as the Soviet Union. Parliament and the state could also play a significant role in further altering the economic base and reversing the power relationship between private and public property. His emphasis on property relations still remained central to his analysis. Although tensions existed between them, Bevan combined these two strands of his thought, representing what Foote described as a 'restatement of Labour Marxism, but presented in a manner appealing to the emotions of labourism'.[106] Bevan and the Labour left could face both the non-Labour left and the Labour right by 'upholding the nineteenth-century radical view'. The left of the party could try to convince people that in a capitalist society, the way to achieve socialism was through the Labour Party acting in the House of Commons.[107]

Yet, as is often case, Bevan's political thought came into conflict with many of Labour's ideological foundations. His advocacy of Parliament, his belief in state power and his plans for a mixed economy fitted comfortably with other Labour politicians and intellectuals within the party. Yet, his views on the purpose of Parliament and critiques of the state and the structure of the mixed economy were different to what had been achieved by

Labour government and to what mainstream Labour thought advocated. Labour struggled to create a counter-hegemonic bloc to challenge the class constraints faced by social democratic parties in democratic capitalist countries.[108] Labour had become firmly institutionalised within the moderate British political tradition. The legacy of the party's development meant that more radical, transformative reforms, such as those championed by Bevan, were not pursued.[109] Coming back to the work of Perry Anderson discussed earlier, he argued that a socialist party that wanted to create a working-class hegemony needed a theoretical underpinning and an understanding of social transformation.[110] However, particularly in the 1950s, Labour leaders were reluctant to follow the more radical ideas of Bevan and his supporters, with Gaitskell's election as leader accentuating a shift within the party that gave the arguments of the right a sharper ideological and political articulation.[111] This gave the left ammunition to accuse the Labour Party of being no different to the Conservatives (p. 344), exactly the criticism that Bevan levelled at those who called for the party to become more 'pragmatic' and 'practical'.

Chapters 1 and 2 have focused almost exclusively on Bevan's analysis of domestic British institutions and conditions. An essential part of Bevan's thought throughout most of his career, however, was concerned with global politics. From the Spanish Civil War to the Second World War, and the fragile international power politics that emerged in their aftermath, Bevan's analysis of other nations also assists in understanding his conceptions of historical development and democracy. The next chapter explores Bevan's analysis of economic and political power in relation to his reflections on international society.

NOTES

1 British Pathé, 'Labour Party Conference (1953)' (2014), *www.youtube.com/watch?v=RKhQRqRjnyk&t=555s* (accessed 5 January 2024).

2 Howell, *British Social Democracy*, p. 10.

3 Francis, *Ideas and Policies under Labour 1945–1951*, p. 230.

4 Miliband, *Parliamentary Socialism*, p. 13.

5 Bevan, *In Place of Fear*, p. 22.

6 Bevan, *Why Not Trust the Tories?*, p. 13.

7 Aneurin Bevan, 'The Tories' prisoner', *Tribune* (18 October 1940), pp. 12–13.

8 Editorial, 'The camouflaged saboteurs', *Tribune* (19 March 1943), p. 2.

9 M.P., 'M.P.s pack Commons to listen to rich men's sad woes', *Tribune* (30 April 1937), p. 7.
10 Aneurin Bevan, 'All is not well', *Tribune* (28 February 1941), p. 1.
11 M.P., 'Prim Neville takes his bow for state profiteering', *Tribune* (23 April 1937), p. 7.
12 Aneurin Bevan, 'A bad break for our Dr Goebbels', *Tribune* (14 April 1938), p. 7.
13 Bevan, 'The Tories' prisoner', p. 13.
14 Bevan, *Why Not Trust the Tories?*, p. 78.
15 Bevan, 'A declaration of class war', p. 4.
16 Aneurin Bevan, 'Two faces of Macmillan', *Tribune* (21 March 1958), p. 5.
17 Bevan, *In Place of Fear*, p. 100.
18 Aneurin Bevan, 'We get a dirty deal from the press', *Tribune* (15 November 1940), p. 13.
19 M.P., 'Spain – and the big guns go booming', *Tribune* (2 July 1937), p. 6.
20 Aneurin Bevan, 'People versus property', *Tribune* (11 February 1938), p. 7.
21 Editorial, 'The challenge of big business', *Tribune* (17 April 1942), p. 2.
22 Aneurin Bevan, 'Bevan on Parliament', *Tribune* (5 June 1959), p. 12.
23 Aneurin Bevan, 'M.P.s' tongues must be loosened', *Tribune* (21 March 1941), p. 7.
24 Aneurin Bevan, 'M.P.'s recall days of August 1914', *Tribune* (8 July 1938), p. 3.
25 Campbell, *Nye Bevan and the Mirage of British Socialism*, p. 48.
26 Coates, *The Labour Party and the Struggle for Socialism*, pp. 141–4.
27 Saville, *The Labour Movement in Britain*, p. 88.
28 Aneurin Bevan, 'Highwaymen in The Upper House', *Tribune* (8 July 1938), p. 7.
29 Ralph Miliband, 'Poulantzas and the Capitalist State', *New Left Review*, 1/82 (1973), *https://newleftreview.org/I/82/ralph-miliband-poulantzas-and-the-capitalist-state* (accessed 5 January 2024).
30 Coates, *The Labour Party and the Struggle for Socialism*, pp. 171–6.
31 Aneurin Bevan, 'The T.U.C.'s two voices', *Tribune* (13 October 1944), p. 7.
32 Aneurin Bevan, 'Can Parliament do it?', *Tribune* (26 November 1954), p. 1.
33 Aneurin Bevan, 'Save democracy – have a general election now', *Tribune* (18 January 1957), p. 5.
34 Tudor Jones, '"Taking Genesis out of the Bible": Hugh Gaitskell, Clause IV and Labour's Socialist Myth', *Contemporary British History*, 11/12 (1997); Peter Riddell, 'The End of Clause IV, 1994–95', *Contemporary British History*, 11/2 (1997).

35 Aneurin Bevan, 'All set for a new thrust forward', *Tribune* (26 September 1952), p. 4.
36 Jackson, *Equality and the British Left*, p. 159.
37 Coates, *The Labour Party and the Struggle for Socialism*, p. 48.
38 Callaghan, 'The Left', pp. 28–9.
39 M.P., 'Why Mr Ernest Brown infuriates opposition and Tory members alike', p. 7.
40 John Strachey, *The Coming Struggle for Power* (London: Victor Gollancz, 1932).
41 Although Bevan is not named in the book, he has been identified as the author of the referenced passage. See Foot, *Aneurin Bevan: 1897–1945*, p. 152.
42 Strachey, *The Coming Struggle for Power*, p. 318.
43 Bevan, *In Place of Fear*, chapter 4.
44 Labour Party, 'Labour Party Annual Conference Report' (1949); Aneurin Bevan, 'Rationed – or "free"?', *Tribune* (29 October 1954), p. 2.
45 Bevan, *In Place of Fear*, p. 29.
46 Aneurin Bevan, 'Blind men are leading us!', *Tribune* (11 October 1940), p. 11.
47 HC Deb, 6 March 1946, vol. 420, col. 377–463.
48 Bevan, *In Place of Fear*, p. 117–18.
49 Aneurin Bevan, 'Ten years – *Tribune*, 1937–1947', *Tribune* (31 January 1947), p. 7.
50 Aneurin Bevan, 'Should we plan wages?', *Tribune* (21 January 1955), p. 1.
51 Aneurin Bevan, 'The fatuity of coalition', *Tribune* (13 June 1952), p. 1.
52 Editorial, 'Coal owners *ueber alles*', *Tribune* (5 June 1942), p. 2.
53 Bevan, *In Place of Fear*, pp. 97–8.
54 Aneurin Bevan, 'Nationalisation and tomorrow', *Tribune* (12 November 1954), p. 12.
55 HC Deb, 23 June 1944, vol. 401, col. 491–582.
56 Aneurin Bevan, 'Britain without Churchill', *Tribune* (8 April 1955), p. 1.
57 Aneurin Bevan, 'Next steps to a new society', *Tribune* (25 October 1940), pp. 6–7.
58 Aneurin Bevan, 'Plan for Work', in Fabian Society (ed.), *Plan for Britain: A Collection of Essays Prepared for the Fabian Society* (London: The Labour Book Service, 1943), pp. 34–5.
59 Thomas-Symonds, *Nye*, p. 165.
60 Campbell, *Nye Bevan and the Mirage of British Socialism*, p. 266.
61 Bevan 1952 cited in Krug, *Aneurin Bevan*, p. 138.

62 Thomas-Symonds, *Nye*, p. 254.
63 Demont, 'Tredegar and Aneurin Bevan', p. 215.
64 Howell, *British Social Democracy*, p. 28.
65 Callaghan, 'The Left', pp. 26–7; Foote, *The Labour Party's Political Thought*.
66 Saville, *The Labour Movement in Britain*, pp. 109–11.
67 Bevan, 'The T.U.C.'s two voices', p. 6.
68 Bevan, *In Place of Fear*, p. 103.
69 HC Deb, 30 April 1946, vol. 422, col. 44–142.
70 Bevan, *Why Not Trust the Tories?*, p. 87.
71 Ellison, *Egalitarian Thought and Labour Politics*; Foote, *The Labour Party's Political Thought*.
72 Bevan, 'Next steps to a new society', pp. 6–7.
73 Bevan, 'Plan for Work', p. 44.
74 Aneurin Bevan, 'Who wants controls?', *Tribune* (29 December 1944), p. 9; Aneurin Bevan, 'The coal board loss', *Tribune* (24 December 1954), p. 1.
75 Bevan, 'Plan for Work', p. 46.
76 Bevan cited in Foot, *Aneurin Bevan: 1897–1945*, p. 492.
77 Bevan, *In Place of Fear*, p. 118.
78 Bevan, 'Who wants controls?', p. 9.
79 Bevan cited in Foot, *Aneurin Bevan: 1897–1945*, p. 349.
80 Bevan, *In Place of Fear*, p. 168.
81 Aneurin Bevan, 'Beware of this Tory trap', *Tribune* (11 November 1955), p. 1.
82 Aneurin Bevan, 'Facts and taxes', *Tribune* (13 January 1956), p. 5.
83 Aneurin Bevan, 'July 5th and the socialist advance', *Tribune* (2 July 1948), p. 7.
84 Bevan, 'Tory gamblers pour £1,500 million down the drain', p. 3.
85 Aneurin Bevan, 'Steel ramp exposed', *Tribune* (30 October 1953), p. 1.
86 Bevan, 'The fatuity of coalition', p. 2.
87 Aneurin Bevan, 'Why we lost West Derby', *Tribune* (3 December 1954), p. 1.
88 Aneurin Bevan, 'Being very, very practical', *Tribune* (24 February 1956), p. 4.
89 Editorial, 'Manchester – the real story', *Tribune* (10 February 1956), p. 7.
90 Thomas-Symonds, *Nye*, p. 193.
91 Anthony Crosland, *The Future of Socialism* (London: Constable, 2006), p. 46.
92 Crosland, *The Future of Socialism*, p. xii.
93 Thomas-Symonds, *Nye*, p. 193.
94 Callaghan, The Left', pp. 30–1.
95 Saville, *The Labour Movement in Britain*, pp. 107–8.

96 Saville, *The Labour Movement in Britain*, pp. 85–7; Coates, *The Labour Party and the Struggle for Socialism*, p. 47.
97 Saville, *The Labour Movement in Britain*, p. 109.
98 Foote, *The Labour Party's Political Thought*, p. 276.
99 Thomas-Symonds, *Nye*, p. 164.
100 Campbell, *Nye Bevan and the Mirage of British Socialism*, pp. 327–30.
101 Krug, *Aneurin Bevan*, p. 255.
102 Thomas-Symonds, *Nye*, p. 193.
103 Campbell, *Nye Bevan and the Mirage of British Socialism*, p. 271.
104 Thomas-Symonds, *Nye*, p. 234.
105 HC Deb, 3 November 1959, vol. 612, col. 860–985.
106 Foote, *The Labour Party's Political Thought*, p. 273.
107 Drucker, *Doctrine and Ethos in the Labour Party*, p. 69.
108 Ralph Miliband, *The State in Capitalist Society* (London: Quartet Books, 1973); Coates and Panitch, 'The continuing relevance of the Milibandian perspective', pp. 72–3.
109 Coates and Panitch, 'The continuing relevance of the Milibandian perspective', p. 73.
110 Wickham-Jones, 'An exceptional comrade? The Nairn-Anderson interpretation', pp. 90–1.
111 Miliband, *Parliamentary Socialism*, p. 332.

3
WAR, INTERNATIONAL RELATIONS, WORLD DEVELOPMENT

> The western powers must reconcile themselves to the fact that the framework of the past has been irretrievably broken, and the second half of the 20th century will see the building of the outlines of the future pattern of society.[1]

BEVAN'S POLITICAL career coincided with significant international conflict. He was active in the trade union movement during the First World War, campaigned vigorously in support of Republican Spain during the Civil War, came to prominence as a parliamentarian during the Second World War, and became shadow foreign secretary in 1956 during a period of considerable international tension. It is no wonder then that Bevan's writings took on a significantly internationalist character. During the Second World War he was arguably the most prominent critic of the National Government in Parliament – a 'squalid nuisance', as Churchill described him.[2] His writings concentrated largely on how society could move from a state of conflict to a state of peace. During the 1950s, Bevan sought solutions to Cold War tensions. This focus meant that international relations were a major component of his political thought.

On international issues, as with most issues being debated within the Labour Party, there have been a variety of opinions, splits and perspectives.

As Rhiannon Vickers has discussed, the Labour Party emerged from an international context in which Britain was a global hegemon.[3] The Labour Party, in government and in opposition, was shaped by Britain's role in the world and its decline over the course of the twentieth century (p. 17). Vickers highlighted three main factors that influenced Labour's foreign policy: 1) Britain's position in the world; 2) that the party emerged later than most European parties and from many different groupings, meaning it did not have a single, united ideology; and 3) the effect of party members: more left-wing out of government, less left-wing when in government and facing the realities of the world situation (p. 19). Bill Jones identified two approaches to foreign policy within the party: realist and idealist. Realists emphasised the importance of military and economic power, while idealists appealed to ideas of good faith in changing the international system.[4]

It is perhaps more difficult to study foreign policy in terms of ideas. Foreign policy is often a response to external events, rather than an application of a particular vision. The British political system lends itself to this reactive type of foreign policy.[5] Nevertheless, Vickers has demonstrated some of the main ideas underpinning Labour's approach to the world. The party's political thought has been marked by a commitment to internationalism, one that is based on the principle that states share common goals and belong in an international 'community'. This outlook maintains that international relations should be based on democratic principles and universal norms, collective security, anti-militarism and working-class solidarity (pp. 6–8). Although there were differences over how this internationalism could be achieved, Vickers argued that it represented a broad understanding of what the party stood for.

While acknowledging the often reactive nature of foreign policy, this chapter explores Bevan's attempt to develop a vision of society that would relegate military power in favour of other concerns. First, it explores Bevan's writings during the Second World War to establish his understanding of war, its causes and its features. Second, the chapter examines Bevan's analysis of power politics that defined post-war international tensions. Then, finally, it considers Bevan's vision for a new pattern of international society based on strong international political institutions and the provision of aid to the developing world. While many of Bevan's discussions see him responding to international events, this chapter nevertheless demonstrates that a relationship exists between core components of his political thought and his analysis of international society.

War

CAPITALISM AND WAR

To understand Bevan's views on war, it is important to reflect on his critique of capitalism, as discussed in previous chapters. It was established that Bevan's conception of society centred on the conflict between the working class and the ruling class. For Bevan, war was tied up with this conflict. He believed that war was simply a consequence of the destructive dynamics of capitalism and would be waged to the advantage of the ruling class. He also argued that war was the inevitable result of power politics between the large nations of the world. In 1938, in the build-up to the Second World War, he wrote that 'the Government had abandoned the policy of Collective Security for which they declared themselves at the General Election, and were now pursuing the old pre-war system of power politics and alliances, which must in the end, result in another blood bath'.[6] Power politics between capitalist nations had thus created the conditions for war.

Although he was opposed to the First World War,[7] Bevan was not a pacifist. He supported the Second World War, viewing it as a defence of democratic values against the rise of fascism. Nonetheless, he suspected that capitalists were exploiting war as an opportunity for increased profit. For example, his assessment of the rearmament programme, which began in the 1930s as a response to the deteriorating international situation, followed this line of argument. He wrote that 'capitalism finds employment for its millions of idle workers – they are put to dig their own graves'. He predicted that:

> The whole industry of the country will be geared to the production of munitions; the one voracious and insatiable consumer for the output of modern scientific industry is found where capitalism was bound to finally find it, in preparations for war on a vast scale.[8]

A *Tribune* editorial reminded readers that wars are caused 'by social maladjustments and we must expect that those who benefit by these maladjustments will try to divert attention from the fact'.[9] Bevan argued that it was the capitalist ruling class that benefited from these social maladjustments.

Throughout the war, Bevan suspected the government of protecting the interests of private enterprise, accusing the Conservatives of wanting to increase the profits of big business from arms production. In 1942 he wrote, 'If the immediate outlook makes them feel apprehensive they take comfort in the knowledge of fat bank balances growing fatter each day by unprecedented profits from the manufacture of arms'. He also commented on the collaboration between the capitalist class and the state: 'First they make enormous profits by supplying arms to the nation and then they make still more money by lending these profits to the Government.'[10] From the outbreak of war, 'the big capitalists dug themselves into every State department ... battening on the nation'.[11] 'In every department of State', a 1942 *Tribune* editorial stated, 'the nominees of monopoly capital are in control. The working classes, on the other hand, have accepted willingly unheard-of disciplines and coercions'. The editorial accused the ruling class of wanting national unity 'in order to persuade the people to abandon their demands upon private interest'.[12] The collaboration between private enterprise and a Conservative-led government was a central feature of Bevan's analysis, which was particularly prominent during the war. His theory of class conflict remained central to it.

Another example of the unhealthy relationship between capitalists and the state was the issue of food supplies. Bevan claimed in 1939 that while military preparations were in the hands of the government, the nation's food supplies were in the hands of private enterprise. He argued that those controlling food had only the profit motive in mind. While private enterprise took no responsibility for the health of the nation, the government was protecting its interests: 'Private enterprise gets us into a war and at the same time is unable to protect us from the threat of starvation consequent upon it.'[13] Bevan believed that this situation was hampering the war effort as workers did not want to struggle for the profit of others. He wrote that, 'The evils of profit-making here stand plainly revealed as barriers to the effective prosecution of the war', arguing that people would 'risk their lives for liberty' but not when liberty included fighting for dividends.[14] Private enterprise and the effective undertaking of the war were not conducive to each other.

Bevan considered rearmament to be the most explicit example of capitalists taking advantage of the war. He wrote in 1938 that 'Preparation for death is the main thing that is keeping economic life going', asserting that 'War and the fear of war afford the only market which the National Government is able to find for the consumption of the product of men's hands, until the men themselves are swallowed by the thing which is fed by their work'.[15] Bevan warned the government that 'the workers are not prepared to let the employers get away with the swollen profits of arms production without a struggle'.[16] He considered it ridiculous to suppose that the government would use the armed forces 'for the furtherance of any of the principles which we have at heart, such as the defence of democracy, or resistance to capitalist exploitation'. He demanded that Labour desist from supporting the arms budget of the government as there 'can be no greater madness than for Socialists to help arm their class enemies'. He was not necessarily against the building up of arms, alongside mainstream Labour thinking by the end of the 1930s,[17] but insisted that if Labour was in power, they would be used 'to protect and not to destroy working class interests'.[18] He maintained that 'It is no argument to say that because I may need a sword in the future that I should therefore put a sword in the hands of my enemy now'.[19] War and its build-up were therefore not immune to class conflict as Bevan saw it existing in Britain.

As well as being used to maintain the dominance of the capitalist system, Bevan also saw war as protecting Britain's imperial interests. Rather than caring about democracy elsewhere, Bevan accused the British government of only being concerned 'with the defence of British Imperialism' and of not caring 'a fig for freedom here or anywhere else'.[20] He was concerned that the war was being fought to preserve the old order:

> In short, if we are to judge by the specific and definite statement made on our behalf by the British Foreign Office and by the Prime Minister himself we are fighting this war, going through all this agony and privation simply in order to put the old world back on its feet again.[21]

Bevan's perception of ruling-class motives during the war was based on his underlying belief in the realities of class conflict. In this instance, he also identified class conflict as a phenomenon taking place throughout the world as the ruling class attempted to protect imperial interests.

FASCISM AND THE RULING CLASS

While detecting an attempt to prop up capitalism, Bevan did, however, recognise that the Second World War was being fought to defeat fascism. As well as criticising the government's appeasement of fascism and the lack of emphasis on collective security throughout the 1930s and earlier, Bevan understood the cause of war to rest with the rise of fascism throughout Europe. By the time war arrived, Bevan argued that his and *Tribune's* prophecies on the impending conflict had come true. He declared that socialists needed to fight against the rise of fascism with vigour:

> Whatever else may be entailed in the present war there is the possibility and avowed purpose of arresting the progress of fascist aggression. So long as that purpose is behind our efforts, every good Socialist will do his utmost to assist the anti-Fascist forces.[22]

Bevan's analysis of capitalism made him see fascism as the attempt of the ruling class to bring order to economic anarchy. He declared that fascism is the 'super-imposition of the collective state upon competitive anarchy inside'.[23] Bevan linked his analysis of fascism with his understanding of poverty, property and democracy, declaring that 'Fascism is, in its very essence, the destruction of democratic government'.[24] Fascism promised 'order, security and exemption from the pain of personal decision' and Bevan suspected that economic disorder between the wars fuelled this insecurity across Europe: 'In short the social machinery which men had been building up since the beginning of the industrial revolution got out of hand and it came to be realised that the most urgent problem of the day was to bring society once more under control.'[25] He believed people were willing to give up freedom to ensure security in a chaotic world (pp. 12–13). The importance of control and predictability is a recurring theme in Bevan's analysis of society (see Chapter 4). Although Bevan certainly supported a war effort to destroy fascism, he also suspected that such elements were emerging in Britain.

Whether it be the maintenance of imperial interests, or of capitalism at home, Bevan argued that power during the war resided with reactionary elements. Whereas Bevan wanted the Second World War to bring about the creation of a new society based on the needs of the people, he accused the ruling class of attempting to maintain its power, denying the fervour for change that he felt existed throughout the country. He argued that 'the

Tories would risk a victory for Hitler rather than that property should suffer any diminution in its power and status'[26] – 'Thus in Fascist and non-Fascist states alike big business remains in control'.[27] Bevan accused the Conservatives of not wanting to create a new world, including seeing nothing wrong with the empire and the social situation that existed before the war. Fascism was 'the future refusing to be born' according to Bevan, and he sensed that reactionary elements within Britain were partaking in this process.[28] Bevan outlined how, in 1944, he supposed that a fascist situation was present as the ruling class attempted to maintain its grip on society:

> All the elements of Fascism are present in such a situation. First, a production crisis arising out of a clash between workers and employers in the most socially mature industries. Second, a powerfully entrenched employing class, able to resist the first attacks on their position and, therefore, to prolong the crisis until other sections of the nation become impatient. Third, a leadership of the workers too weak or too involved to mobilise their forces for a final assault, and, therefore, led to reproach their own followers in an attempt to resolve the crisis by sounding the retreat. Fourth, a sullen and confused mass of workers ripe for exploitation by Fascist demagogy.[29]

Bevan was discussing the situation in the mining industry, and while he believed that the miners could fight against this exploitation, since they were 'the most advanced section of the workers', he worried that the same conditions 'in a number of other industries with less politically educated workers ... [were] the ideal ingredients for British Fascism' (p. 7). Bevan argued that property would attempt to destroy democracy when poverty attempted to take control of the functions of property. Bevan's analysis above demonstrates that he saw this as the onset of fascism.

Bevan warned that the Conservatives could not be allowed to lead on planning for future relations in Europe as they would seek to keep reactionary elements in power. He predicted that if a social revolution came, then Wall Street and the City would attempt to starve and suppress it:

> If a revolutionary movement seizes power Wall Street and the City will be tempted either to starve it into submission or suppress it

> by force of arms under the pretext of preserving order and civil conditions. What starts as a campaign of liberation will tend to develop into a counter-revolutionary occupying force. Nor are we entitled to be surprised if and when this happens. If the people of Europe declare the railways, the land, the banks, the mines and the factories public property the owners of similar properties here and in America will take alarm and will try to suppress a revolution which might have unpleasant repercussions for them.[30]

The previous war had produced the Russian Revolution, which, Bevan argued, had been starved at birth by capitalists. He insisted that this war could 'give us the European Revolution if the arm that strikes down the Nazis is not allowed to crush the insurgent spirit of Europe' (p. 7). He stressed the need to fight fascism and warned that the ruling class could lead Britain to a fascist state if an attempt was made to challenge property. Thus, Bevan saw the attempt to preserve capitalist principles as the onset of fascism, not just elsewhere in Europe but also in Britain.

THE POST-WAR WORLD

Although Bevan was critical of the way in which the government conducted the war effort, he argued that behind Churchill was 'a united nation in a sense that has never before been achieved'.[31] *Tribune* warned, however, that the Conservatives stood 'for the maintenance of the existing order, therefore they pretend that national unity and defence of Toryism are made one and the same thing'.[32] Bevan demanded that the war needed to be conducted in the interests of the people. A *Tribune* editorial in 1942 stated: 'We shall not have won the war, if, in the waging of it, the individual man and woman falls out of the picture and their place is taken by an empty generalisation.'[33] The people needed to be at the heart of shaping military strategy.

Bevan claimed that the war had shifted the mood of the country significantly to the left. He suspected, however, that the National Government was not following that change of mood: 'the stubborn and decaying class which governs us confines the spirit of this country in the old mould.'[34] To capture this mood, Bevan wanted the war to be directed by leaders with a socialist mind-set; leaders who would have the concerns of the people as their main priority.[35] He even suggested that the Labour Party needed to join forces with other groups on the left, such as the Communist Party and the Liberal Party. He argued that the main task of the Labour Party was 'to construct a People's Government, through the instrumentality of what I have called a Coalition of the Left'. He believed that it should have been possible 'to make concessions so as to harness many diverse currents in progressive politics'.[36] To combat the capitalist approach to war, Bevan wanted to see socialist principles applied, such as coalmines being taken over and run in the interests of the workers and the nation.[37] Bevan was thus identifying the importance of public ownership during wartime.

A central component of Bevan's political thought was his desire to develop a plan for the post-war world. *Tribune* declared in 1942 that 'A modern army needs modern weapons, but it also needs the confidence that it is led by men with modern ideas'.[38] A year later it stated that there was a 'growing demand that immediate plans should be made for dealing with the post-war world' due to the fear of returning to the pre-war situation.[39] Bevan claimed that a conception of the war based on democratic principles 'inspired the common people of Britain', while at the same time it 'frightened the devotees of the old social order who still had their hands on the levers of power'. He identified a connection between the structure of society and the way war strategies were carried out. He claimed that the war was being waged in the interests of the ruling class, therefore proving 'that political considerations lie at the base of all military plans and ... that the pattern of war follows inevitably the structure of the society which wages it'. Bevan wrote that the ruling class was confronted with 'a revolutionary Europe' for which they had no vision.[40] Socialists could provide that vision of a new society to replace the dominant capitalist principles that had prevailed for many years.

Bevan consistently argued for the principles of democracy to be maintained during wartime. He wrote that war had been a constant theme throughout human history and had shaped the way societies had developed:

> Men have never been able to go about the ways of peace without keeping an eye on their enemies. War, either active or imminent, always troubled their minds and if they laid the sword aside for a moment it was never far away. It has therefore never been possible for men to turn away from the thoughts of war and dedicate

> themselves wholly to peaceful pursuits, for both war and peace are woven together inextricably in the patterns of human history.[41]

If war has always been a consideration throughout human history and 'if in times of peace the shadow of war marches by our side', then 'so also in time of war we must never abandon the dreams, ideals and ambitions of peace. To do so would be to give war a mastery it has never had' (p. 12). Bevan declared that victory would not be achieved in a narrow military sense but would come 'by calling to our aid millions of ordinary people all over Europe, to rise against their tyrants'.[42] Bevan's belief in democracy was fortified by his analysis of the military situation.

Bevan accused the government in 1937 of silencing the voice of the people. He wrote that the 'fear of Hitler is to be used to frighten the workers of Britain into silence. In short, Hitler is to rule Britain by proxy'.[43] He was critical of the powers that the government possessed, believing that the Home Secretary had been given the ability to arrest people at will with no defence and to declare legitimate strikes as sabotage. In 1939 he argued that 'the first major casualty of war was the liberty of the British people', accusing the government of trying to limit political discussion and attempting to establish in Britain 'those very principles which we are supposed to be fighting to destroy'. Bevan lamented that on the Home Front, 'a real blow for the defence of liberty had been struck'.[44] His faith in Parliament led him to fight for democratic values at home, while they were being fought for abroad on the battlefield. His defence of democracy came to the forefront during this period.

War, Bevan predicted, could have an educational effect on the British people, allowing them to see clearly the life they were leading. He wrote that 'They [the British people] have been brought to see that the vicissitudes they suffer are not implicit in an immutable pattern of life, but are the direct consequences of a particular kind of social organisation, and, therefore, capable of being dealt with by social action'. He trusted that the war had created a new state of mind, which believed that all the economic and social ills of society were preventable:

> This is a state of mind that I call deeply optimistic ... It sees that poverty, ill-health, economic insecurity, unemployment, and war are socially preventable evils. It believes in the secular origin of

man's fate, and that, when you come to think of it, is the biggest revolution that has occurred for thousands of years.[45]

The task for socialists, Bevan maintained, was to develop economic planning while preserving personal liberties after the war. This involved reiterating that public ownership was vital to creating a new society. Bevan's writings on war and the post-war world were again informed by his desire to reverse property relations: 'the area of private property must be drastically restricted, because power over property is the instrument of economic planning.' Bevan was careful to emphasise that democratic liberties needed to be maintained: 'The supreme test for democratic institutions is whether they can bring about a planned economy whilst at the same time preserving the decent personal liberties which were the best products of the Liberal Revolution.' He saw socialism as being the only option, asking, 'Can the state be given power over our work without the same power swallowing the whole of our life? That is the question millions are asking. I believe it can be done' (p. 11). Bevan argued that Labour ministers in the National Government needed to realise 'that the principles of national ownership and public control that they claim to believe are not only the programme of a Party. They are the indispensable conditions for the successful prosecution of the war'.[46] The war therefore strengthened Bevan's faith in Parliament and his belief in public ownership.

As a step to creating a better post-war society, Bevan endorsed the proposals of the incredibly popular Beveridge Report, published in 1942. He was extremely vocal in his criticism of what he saw as the Conservative Party's attempt to delay the report's implementation, as it, he argued, did not want to see a social revolution happen in Europe that would alter the fabric of society.[47] If Britain showed that it had the 'courage, imagination and resilience to embark on a social experiment of such a magnitude in the midst of war, then she may once more assert a moral leadership which will have consequences in every sphere of her activities'.[48] Bevan argued that the post-war world could only be tackled by forming a new government to fix the 'future pattern of our lives'.[49]

An important aspect of Bevan's post-war vision concerned the international arena. He envisioned a post-war world where nations would work in co-operation with each other. Reflecting on the First World War, Bevan interpreted it as a war fought for national self-determination, or 'in plainer words, national freedom. We now see how wrong that aim was'. He stressed that the Second World War needed to be fought 'for the right of individual self-determination, of individual freedom'. This desire was the same all over the world. It required co-operation as the 'nations of the world are so closely interwoven that the welfare of one is determined by the behaviour of another. There cannot be any absolute national freedom'.[50] Bevan appreciated the importance of national sovereignties in the post-war world but envisioned an international society based on collective action.

Ultimately, Bevan argued that war needed to lead to victory for the 'Socialist and Internationalist Cause'.[51] The Second World War provided a new fervour to the peoples of Europe and highlighted the competing conceptions of society envisioned by socialists and capitalists. While Bevan accused capitalism of trying to profit from war, he believed it offered a new chance for socialist principles to emerge. His rejection of military power is consistent with his ambitions for society as analysed in the previous chapters. Bevan attempted to articulate a vision of post-war international society that was based on democratic socialist principles. This vision also contained his emphasis on radically altering property relations as a means to bring about social revolutions, both in Britain and throughout the world.

International Order

POWER POLITICS

Bevan saw the end of the Second World War as potentially ushering in a new period of international co-operation. But, in reality, post-war international society became merely an extension of the fragile position that had developed pre-war. The world was now divided into two hostile camps, each reflecting different ideologies: the capitalist United States versus the communist Soviet Union. The build-up of armaments undertaken by the world superpowers after the Second World War, and also by Britain itself, led Bevan to suspect that the same level of hostilities would just be perpetuated post-war.

Bevan urged the major powers to forget about the old world and work together to forge a new one. He argued that the 'western powers must reconcile themselves to the fact that the framework of the past has been irretrievably broken, and the second half of the 20th century will see the building of the outlines of the future pattern of society'.[52] The 'reality of the modern world', Bevan declared, was 'that power [had] stalemated itself. The price of glory is too high. The great powers confront each other with mutual respect born of mutual fear. They are poised for war and afraid to strike'.[53] In urging for this new world, Bevan wanted Labour to commit to a policy that rejected power politics.

Power politics was taking place primarily between two ideological blocs, communism and capitalism. Bevan's understanding of these ideologies is analysed in greater detail in the next chapter, but it is important to highlight his view that the world was being framed increasingly as a battle between these two ideologies and their representatives, the Soviet Union and the United States. He argued that as long as the United States remained 'convinced that the chief danger to peace is the military aggressiveness of the Soviet Bloc', encouraging those in the United States who wanted war with the Soviet Union, then 'the danger of war will be immediately upon us'. Due to wealth being 'tied up in the war machine', economic and financial pressures would worsen the situation, thrusting the world 'either into military action or the continuation of arms production on a self-defeating scale'.[54] Bevan argued that the Cold War was being driven by anti-communist sentiment as much as by a rational analysis of Soviet intentions. Attitudes towards the Soviet Union within the Labour Party were more mixed.[55]

A central theme in Bevan's analysis of the Soviet Union was the mistake in attributing aggressive intentions to it. He argued that there was 'no evidence to show that the Soviet Union wants a trial of strength'.[56] He was critical of previous Soviet expansion – commenting on Russian influence in Czechoslovakia, Bevan wrote that 'in coming so far to the West she overran her sociological frontiers. She could occupy but she has not been able to digest'.[57] However, Bevan felt that a hostile reaction to the Soviet Union was unwarranted and unhelpful in striving for world peace. He argued that far from solving international issues, the United States' military aggressiveness was 'feeding the peril of Communism as much as they [were] combating it'.[58] This distrust led to the development of an international society focused on an escalating arms race: 'Behind the weapons are the causes of international tension, and these must be tackled successfully before the nations will be disposed to approach even partial disarmament in a favourable climate of world affairs.' Failure to reach an agreement on the development of arms would lead to serious consequences for the world.[59] Mutual suspicion and fear were driving nations to build-up armaments and to the brink of war.

ARMS

Just as he did in the lead up to the Second World War, Bevan argued that the increase in arms was being driven by economic considerations. He suggested that economies had relied on war to keep private enterprise strong. States and businesses, therefore, were reluctant to see that end. Bevan admitted that shareholders were perhaps not *actively* seeking war, yet he suspected that they would certainly be concerned about their profits if armaments were reduced. He wrote in 1953 that:

> Arms production has operated like a great public works programme – as indeed it is – to underpin the economies of the West, providing markets and postponing the depression which has come to be regarded almost as a natural phenomenon in private enterprise economy.[60]

Bevan contrasted this with the Soviet Union, which he believed was not concerned with principles of business when considering war production: 'Whatever else makes Russia compelled to make arms, it is not in order to make profits. There is no economic vested interest in the war machine' (p. 4). A few years later in 1958, Bevan wrote that, 'Obsessed by the immediate fear of trade recession and unemployment, the larger danger that an intensification of the arms race might lead to the destruction of our whole world appears to be a mere background consideration'.[61] Again, Bevan attributed economic considerations to the build-up of arms, reflecting his analysis of the relationship between economics and the resulting social implications.

Whatever the reasons for the increase in arms production, Bevan urged for an international programme of disarmament. Weapons had become 'a nonsensical and intolerable burden; therefore, what is now required is an agreed way of dismantling the war machine'.[62] Disarmament provided an opportunity for the world to change and should have been seen 'as a message of hope and deliverance and not as a harbinger of economic chaos accompanied by mass unemployment'.[63] Coupled with this desire to see an end to nuclear weapons was Bevan's consideration of German reunification as an arena that perpetuated international tensions. Bevan insisted that the reunification of Germany was vital, but he did not want the matter to be separated from the issue of disarmament. He maintained that reunification could not take place at the same time as West Germany was being rearmed.[64] He saw the desire of the West to number Germany among its military assets as the chief obstacle to a united Germany, concluding that 'Unity on the basis of neutrality: that seems the only way out'.[65] A full, not a partial, solution to world problems was needed. Bevan was critical of the rearming of West Germany as it raised an obstacle to rapprochement with the Soviet Union, thus harming the prospect of peace.[66]

The central concern defining Bevan's attitude to armaments during the 1950s was the development of the hydrogen bomb. Bevan's writings demonstrate a desire to stop international relations being reduced to military strength and the possession of weapons. He urged world powers to stop testing nuclear weapons and to step away from the brink of war. Bevan argued that 'the existence of nuclear weapons can no longer be regarded as a deterrent to war, but as making war a certainty'. He wrote in 1957 that 'so long as weapons of this character are in the possession of governments' then 'decisions about life or death, about the future of the human race, have passed out of the control of the civil political institutions'. 'The conclusion', he wrote:

> is inescapable. If the people are to recover control over those issues that are central, not only to the future of civilisation but to its proper functioning, then we must apply our minds to the destruction of nuclear weapons before they have the chance to destroy us.[67]

Bevan insisted that it was 'not enough to halt on the edge of the precipice and remain poised there. We must draw back further and further until we reach a place where the nations can settle down in peaceful intercourse'.[68] Nuclear weapons needed to be destroyed, Bevan claimed, in order to remove military calculations from international relations.

The hydrogen bomb was the subject of arguably the most infamous moment in Bevan's career and his time as shadow foreign secretary. Responding to a proposal for unilateral disarmament at Labour Conference in 1957, Bevan rejected it, calling it an 'emotional spasm'. He believed that possessing the bomb would be useful as a bargaining tool for negotiations with other nations and would give Britain status and a measure of foreign policy independence from the United States.[69] Bevan had previously stated in 1956 that he saw the benefit of Britain possessing nuclear weapons because the United States and Soviet Union had them.[70] He stressed that his opinion was not based on support for nuclear weapons, however. Nonetheless, his attitude did seem to reflect a reversion back to traditional power politics based on the possession of weapons that he had previously criticised. This conflicts with his writing during this period. Yet, while this incident (reported on extensively in biographies and Labour histories) does seem to suggest Bevan abandoning previously held beliefs on the status of nuclear weapons, it supports his position that Britain should act as a mitigating presence in international affairs, or even as part of a third force (as discussed below).

There were instances when Bevan held hope that things were changing, suspecting at one time that Soviet leaders were beginning to depart from an arms race. In 1958, he wrote that:

> The economic exploitation of a modern advanced industrial community by military garrisons imposing an alien ideology is wholly impracticable. The Russians are beginning to learn this at the very time when the West is beginning to forget it ... Unless many of the leaders of Western opinion can disentangle themselves from this ideological cats' cradle, they will never be able to think clearly about the inner nature of the problem facing the world today.[71]

As the end of the 1950s approached, however, Bevan saw no signs that the situation was improving,[72] despite insisting that the 'concept of massed armies, armed with conventional weapons, traversing great distances surrounded by hostile populations, belongs to the past'.[73] Bevan's desire for an international society of co-operation appeared to be a far-off reality.

THE 'THIRD FORCE'

Bevan's writings reflect a desire to see Britain detach itself from the politics of power blocs. He argued that British policy 'should align itself with all those forces in the world that make for a peaceful solution to problems'.[74] He pointed to countries such as India as achieving success after separating itself from the two world blocs, arguing that neutrality did not mean ineffectiveness. For instance, Bevan attributed a strong role to India in ending conflict in Korea: 'India has proved that military weakness is not the same thing as international impotence.'[75] He also praised communist countries such as Yugoslavia and China for forging their own paths in foreign policy.[76]

Bevan's denouncement of unilateral disarmament appeared to put him in the power politics camp, but as noted above, he did qualify his statement by referring to Britain as a moderating force.[77] Bevan wanted Britain to align itself with countries that were standing aside from the machinations of power politics.

It has been claimed by several authors that Bevan advocated a 'third force' in international relations. Campbell described Bevan's position as wanting Britain to be a third power, charting an independent course from the foreign policy of the United States.[78] Campbell argued that Bevan and the Left demanded a peaceful settlement to world tensions, advocating a third-way foreign policy and a non-aligned faction that would include anti-colonial movements around the world (pp. 28 –5). Thomas-Symonds noted that Bevan distinguished between a 'third force' (which he advocated) and a 'third bloc' (which he saw as dangerous), although the precise difference between the two is not made clear.[79] Jonathan Schneer attributed the development of the Third Force movement to the Keep Left group that emerged during the period 1945–51. Led by *Tribune* MPs such as Jennie Lee and Michael Foot, it became the nucleus of the Bevanite movement.[80] Further evidence for the claim that Bevan advocated a 'third force' appears in a speech Bevan made to the Indian Parliament on a visit in 1953. He was reported as stating:

> I believe that not only for you but for mankind it is necessary that there should be a re-alignment of the forces of the world, that there should emerge a third bloc of nations holding the world balance of power and compelling the two giants (the United States and Russia) to listen to what they have to say.[81]

This comment was criticised by Indian Prime Minister Jawaharlal Nehru, who declared that the:

> idea of a third bloc, or third force, frightens or embarrasses people. Let us rather work to get as large an area as possible of countries which do not want to encourage any tendencies to war, who wish to work for peace, and do not want to align themselves with any bloc.[82]

This comment foreshadowed the non-alignment movement established in 1961.[83]

The Times later reported that Bevan insisted that he 'had never suggested the establishment of a "third force" between Russian and American blocs', contradicting Thomas-Symonds' assessment above. Instead, he was reported as declaring to the Indian Council of World Affairs that 'They have been attributing to me a phrase called "third force", but I have always been careful to say that I am not speaking of a third bloc'. What Bevan was actually arguing for, according to *The Times* report, was the prevention of 'other nations from lining up with either bloc or getting sucked into the cauldron'.[84] Foot, reporting on this incident, believed that Bevan's views were not so different to Nehru's: Bevan did not argue for a third bloc, but in fact restated the idea of a group of non-aligned countries who refused to sign up to either bloc.[85] Thomas-Symonds emphasised that Bevan's 'third force' idea was linked to his 'contacts with non-aligned countries, such as Yugoslavia and India, which were key to his strategy'.[86] Rather than analysing these views in terms of 'blocs' or 'forces', it could be argued that Bevan's attitude represents a precursor to the non-aligned movement, or at least support for its stance.

Bevan did not see an issue with Western nations discussing security needs through an organisation such as NATO. Nonetheless, he argued that any international body that requires the giving up of sovereignty must have as its aim the lessening of tensions and the pursuit of morally beneficial consequences, not military ones. He wrote that 'We must be told what steps are contemplated to seek a lessening of the tensions which have led to the creation of this unprecedented military apparatus'. Bevan insisted on the need for nations to develop foreign policy with a level of independence:

> We should refuse to surrender the ability to act independently, except in a cause which promises wider and moral beneficial consequences than are likely to be obtained by adherence to our

> traditional powers ... It is not that we should seek to act alone, for that is neither permissible nor practicable in the world as it is today ... But if we are asked to merge our sovereign rights with those of other nations, we should be clear, not only about the conditions on which it is done, but on the objectives at which we are aiming.[87]

Just as Bevan argued for smaller nations to create a movement separate from the two main power blocs, he encouraged them to 'concert among themselves to defy a leadership so myopic, so smugly self-satisfied, so dangerous, and so unequal to the imperious needs of the time'.[88] Although Bevan was discussing the need for integration, he still envisioned nations acting independently, not being obliged to act within the confines of traditional power politics and refusing to accept the dominance of larger nations.

It is certainly true that Bevan sought to abandon power politics. His relationships with the likes of Nehru in India and Tito in Yugoslavia give credence to the view that Bevan sought allies throughout the world beyond the traditional powers, thus supporting the thesis that Bevan was an early advocate of the idea of a non-aligned movement. It must be kept in mind, however, that describing the strategy as developing a 'third *force*' is problematic, particularly when it is not clear how a 'force' or a 'bloc' is defined. It is doubtful that Bevan was arguing for a third 'force' or 'bloc' as a *military* balance against Soviet and American hostilities; although his 'emotional spasm' comments may suggest that he was committing the Labour Party to traditional power politics. Bevan's vision was for nations to not be sucked into this game. Instead, he envisioned nations working together through strong international institutions.

Rather than continuing on the path of dangerous power politics, Bevan called for an international order based on peace and co-operation. To achieve this, he called for a series of measures that would bring the nations of the world closer together. During the Second World War he began to argue for the internationalisation of many aspects of the world economy, believing that in the future national sovereignties 'must be limited, and part of their powers vested in an over-riding international authority'.[89] He wanted to apply socialist principles across nations, hoping that a way would be found 'to reconcile the claims of cultural independence with the needs of cross-frontier economic planning'.[90] There needed to be a world conference immediately after the war to 'reach agreement on the framework of future international society'. Therefore, 'out of the agony of war the new world takes shape after the fashion of the old and the dear hope that millions began to hold of a future of assured peace and plenty fades once more before the reassertions of greed and power'.[91] Bevan argued that the world was 'weary of war and the ways of the war-makers. It is time the architects of peace took charge'.[92] Bevan contended that after the Second World War, national sovereignties needed to be consigned to the past in favour of international co-operation.

The creation of this new world order needed to be based on stable international organisation, not on alliances and treaties. Alliances would simply 'breed fear and fear will pile up rival war machines once more until the whole world will groan under an intolerable burden of war preparations'.[93] It could not be based on the motives of profit and private enterprise either. Bevan did not want for 'our dead [to have] died in order to make the world safe for foreign investment'.[94] This is why Bevan would later reject the idea of the European Common Market, which he interpreted as 'an escapist conception in which the play of market forces will take the place of political responsibility'.[95] A new international organisation needed to move away from the dominance of global market forces and capitalism, to instead be based on democratic principles.

World Development

THE UNITED NATIONS

To achieve this new world order, Bevan put his faith in the United Nations (UN). He argued in *In Place of Fear* for an 'increasing emphasis on the role of the United Nations' as regional pacts 'tend to wear the appearance of instruments of dominant Powers'.[96] Whatever was to be decided for the future of the world, it needed to 'command the resources of idealism ... to surmount the fears and limited ambitions in which international relations are now snarled'. Bevan continued, the 'instrument for the task cannot be one nation, nor a limited combination of nations. It must be the Assembly of the United Nations itself. Otherwise we shall start off in a climate of mutual suspicion' (p. 144). The UN presented an opportunity to create a world of co-operation rather than mutual distrust.

Bevan cautioned that the UN must not be used as a military organisation to further the interests of larger nations. Instead, it needed to be a vehicle for peace. Bevan's reaction to the Suez crisis highlights his vision of the UN's role. In 1956, Egyptian President Gamal Abdel Nasser nationalised the Suez Canal. Britain and France followed Israel in invading Egypt but after the United States, the Soviet Union and the UN exerted pressure, they were forced to withdraw. The incident was a humiliation for Britain, and Bevan was vocal in his opposition. He proclaimed that the arrival of UN troops was 'the physical manifestation of a moral idea', not a symbol of a future war machine. The UN was there in Egypt to facilitate peace, not to further the interests of the world's largest powers. The people of Egypt needed to see this: 'Peace ... can succeed only if the area of fear is made steadily to contract and give place to confidence and hope.'[97]

Bevan argued that 'The Arab nations will not continue to respect the authority of the U.N.O. Police if they merely symbolise an effort to make them peacefully endure feelings of outraged national pride, unnecessary poverty and imperial exploitation' (p. 1). He reiterated this view the following month: 'The strength of the United Nations in the Middle East, in the strictly moral sense, may well depend on the extent to which the Arab nations can regard it as untainted by any suspicion of being an indirect instrument of Western imperialism.'[98] The UN needed to possess the same functions as Parliament, providing a voice to all nations of the world. Just as he argued for Britain, Bevan saw democracy as the solution to exploitation by a ruling class.

Despite high hopes, Bevan admitted that there were issues with the UN. He argued that due to the veto power possessed by some states in the Security Council, power politics was still being played out. In the event of the veto being a stumbling block, nations would still bypass the UN. The Suez invasion was an example of this kind of disregard for international authority. Bevan concluded that it undermined the purpose of the UN, Britain and France being guilty of 'destroying the one single institution that offers the hope of guiding mankind into more civilised ways'. Again, Bevan urged for the principles of democracy to be extended to the international stage:

> The essence of democracy is government by discussion. The extension of the same principle to international affairs is not only logical but a pre-condition for the preservation and strengthening

> democratic processes as it is also for the maintenance of peace between the nations.[99]

The UN would only be a successful institution if it was guided by the principles of democracy.

By 1957, Bevan lamented that collective action through the UN had not been realised. He concluded that the UN had simply become an arbitration court between the views and claims of competing nations. This contrasted with his ambitions for the UN to be 'an arena of contending nations where the more civilised statesmen are attempting to build up a code of international conduct which, we must all hope, will eventually win universal approval and acceptance'. The role of the UN was not to freeze the relations of nations where they were, 'but to change and mould them in a way in which force, or the threat of force, becomes progressively infrequent'.[100] The UN had been unable to prevent the power politics that had been the hallmark of international relations, undermining Bevan's vision.

Although in effect the UN had struggled to prevent the waging of power politics, Bevan envisioned it as an organisation that could forge a new path in international relations. It could act as a promoter of peace and foster co-operation between nations. If the role of the UN was to bring all the nations of the world together, how could this be achieved? Bevan's vision was for the UN to play a major part in the economic and social development of the world.

WORLD DEVELOPMENT

Instead of asserting dominance, Bevan wanted larger nations to foster world development. Foot wrote that Bevan applied his domestic analysis of Marxism to smaller nations going through their own industrial revolutions, which needed to be given support and aid.[101] Bevan argued that 'white imperialism' had been inflicted on people for centuries alongside economic exploitation.[102] To right these wrongs, economic resources needed to be organised through the UN to benefit poorer nations. For example, Bevan predicted that there might have been 'immense deposits of precious metals and minerals yet to be surveyed and discovered'. Yet, he argued for their discovery not to be conducted by private adventure but:

> by some agency of the United Nations acting for the whole world, so that they could be extracted under reasonable conditions for the nations and peoples immediately concerned, and shared among the consuming countries in accordance with some carefully worked-out plan of priorities.[103]

This, Bevan argued, would go some way to preventing exploitation driven by private greed.

Bevan pointed to instances where the interests of capital had negatively affected smaller countries. He referred to the West's, including Britain's, reliance on the Middle East for oil, which led to 'private greed and ambition exacerbate[ing] a situation already dangerously complicated'. He continued: 'When to these ingredients you add ostentatious opulence, cheek by jowl with appalling poverty and ignorance, gimcrack political constitutions, religious bigotry and flaming nationalism, it is scarcely conceivable that the whole area will not blow itself up.' He summarised the situation thus:

> Where international co-operation is manifestly a paramount necessity, we have instead intense rivalry and, most insane of all, competition in the supply of arms to nations that do not murder themselves and others only because so far they have lacked the means to do so.[104]

Bevan warned that unless problems were brought 'under effective control, it is quite certain that some day one of them will set the world alight' (p. 5). He predicted that American imperialism fuelled by capitalism would lead to the eruption of conflict in the area.[105] To prevent this, he maintained that 'the medium of the United Nations offers the greatest hope. It enshrines a conception of the world which gives hope for people everywhere'.[106]

Instead of creating conflict, Bevan wanted larger nations, led by the UN, to foster social revolutions taking place 'in nations which have lain dormant for thousands of years'. 'Our task', he stated, was to 'accommodate them within a general pattern of world co-operation'. He argued that 'World leadership must take account of world movements or it condemns itself to futility'.[107] According to Bevan, these revolutions were developing largely in agrarian countries. He insisted that it was the duty of developed countries to provide assistance, asserting that the 'advanced industrial communities of the West' could make little progress themselves 'without sharing the achievements of their industries and sciences with the rest of the world' (p. 136). Bevan pointed out that whereas social revolutions had historically been starved at birth by the lack of investment from private enterprise, the UN needed to step in and offer aid to developing countries: 'It will not be easy to achieve, but it is preferable to sitting with folded hands while democratic Socialist experiments are throttled at birth.'[108]

Bevan insisted that the UN should be the organisation to direct aid to developing countries. This would mean that its distribution was not dependent on the foreign policy concerns of each of the major nations.[109] He 'always insisted that inter-governmental funds for the development of the backward countries should be canalised through an international agency, preferably one set up by the United Nations'.[110] Private capital could not be relied on to do this as it would not 'flow in sufficient volume to backward countries without guarantees against revolutionary action, and these cannot be provided without, at the very least, appearing to infringe the newly won sovereign rights'.[111] Bevan warned that unless something was done to help poorer nations, 'millions of people will be watching each other starve to death through expensive television sets'.[112] Bevan wanted redistributive principles applied internationally to prevent this.

Bevan's solution was for arms spending to be redirected towards development. In 1952, he urged for a reduction in arms spending and for 'realistic international discussions [to] take place for the substitution of an ambitious plan of world development to replace a substantial proportion of the expenditure on arms' (p. 146). He reiterated this point the following year when he argued for a 'Pool of Mutual Aid'.[113] Further, in 1955 he set out his proposal for diverting funds from armaments to international aid:

> There are two main aspects of it, intermingled; the nations providing aid and the nations receiving it. Both have to be prepared, and it could prove the greatest economic operation ever carried out by man. It would be ten thousand pities if, for lack of effective preparation, it turned out to be a source of misery to both giver and receiver.[114]

Thus military machinations could be redirected to provide nations with economic power.

To ensure democracy was adopted in these countries, Bevan argued that they needed to be helped economically. Here, Bevan applied his understanding of democracy to the rest of the world. He argued in 1956 that the greater part of the world had 'lagged behind the other in the application of the industrial sciences ... The psychology of the situation is made worse by the fact that the part which has lagged behind was for centuries the prey of the nations which have advanced'. The solution again offered by Bevan was that economically developed countries needed to pool resources together through the UN. Then, the 'surpluses of the advanced nations should be made available to those which are backward, but it should be done in a way that avoids any taint of national subordination on the one hand or "big nation" condescension on the other'. Summarising his view on the need for peaceful institutions, Bevan wrote: 'It is no use only praying for peace. The institutions of peace must be strengthened and clothed with power and dignity, so that all men can see in them both the source of their material well-being and the hope of its continuance.'[115]

He predicted that this support would contribute to the establishment of democratic institutions. To develop democracy throughout the world, assistance was needed from the West:

> If democratic institutions are to be helped to take root in the Orient, it can be done not by sending professors to teach the virtues of democratic constitutions, but by sending the means to raise their material standards. Man must first live before he can live abundantly.[116]

Further, Bevan wrote that collective action:

> against aggressive war is certainly essential if mankind is to survive. But it is only one half of the answer. The social revolutions of the East will overspill national boundaries and take on the nature of aggressive acts unless their economic tensions are eased by assistance from the West. (p. 40)

As a result he hoped that emancipated nations would:

> put their faith in the institutions of political democracy after the fashion of the West ... But these depend on popular support, and this will not be forthcoming to a government which appears unable to provide for an improvement in the material conditions of its people.[117]

The materialist conception of history is evident in Bevan's reflections on societal development; again, he highlighted the influence of economic conditions on political structures. The transformation of a nation's economic base would have profound effects on its political structure.

While a general theory of societal development is evident in Bevan's writings, he appreciated that the nature of social revolutions needed to be considered within the unique context and conditions of a particular society. In relation to China, for example, Bevan stressed that while 'the struggle of the British workers in their own country against the forces of capitalism causes them to sympathise immediately with the struggles of the workers in other countries', it must be remembered that the struggle 'takes various forms because it is fought under different historical conditions'. These conditions impact on the way socialism is achieved. The main difference between the struggles in Britain and in China was the existence of democratic institutions in Britain, converting 'the political franchise into a revolutionary instrument if it is used with vigour and determination'. Bevan, speaking to the Chinese Communist Party in 1954, declared that 'In the opinion of British Socialists it is this failure to recognise the challenging character of representative parliamentary institutions which has been responsible for much of the political sterility of people who regard themselves as revolutionary'.[118] He saw democracy as capable of playing a large role in transforming societies, as he believed it did in Britain. While recognising different circumstances, Bevan still proclaimed the superiority of British parliamentary democracy.

Bevan admitted that Britain's industrial and democratic revolution had been aided by the exploitation of poorer countries. He insisted that young dominions could not achieve their industrial revolutions through the surpluses of exploitation as Britain had. Bevan argued that these countries needed to develop industry with the active involvement of the people, but also through state control. In order for them to choose a democratic socialist course to industrial development, Bevan insisted that larger nations needed to provide help. This way, 'our way of life' (Britain's) would be developed. By 'our way of life', Bevan meant 'the urbanities, the tolerance, and the free institutions to which we are accustomed'. These could only be defended 'by economic policies which assist the peoples of the young Dominions to win their way to better material conditions without suffering intolerable privations'.[119] Bevan believed that in order to develop democratic institutions, material conditions needed to favour the masses. The importance of economic planning and the state is again evident.

Bevan acknowledged the difficulties involved with carrying out massive industrial development while simultaneously preserving democracy. He raised the question, can 'an economically backward nation ... build up its capital equipment and technical resources and at the same time enjoy democratic institutions?' It certainly was not achieved this way in Britain: he wrote that the British people 'achieved their industrial expansion in a different century, under totally different conditions'. He pointed out that it 'should not be forgotten that the workers of Europe did not enjoy the full range of political liberty' when going through their industrial revolutions. Instead, the 'building of the capital equipment of Europe was largely an involuntary act by the workers of Europe'. Fundamentally transforming an economy while ensuring democratic rights was difficult to achieve, but Bevan suggested that nations such as India had demonstrated that it was possible.[120] The dominance of private property meant that economic development was halted, highlighting the need for democratic institutions to alter prevailing power and property relations.

Bevan believed that establishing or maintaining democracy was particularly difficult due to the nature of change taking place in former colonies. Bevan wrote that when 'the colonial power is withdrawn by agreement ... or driven out by successful revolt, the change is profound – so profound as to constitute for a while almost a trauma'. This is due, Bevan supposed, to the 'sudden onrush of responsibility ... [that] finds many of the emancipated people unprepared'. He wrote that 'After the first rejoicings over independence comes a sober realisation of the tasks ahead'. He again asserted that 'recently emancipated colonial peoples can rarely hope to continue to enjoy personal liberty as well as national independence unless some aid from outside is available'. He continued, 'Political liberty, as distinct from national independence, is rooted in economic surplus. The flower of liberty does not flourish on barren soil'. Bevan argued that if Western nations wanted to see democracy extended, then they 'must be prepared to compensate for the years of neglect, and to underpin the political institutions of the new nations with part of their own wealth'.[121] Democracy could only flourish as a result of improved economic conditions, which Bevan argued could only be created as a result of assistance from wealthier nations: 'Freedom is the by-product of economic surplus',[122] a phrase that encapsulates Bevan's attitude towards societal development.

Bevan warned of the dangers associated with trying to suppress social revolutions. Referencing the United States' attempt to prevent China's revolution, he wrote:

> The way to treat a revolution in an agrarian country is to send it agricultural machinery, so as to increase food production to the point where the agricultural surplus will permit of an easier accumulation of the industrial furniture of modern civilisation. (pp. 41–2)

He stressed that one 'cannot starve a national revolution into submission'. It could only be starved 'into a repressive dictatorship' and 'to the point where the hellish logic of the Police State takes charge' (p. 42). The way to peace was not 'to treat great nations as political pariahs, but to bring them within the community of nations and by social intercourse and economic co-operation seek to heal the wounds inflicted by civil strife'.[123] He predicted that if this was to continue, nations would be forced into the arms of the Soviet Union to rely on aid and investment. In 1956, Bevan wrote that as the United States was 'cutting back economic aid to backward countries, Russia is emerging on the scene bearing gifts' in the form of industrial and technological expertise.[124] By failing to deliver economic aid, Bevan argued that smaller nations would look 'more and more to the expanding production of the Soviet Union'.[125]

In Bevan's mind, 'most, if not all, the peoples of the world are linked together in an endless variety of reciprocal activities'. Therefore 'the condition of each one of us, becomes the concern of all of us'. He saw exploited peoples 'as our countrymen in the sense that our industry is interlocked with theirs'.[126] Bevan maintained that developing collective action, the main goal in building international society could be achieved. He saw that goal as being 'the defeat of hunger in the most literal physical sense'. He wrote that 'Until hunger has been left behind as a racial memory, it will not be possible to say that man has won the decisive victory in his long struggle with his physical environment' (p. 144). The rejection of power politics and the development of international organisations had as its aim the creation of a new world of peace, co-operation and the development of the material resources of the world. This was how Bevan envisioned international society moving beyond military strength to focus on economic development. The relationship between the base and superstructure underpins Bevan's writings on world economic development.

NATIONAL SOVEREIGNTIES

Bevan identified several challenges to creating this new international society based on peace and co-operation. Pooling resources through the UN was important, yet there still existed the issue of how to marry independence and national sovereignties with international co-operation. During the Second World War, Bevan began to argue that nations would have to give up their sovereignty after the war. 'No one really believes', he wrote in 1941, 'in the possibility of sovereign independent states after the war'. This did not mean that nations would be subsumed by larger nations; rather, the war was about 'making a peace which will embody the best contributions of the most diverse cultures'.[127] Despite this, following the end of the Second World War, Bevan observed a desire for national independence, particularly throughout the British Empire. He saw this as a potential danger to his plan for international co-operation.

As we have seen, Bevan assigned the UN with the responsibility of bringing nations together, while respecting the national independence and goals of each of them. The aim of the UN was to 'persuade nations to put such inhibitions upon their sovereign powers as will eventually build up a code of conduct that will operate with the force of law'.[128] Collective action through international organisations could not sacrifice the goals and ambitions of individual nations. National independence was therefore an important consideration in Bevan's writings.

For this to be achieved, Bevan called for larger nations to refrain from asserting dominance on the rest of the world. He was concerned that imperialistic action from nations such as Britain and the United States was fuelling 'aggressive nationalism'.[129] This aggressive nationalism would fuel social revolutions, he warned, unless a new order of society could be created with the end of colonial exploitation as its basis. He argued that peace 'cannot be based permanently on colonial exploitation' and that the 'rule of collective peace in the world must provide for social progress and for the attainment of self-government by subject peoples. Otherwise their legitimate struggles for nationhood will endanger peace. Peace and injustice can never live long together'.[130]

In Asia, Bevan considered China to be waging a 'struggle for independence against imperialism'.[131] This was also the case in Eastern Europe where Bevan felt the Soviet Union was infringing on national independence, for example in Hungary.[132] Although sovereignty needed to be restricted in the case of international relations, this did not mean large powers imposing values on smaller nations. For Bevan, national independence did not preclude international co-operation.

A clear indication of Bevan's attitude to international society and national independence can be seen through his analysis of the Suez crisis, discussed earlier. It was a situation that saw the old power politics collide with demands for national independence.[133] The behaviour of Britain and France had converted the crisis into 'the old arid struggle between imperialism and the new nations'.[134] Power politics was bankrupt and the 'moral sense of the world was outraged by the very brutality of the attempt by great powers to impose their will by armed force on a weaker nation'.[135] Suez was a clear example of the deficiency of power politics and the need for a new attitude to national independence and sovereignty.

At the same time as respecting Egypt's right to sovereignty, however, Bevan argued that Nasser's actions were not the precursor for a social revolution. In fact, he argued that Nasser's movement was largely nationalistic as it 'derived its driving power from resentment against Western imperialism', rather than on improving social and economic conditions, which Bevan argued national movements needed to be based on: 'If a social movement elects to take the path of revolution, it must pursue it to the end, and the end is a complete transformation of society, accompanied by a transference of power from the old to the new social forces.'[136] The issue that Bevan had with Nasser's revolution in Egypt was that 'from the beginning, the Movement was strongly nationalistic, with social and economic objectives playing a secondary role' (p. 5). Bevan considered this to be an inevitable outcome of Western aggression towards Egypt.

Instead of redistributing property, Bevan accused Nasser and his colleagues of focusing only on nationalist sentiment. He admitted that Nasser and his military generals 'resented the extremes of wealth and poverty around them'. However, he believed that they 'saw the solution not as beginning with a root and branch redistribution of property, but as depending upon the building up of a modern state, to a large extent with outside aid'. He argued that 'Nationalist resurgence could have been canalised for social and economic purposes'. Unfortunately for Nasser, Bevan argued, he had 'not realised that to keep on stirring the pot of nationalist passions is not conducive to the creation of conditions favourable to long term economic projects'. Bevan also lamented that the canal was not an international waterway, the situation preventing collective decision-making. He insisted on the importance of national independence but maintained that nations also needed to co-operate with the international world: 'Nations should be set free so that they may freely come together. National independence is the basis for international co-operation, not for the indulgence of rabid nationalist excess' (p. 5). Bevan looked at Egypt as proof of the consequences of imperialist power on smaller nations.

These articles written by Bevan at the height of the Suez crisis reveal his attitude towards national independence, class and international organisation. National independence was a worthy cause, Bevan argued, if it could break the yoke of imperialism, but it needed to have as its aim the material improvement of the people of that country. For instance, Bevan saw in Yugoslavia a positive example of socialism and national independence being combined. Yugoslavia, he argued, developed an independent strategy during the war, a strategy that combined the ambitions of the peasantry and the urban worker. 'For them', Bevan wrote, 'the war was essentially a struggle for national independence'. What was important about this struggle, in Bevan's view, was that it combined national independence with socialist ambitions:

> The passionate desire for national freedom, which is the centuries-old tradition of the peoples of Yugoslavia, merged during the war with the revolutionary aims of the Yugoslav Communists. There was therefore a clear understanding between the two. For

> the urban workers, Socialism, for the peasants, land, and for both national independence.[137]

Thus, Yugoslavia was able to chart a course of action based on national independence but with socialism at its core, avoiding what Bevan would have seen as the pitfalls of purely nationalist sentiment.

Bevan maintained that co-existence involved 'co-operation including cultural, commercial and economic intercourse'. He insisted that policies must not be based on 'the leadership of this or that nation ... but on the equality of all nations, great or small. Not on blocs of nations seeking to establish uniformity amongst themselves, but on diversity and mutual interplay of natural differences'.[138] There were tensions in the struggle between national independence and co-operation, but Bevan believed that these could be reconciled to ensure peaceful co-existence. Yet, there is also evidence that this was a tension in Bevan's thought.

Bevan also insisted that for international co-operation to be successful, a nation's domestic society needed to be based on democratic socialist principles. He reflected in *In Place of Fear* that 'the nation is too small an arena in which to hope to bring the struggle [for power] to a final conclusion', arguing that 'National sovereignty is a phrase which history is emptying of meaning'. He admitted that this led many to 'turn away from the difficult task of establishing Socialism in their own country', as it would mean only partial victory.[139] Nevertheless, Bevan insisted that if 'you are going to plan the world you must first of all control the part of it that you will want to fit into the whole' (pp. 170–1). He wrote that while this 'was not an argument against international co-operation', this co-operation 'would be given greater reality in action, if governments of the world could speak with authority for the economic behaviour of their own peoples'. He concluded by insisting that 'the principles of democratic socialism are the only ones broadly applicable to the situation which mankind now finds itself' (p. 171). Democratic socialism within a nation is a crucial consideration of the next chapter.

Conclusion

This chapter has detailed Bevan's reflections on war and international relations, highlighting the importance he attached to the dynamics of capitalism in creating social and political conditions. Throughout the 1930s and during the Second World War, Bevan argued that fascism was an extreme form of capitalism, representing an attempt by the capitalist class to destroy democracy and to maintain its power. The struggle between poverty, property and democracy was given considerable emphasis in Bevan's writings during this period, particularly in the context of fascism. The conflict within property relations was also continuously highlighted by Bevan as he accused the ruling class of defending its interests against attack from the masses, and even using the war to benefit its position. There is an important link in Bevan's political thought between property relations and the international arena.

This chapter has also identified Bevan's hopes for a post-war international society that rejected great power conflict. While Bevan hoped for a peaceful post-war settlement, conflict between the United States and the Soviet Union prevented this from developing. Military power was viewed by the largest nations as essential in the post-war world, leading to the accumulation of armaments and the inflaming of international tensions. Bevan's writings during this period stressed the need to reduce armaments, although his actions betray this desire somewhat. His emphasis on the need for Britain to possess the hydrogen bomb as a bargaining tool in discussions with the United States and the Soviet Union suggests that Bevan was being sucked into a pattern of international relations that he wished to see changed. His desire to reach out to non-aligned nations does suggest, however, that Bevan was seeking an alternative to a world divided into two competing power blocs.

Although his interpretation of the international environment identified mutual distrust between competing states, in seeking solutions to international tensions, Bevan articulated an idealist vision. This chapter has acknowledged the emphasis that Bevan placed on strong international organisation, wishing to see principles of collective action at an international level, backed up by a strong UN. He also wanted larger nations to abandon their previous hostility and work towards developing the economies of the poorer nations that they had historically exploited. Bevan wanted democratic institutions to develop in these nations, and argued that the only way to do this was for large nations to provide aid so that material conditions were strengthened. The relationship between the economic base and the political and social structure of society, identified in previous chapters, was applied by Bevan to the international stage.

Bevan's ambitions were often opposed to those of his colleagues. Post-war, Labour appeared to be continuing some of the policies enacted by the coalition government; policies that ran contrary to Bevan's own vision. For instance, Ernest Bevin as foreign secretary continued coalition policy in Greece, Spain and Indonesia, with Conservatives applauding his attempts to protect Britain's imperial interests.[140] Despite the commitment of Labour and Labour leaders to a new post-war settlement, experience of the wartime coalition made the likes of Attlee and Bevin more moderate and reactive when it came to international affairs. Attlee urged a closer relationship with the United States post-war, while Bevin emphasised Britain's commonwealth and empire commitments. Labour appeared to be abandoning its ambitions for the post-war world, arguing that there was a national interest that ran counter to the visions of internationalism.[141]

Winston Churchill went so far as to say that the Conservative Party and the Labour Party were aligned on foreign policy (pp. 151–2). When it came to power politics, Labour, when in government and in opposition, was supportive of – some would argue subordinate to – the United States, drawing criticism from the left of the party who argued that Labour had failed to develop an alternative vision for foreign policy (pp. 173–81). The Labour Party, throughout its history and particularly during the Second World War and the 1950s, was supportive of the special relationship between Britain and the United States. Saville accused the Labour Party, and the Left, for joining in with anti-communist hysteria in its attempts to foster this special relationship.[142] The post-war Labour government relied heavily on Marshall Aid from the United States, with Ernest Bevin a willing partner to the Americans.[143] However, Bevan's increasingly critical sentiment towards US foreign policy went against the stance of the Labour leadership. Foote asserted that Bevan's criticisms of the government in the 1930s, regarding the class elements of its foreign policy, had abated in the 1950s and that Bevan did not see Britain and the United States as imperialist powers.[144] An analysis of Bevan's writings demonstrate that this was not the case. Bevan spent much of the 1950s arguing that military power and confrontational power politics were being pursued by the ruling class and therefore needed to be rejected.

Labour's attitude towards the Soviet Union was perhaps more complicated, as the party contained within it many different voices and opinions.[145] Important Labour intellectuals, such as Beatrice and Sydney Webb, looked favourably on the Soviet Union during the 1930s (pp. 18–22). Bevan himself spoke of the rejoicing that greeted the Russian Revolution by British workers:

> I remember so well what happened when the Russian revolution occurred. I remember the miners, when they heard that the Czarist tyranny had been overthrown, rushing to meet each other in the streets with tears streaming down their cheeks, shaking hands and saying: 'At last it has happened.' Let us remember in 1951 that the revolution of 1917 came to the working class of Great Britain, not as social disaster, but as one of the most emancipating events in the history of mankind. Let us also remember that the Soviet revolution would not have been so distorted, would not have ended in a tyranny, would not have resulted in a dictatorship, would not now be threatening the peace of mankind, had it not been for the behaviour of Churchill, and the Tories at that time.[146]

However, opinion started to change during Stalin's show trials.[147] Criticism of the Soviet Union remained muted during the war, but over time, and especially since the appointment of Bevin as foreign secretary, a more hard-line attitude developed towards it. Bevan was certainly critical of the Soviet Union. However, this criticism, as we have seen, was qualified by his understanding of power politics and of the Soviet Union's economic development.

In summarising the post-war period, Saville was critical of Labour's approach towards international relations. He argued that Labour's foreign policy continued to maintain existing imperial attitudes, invented a special relationship with the United States, was anti-Soviet Union, anti-national liberation and gave too much importance to military expenditure when reducing this would have helped fund domestic initiatives. Saville contended that Ernest Bevin, as the shaper of post-war Labour foreign policy, had no concept of a distinct Labour approach to international affairs, and was quite happy to continue the foreign policy of the wartime coalition government.[148] Bevan's infamous declaration at Labour conference in 1957 over the H-bomb demonstrates the complexity in setting out a socialist/labourist approach to foreign policy. Internationalism can be both utopian and confined by the international situation.

Considering Labour's position on foreign policy, it could be argued that Bevan's views, particularly in the 1950s, did not depart significantly from his colleagues and ideological rivals. For instance, as leader Gaitskell set out the aims of a democratic socialist foreign policy, arguing for a world based on international law, racial equality, independence and richer nations giving to the poor.[149] Bevan's views reflected those of the revisionists, being based on 'internationalism, a commitment to the UN and the international rule of law'.[150] Thus, in many ways Bevan's emphasis on internationalism fitted comfortably within the Labour Party.

Although these principles are evident in Bevan's writing, this chapter has also highlighted the centrality of alternative key themes in Bevan's political thought: his criticism of capitalism; the existence of class conflict; the relationship between economic conditions and the structure of society; and his belief in the principles of democracy and representative institutions. While similar to the internationalism of others in the party, Bevan's economic and political analysis cannot be separated from his analysis of international affairs, which, as we have seen, differed from many of his colleagues. His conception of internationalism acknowledged the importance of industrial development to improving the material conditions of the masses throughout the world. While rhetorically Labour was committed to this, the foundation of Bevan's economic analysis differed. Bevan's conception of internationalism also envisioned political power through democracy acting as a revolutionary tool to radically improve these conditions. While reflecting traditional internationalist ambitions of the Labour Party, Bevan's mistrust of American capitalism, and his less critical view of Soviet intentions, set him apart from the Labour leadership in many respects.[151] His view of international society was rooted firmly in his critique of capitalist exploitation.

Bevan's reflections on international relations and military power encompassed the competition between nations and ideologies. He saw the struggle between different ideas as a major cause in fanning the flames of international tensions, demonstrating an understanding of the power of ideas in shaping social organisation. Therefore, he wanted to see the principles of democratic socialism followed in international relations and in nations throughout the world. Bevan's conception of democratic socialism is considered in the next chapter.

NOTES

1 Aneurin Bevan, 'The second Cold War', *Tribune* (23 December 1955), p. 4.
2 HC Deb, 6 December 1945, vol. 416, col. 2544.
3 Vickers, *The Labour Party and the World, Volume 1*, p. 16.
4 Bill Jones, *The Russia Complex: The British Labour Party and the Soviet Union* (Manchester: Manchester University Press, 1977).
5 Vickers, *The Labour Party and the World, Volume 1*, p. 2.
6 Aneurin Bevan, 'Schoolmates cheer a slapstick act', *Tribune* (8 April 1938), p. 7.
7 Thomas-Symonds, *Nye*, p. 26.
8 Aneurin Bevan, 'Giant strides to the next war: we must oppose arms plan root and branch', *Tribune* (19 February 1937), p. 8.
9 Editorial, 'Revenge or reason?', *Tribune* (16 January 1942), p. 2.
10 Aneurin Bevan, 'Eight hundred million pounds go up in – smoke!', *Tribune* (24 February 1939), p. 9.
11 Editorial, 'Labour has been tricked', *Tribune* (13 February 1942), p. 2.
12 Editorial, 'Big business at the wheel', *Tribune* (22 May 1942), p. 2.
13 Aneurin Bevan, 'What is happening to the people's food?', *Tribune* (14 July 1939), p. 9.
14 Aneurin Bevan, 'A plan for air raid warnings', *Tribune* (6 September 1940), p. 13.
15 Aneurin Bevan, 'Britain's 1,700,000 forgotten men', *Tribune* (20 May 1938), p. 8.
16 M.P., 'Prim Neville takes his bow for state profiteering', p. 7.
17 Vickers, *The Labour Party and the World, Volume 1*, pp. 117–19.
18 M.P., 'M.P.s' doubts and fears as they depart for their holidays', *Tribune* (30 July 1937), p. 6.
19 Bevan, 'Giant strides to the next war', p. 9.
20 Aneurin Bevan, 'Our reply to Anderson', *Tribune* (9 December 1938), p. 1.
21 Editorial, 'Hatching vein empires', *Tribune* (13 November 1942), p. 2.
22 Aneurin Bevan and Stafford Cripps, 'Our duty!', *Tribune* (8 September 1939), p. 1.
23 HC Deb, 10 July 1933, vol. 280, col. 815.
24 HC Deb, 4 December 1933, vol. 283 col. 1318–1319.
25 Aneurin Bevan, 'Freedom is not enough', *Tribune* (26 July 1940), p. 12.
26 Aneurin Bevan, 'Conscription: why MPs revolted', *Tribune* (5 December 1941), p. 12.
27 Editorial, 'Big business at the wheel', p. 2.
28 Bevan, 'Freedom is not enough', p. 13.

29 Bevan, 'Are miners different?', p. 7.
30 Aneurin Bevan, 'We and the Germans', *Tribune* (25 June 1943), p. 7.
31 Aneurin Bevan, 'Beaverbrook: and what next?', *Tribune* (9 August 1940), p. 12.
32 Editorial, 'Let the dead past', *Tribune* (18 September 1942), p. 2.
33 Editorial, 'No one is all alone', *Tribune* (24 July 1942), p. 2.
34 Editorial, 'What Churchill stands for', *Tribune* (30 January 1942), p. 2.
35 Editorial, 'The palace revolt against Churchill', *Tribune* (24 April 1942), pp. 1–2.
36 Bevan, 'Are miners different?', p. 7.
37 Editorial, 'Consider coal', *Tribune* (20 March 1942), pp. 1–2.
38 Editorial, 'Grigg's responsibility', *Tribune* (10 April 1942), p. 2.
39 Editorial, 'The old dealers return', *Tribune* (8 January 1943), p. 1.
40 Aneurin Bevan, 'The politics of strategy', *Tribune* (3 September 1943), p. 7.
41 Aneurin Bevan, 'A job for the trade unions', *Tribune* (23 August 1940), p. 12.
42 Aneurin Bevan, 'Choose now, to live or die', *Tribune* (7 February 1941), p. 1.
43 Aneurin Bevan, 'The man who cried out with a loud voice', *Tribune* (19 November 1937), p. 6.
44 Aneurin Bevan, 'A bandage for wounded liberty', *Tribune* (3 November 1939), pp. 4–5.
45 Bevan, 'Blind men are leading us!', pp. 10–11.
46 Aneurin Bevan, 'Gentlemen, do read Hansard!', *Tribune* (10 January 1941), p. 9.
47 Editorial, 'The art of political assassination', *Tribune* (27 November 1942); Bevan, *Why Not Trust the Tories?*.
48 Editorial, 'Parliament on trial', *Tribune* (15 January 1943), p. 2.
49 Aneurin Bevan, 'A Labour plan to beat the Tories', *Tribune* (11 February 1944), p. 7.
50 Aneurin Bevan, 'Stop that nonsense now!', *Tribune* (20 December 1940), p. 13.
51 Aneurin Bevan, 'To any Labour delegate', *Tribune* (11 June 1943), p. 6.
52 Bevan, 'The second Cold War', p. 4.
53 Aneurin Bevan, '"The Times" gets a bad attack of nostalgia', *Tribune* (31 August 1956), p. 5.
54 Bevan, *In Place of Fear*, p. 145.
55 Jones, *The Russia Complex*.
56 Bevan, *In Place of Fear*, p. 127.

57 Aneurin Bevan, 'In place of the Cold War', *Tribune* (17 July 1953), p. 4.
58 Bevan, *In Place of Fear*, p. 123.
59 Aneurin Bevan, 'Churchill confesses', *Tribune* (11 March 1955), p. 3.
60 Aneurin Bevan, 'No settlement of the German problem unless we disarm', *Tribune* (31 July 1953), p. 4.
61 Aneurin Bevan, 'Arms and the slump', *Tribune* (31 January 1958), p. 5.
62 Aneurin Bevan, 'The disarmament breakdown', *Tribune* (11 May 1956), p. 5.
63 Aneurin Bevan, 'Verdict on Geneva', *Tribune* (29 July 1955), p. 2.
64 Aneurin Bevan, 'Western double-talk', *Tribune* (28 January 1955), p. 1.
65 Aneurin Bevan, 'We must not despair', *Tribune* (12 February 1954), p. 2.
66 Aneurin Bevan, Now we know', *Tribune* (10 April 1959), p. 5.
67 Aneurin Bevan, 'Destroy the bombs before they destroy us!', *Tribune* (24 May 1957), p. 1.
68 Aneurin Bevan, 'Cut arms to save peace – not to balance the budget', *Tribune* (31 May 1957), p. 7.
69 Thomas-Symonds, *Nye*, p. 173.
70 Aneurin Bevan, 'Arms: there is real hope now', *Tribune* (6 April 1956), p. 1.
71 Aneurin Bevan, 'Communism or suicide? That's not the real choice', *Tribune* (14 March 1958), p. 5.
72 Aneurin Bevan, 'Eisenhower and Khrushchev', *Tribune* (28 August 1959), p. 12.
73 Aneurin Bevan, 'A nuclear free zone in Europe would be a benediction', *Tribune* (14 November 1958), p. 12.
74 Aneurin Bevan, 'We asked for it', *Tribune* (18 September 1953), p. 1.
75 Aneurin Bevan, 'The year of hope', *Tribune* (1 January 1954), p. 4.
76 Aneurin Bevan, 'Farewell to the Trojan Horse', *Tribune* (27 April 1956), p. 5.
77 Vickers, *The Labour Party and the World, Volume 2*, p. 42.
78 Campbell, *Nye Bevan and the Mirage of British Socialism*, p. 192.
79 Thomas-Symonds, *Nye*, p. 213.
80 Jonathan Schneer, 'Hopes Deferred or Shattered: The British Labour Left and the Third Force Movement, 1945–49', *Journal of Modern History*, 56/2 (1984), 206.
81 'Two "giants"', *The Western Mail*, 17 February 1953.
82 'Indian initiative in peace', *The Times*, 17 February 1953.
83 Lorenz M. Lüthi, 'The Non-Aligned Movement and the Cold War, 1961–1973', *Journal of Cold War Studies*, 18/4 (2016).
84 'Dangers of power blocs', *The Times*, 2 March 1953.

85 Foot, *Aneurin Bevan: 1945–1960*, p. 392.
86 Thomas-Symonds, *Nye*, p. 253.
87 Aneurin Bevan, 'Platitudes won't save mankind', *Tribune* (13 December 1957), p. 5.
88 Aneurin Bevan, 'Dulles must be defied', *Tribune* (15 August 1958), p. 7.
89 Aneurin Bevan, 'Why is Duff Cooper so bad?', *Tribune* (4 April 1941), p. 13.
90 Aneurin Bevan, 'War aims begin at home', *Tribune* (4 October 1940), p. 12.
91 Editorial, 'Passports to insanity', *Tribune* (12 March 1943), p. 1.
92 Aneurin Bevan, 'What Eden cannot do', *Tribune* (14 April 1944), p. 7.
93 Editorial, 'Anglo-American back chat', *Tribune* (5 January 1945), p. 2.
94 Aneurin Bevan, 'We can't leave it all to the Russians', *Tribune* (19 August 1955), p. 8.
95 Aneurin Bevan, 'Back to free markets – and the jungle', *Tribune* (30 August 1957), p. 5.
96 Bevan, *In Place of Fear*, p. 133.
97 Aneurin Bevan, 'Wanted: a new bold policy for peace – that will save Hungary', *Tribune* (16 November 1956), p. 1.
98 Bevan, 'How Ike can take the lead', *Tribune* (21 December 1956), p. 12.
99 Aneurin Bevan, 'Aneurin Bevan asks: do they want to wreck the United Nations?', *Tribune* (14 September 1956), p. 2.
100 Aneurin Bevan, 'Crisis time for United Nations', *Tribune* (1 February 1957), p. 5.
101 Foot, *Aneurin Bevan: 1945–1960*, p. 584.
102 Aneurin Bevan, 'Britain will not fight in Indo-China', *Tribune* (23 April 1954), p. 2.
103 Bevan, *In Place of Fear*, p. 164.
104 Aneurin Bevan, 'The clash of the giants', *Tribune* (23 August 1957), p. 5.
105 Aneurin Bevan, 'Bevan on the crisis', *Tribune* (25 July 1958); Aneurin Bevan, 'Britain in the Middle East', *Tribune* (22 May 1959).
106 Aneurin Bevan, 'Dollar diplomacy? That's no answer', *Tribune* (4 January 1957), p. 2.
107 Bevan, *In Place of Fear*, p. 142.
108 Aneurin Bevan, 'It's naked and brutal imperialism', *Tribune* (19 October 1956), p. 12.
109 Aneurin Bevan, 'The United Nations should send aid', *Tribune* (6 January 1956), p. 4.
110 Aneurin Bevan, 'Suez: now what?', *Tribune* (17 May 1957), p. 3.

111 Aneurin Bevan, 'Give the United Nations a real job to do', *Tribune* (5 October 1956), p. 4.
112 Bevan, *In Place of Fear*, p. 164.
113 Aneurin Bevan, 'Here is a real plan to put the war machine in reverse', *Tribune* (7 August 1953), p. 4.
114 Bevan, 'Verdict on Geneva', p. 2.
115 Bevan, 'Give the United Nations a real job to do', p. 4.
116 Bevan, *In Place of Fear*, p. 40.
117 Bevan, 'Give the United Nations a real job to do', p. 4.
118 Aneurin Bevan, 'Do not dismiss our ideas of freedom', *Tribune* (3 September 1954), p. 2.
119 Aneurin Bevan, 'Tory financial policy could smash the Commonwealth', *Tribune* (28 June 1957), p. 1.
120 Aneurin Bevan, 'We must save India – or lose democracy's hope', *Tribune* (5 September 1958), p. 5.
121 Aneurin Bevan, 'Independence – then hard work: how to maintain the frontiers of liberty', *Tribune* (21 November 1958), p. 5.
122 Bevan, *In Place of Fear*, p. 39.
123 Aneurin Bevan, 'Why we are going to China', *Tribune* (4 June 1954), p. 2.
124 Aneurin Bevan, 'Eisenhower's greatest blunder', *Tribune* (17 February 1956), p. 4.
125 Aneurin Bevan, 'Russia's proposals put Eisenhower on the spot', *Tribune* (11 April 1958), p. 5.
126 Bevan, *In Place of Fear*, p. 137.
127 Aneurin Bevan, 'Complacency will not win the war', *Tribune* (5 September 1941), p. 13.
128 Aneurin Bevan, 'No double standards at UN', *Tribune* (15 March 1957), p. 5.
129 Bevan, '"The Times" gets a bad attack of nostalgia', p. 5.
130 Aneurin Bevan, 'America must be told: "You go it alone"', *Tribune* (16 April 1954), p. 1.
131 Bevan, 'Do not dismiss our ideas of freedom', p. 2.
132 Bevan, 'Wanted: a new bold policy for peace – that will save Hungary', p. 1.
133 Aneurin Bevan, 'Two crimes we can never forget', *Tribune* (9 November 1956), p. 12.
134 Bevan, 'Aneurin Bevan asks: do they want to wreck the United Nations?', p. 2.
135 Bevan, 'How Ike can take the lead', p. 1.
136 Aneurin Bevan, 'It must be world control for all the commercial waterways', *Tribune* (3 August 1956), p. 5.

137 Bevan, *In Place of Fear*, p. 16.
138 Bevan, 'Do not dismiss our ideas of freedom', p. 2.
139 Bevan, *In Place of Fear*, p. 170.
140 Jones, *The Russia Complex*, pp. 116–18.
141 Vickers, *The Labour Party and the World, Volume 1*, pp. 149–51.
142 Saville, *The Labour Movement in Britain*, p. 102.
143 Coates, *The Labour Party and the Struggle for Socialism*.
144 Foote, *The Labour Party's Political Thought*, p. 281.
145 Jones, *The Russia Complex*.
146 Aneurin Bevan, *Labour Party Annual Conference Report (1951)*, p. 121 cited in Vickers, *The Labour Party and the World, Volume 1*.
147 Jones, *The Russia Complex*, pp. 53–4.
148 Saville, *The Labour Movement in Britain*, pp. 93–101.
149 John Callaghan, *The Labour Party and Foreign Policy: A History* (London: Routledge, 2007), pp. 193–4.
150 Vickers, *The Labour Party and the World, Volume 2*, p. 29.
151 Callaghan, *The Labour Party and Foreign Policy*, p. 199.

4

IDEAS, HEGEMONY, DEMOCRATIC SOCIALISM

> Society is not a protean mass moulded by dominant ideas, but rather a living organism absorbing ideas, giving varying degrees of vitality to some and rejecting others completely.[1]

A CRUCIAL aspect of Bevan's analysis of economic, political and military power was the importance of ideas and values in shaping societies. Both domestic societies and the international arena were underscored by competing ideologies and struggles over symbols, values and visions. Bevan was aware of the power that ideas had to shape people's lives and the dominant values of a nation. He was especially concerned about an impending conflict between Russian 'Moscow Communism' and American 'Washington Capitalism', which he predicted would destroy social democracy.[2] The preceding chapters emphasised Bevan's interpretation of the relationship between the economic conditions of society and what he called its social organisation. This encompassed not just political structures but also prevailing modes of thought. These are now analysed.

This chapter examines the value that Bevan attached to ideas in shaping society. It begins by outlining his critique of capitalist and communist modes of thought, both of which he rejected in favour of democratic socialism. Following this, the chapter explores Bevan's view on the way in which the ruling class attempted to merge its values with those of the rest of society in order to maintain its power. It also considers the methods that the working class needed to employ to capture symbols central to national life. Finally, this chapter analyses the values that Bevan wished to see shape people's lives. It concludes by emphasising the importance that Bevan placed on the relationship between economic conditions and the prevailing ideas and values of society.

Ideologies

CAPITALISM

Despite the development of the franchise in Britain, Bevan maintained that capitalism's dominance still created a society based on competitive principles. Bevan attributed this to the primacy of private property. Proponents of capitalism were able to enshrine values of competitiveness and self-interest, which, Bevan argued, were not conducive to creating a civilised society. He contended that the drive for increased production 'takes on the appearance of an enemy of social stability'.[3] Chapter 1 demonstrated Bevan's recognition of the benefits arising from the technological advances of capitalism. Nevertheless, he argued that the consequences of this development were harmful to society's values.

Bevan criticised capitalism for failing to create 'a discernible order of values'.[4] He viewed capitalism as being centred purely on self-interest, writing that the:

> kind of society which emerges from the sum of individual choices is not one which commends itself to the generality of men and women. It must be borne in mind that the successful were not choosing a type of society. They were only deciding what they thought could be bought and sold most profitably. Nothing was further from their mind than making a judgement on the kind of society that mankind should live in. (p. 60)

Bevan wrote that the 'amoral climate of the business world exposes the psyche of the individual to unreasoning compulsions inherited from the remote past' (pp. 47–8). He expressed the view that capitalism was the assertion of individual choices, creating an environment of competitiveness and the disregard of ordered values conducive to a flourishing society.

Bevan quoted the American economist and sociologist Thorstein Veblen, a critic of capitalism, who described the 'systems of make-believe' that were characteristic of the 'Competitive Society' and that, as Bevan recognised, 'still pervade[ed] our thinking' (p. 43). These systems of make-believe rejected 'Collective action' – considered 'anathema' to the competitive society – leaving 'the individual to pursue what he considers to be his own advantage in industry and commerce' (p. 44):

> Material success, in this philosophy, is the prize awarded by society to the individual who has served it best, so the zest for profit is really a search to discover the wishes of the community. Though the motive may be selfish the general welfare is served. (p. 44)

Bevan argued that this philosophy resulted in people falling into poverty. Capitalism, he wrote:

> failed to produce a tolerable home and a reputable order of values for the individual man and woman. Its credo was too grossly materialistic and its social climate too feverish. It converted men and women into means instead of ends. They were made the creatures of the means of production instead of the masters. The price of men was merely an item in the price of things. Priority of values was lacking because no aim was intended but the vulgar one of the size of the bank balance. (p. 45)

Bevan argued that 'efficiency' was the final arbiter of the competitive society, 'as though loving, laughing, worshipping, eating, the deep serenity of a happy home, the warmth of friends, the astringent revelation of new beauty, and the earth tug of local roots will ever yield to such a test' (p. 45). Capitalism was unable to appreciate these values.

COMMUNISM

Alongside his rejection of capitalist values, Bevan also rejected communism as an alternative. Attitudes towards communism shifted and changed over time within the British labour movement. Even if revolution was not pursued within labourism, there was still general support for the Bolshevik revolution in Britain, with Labour not supporting the export of communism but advocating Lenin's experiment as long as it stayed within Russia.[5] Bill Jones in his study of the Labour Party's relationship with the Soviet Union identified three strands of thought within the party: pacifist; fellow-travellers; and radical idealists (p. 210). Over time, particularly after the heroics of the Red Army during the Second World War, Labour became more accepting of the Soviet Union, demonstrated by the fact that the National Executive Committee did not expel those who spoke on platforms with communists (including Bevan) (p. 65). Over time, however, the centre of the Labour Party became increasingly hostile and distrusting towards the Soviet Union (pp. 158–9). As foreign secretary, Ernest Bevin did everything he could to stop the spread of communist influence throughout the world.[6]

Bevan was also highly critical of communism, accusing communist parties around the world of sticking too closely to what he regarded as outdated Marxist dogma, which he argued was irrelevant to real existing conditions and incompatible with democracy. His criticism of communism centred on its dismissal of parliamentary institutions. Bevan's experience in Britain proved to him 'how democratic institutions could be used to ... solve the economic problems of the post-war world'.[7] Parliamentary institutions were vital to Bevan's conception of political power; therefore, he rejected ideas that did not allow for them to be prominent. For instance, he was scathing of the Soviet Union's removal of non-Communist socialist parties in Eastern Europe, arguing that the Communist Party was the 'sworn inveterate enemy of the Socialist and Democratic Parties', the communist looking upon the socialist 'as a dupe, as a temporary convenience, and as something to be thrust ruthlessly to one side when he has served his purpose'.[8]

Bevan interpreted communism as a dogmatic ideology that stuck too closely to Marxist orthodoxy and was unable to adapt to concrete conditions. In 1956 he argued that Soviet leaders, rather than undertaking an 'austere and objective analysis of the relations between men and their social institutions', had substituted for it 'a sort of third rate theology'. He maintained that despite flaws, Western democracy had established 'the separation of the judiciary from the executive authority ... and the existence of more than one political party'.[9] This separation was vital to Bevan. He described the political institutions of communist countries as 'too rigid' and concluded that the 'doctrine of the inevitability of revolution in the West has received too many dents for it to have its old potency'.[10] Bevan saw this as a failure of the Soviet Union to adapt Marxist theory to objective realities.

Bevan considered that throughout the world the 'outstanding fact ... is the failure of the Communist practice and theory to adjust themselves successfully to the democracies of the West'. As a result of this, Bevan declared, communists 'paralysed working class action rather than provided it with a cutting edge'. Communist parties in Western nations had been guided too heavily by Russian policy: 'In addition to all this, they have found their domestic policies fatally affected by Russia's internal situation.'[11] Bevan argued that communists would not be successful if they did not understand the potential of parliamentary institutions.

Bevan further criticised the adherence to Soviet interpretations of Marxism by communist parties, insisting that they needed to tailor policy to national needs and conditions: 'In short, what they need most of all is just "Revisionism".' Good Marxism, Bevan argued, is when it goes beyond polemics to be about the material world: 'all this talk of true and false Marxism is not so much a case of philosophical interpretation as it is of pressing material conditions.' He stated that the 'realities behind the argument are more substantial than the argument itself. That, at any rate, is in accordance with good Marxism'.[12] Bevan stressed that ideas needed to have their foundation in the economic realities of society.

Despite criticism, Bevan saw signs of the Soviet Union developing on democratic lines, reflecting his understanding of the relationship between the economic base and the political superstructure. His analysis illustrates how he envisioned the transformation of society as a result of economic planning. A 1942 *Tribune* editorial declared that since:

> industrialisation of the Soviet Union began in 1928 with the beginning of the first Five Year Plan ... [Russia] has probably made more progress in the creation of heavy industry than even America can show, or Great Britain in the expanding years of the 19th century.[13]

Even though Bevan considered Stalin to be a tyrant, he praised Russia's economic development under his rule. In 1953 Bevan argued that in 'the course of his [Stalin's] lifetime the pattern of Russian society was transformed'. Bevan identified the development of new 'professional and technical classes', recognising that their members 'enjoy considerable prestige, even some measure of power and influence in their respective spheres'. He maintained that only 'a small section of the Russian people felt suppressed; young people, teachers, scientists, and technicians believed they had already been liberated – liberated from illiteracy'.[14] Far from viewing the Soviet Union as a fractured society, Bevan's analysis emphasised its positive progress. Despite hostility towards the Soviet Union, key figures within the Labour Party, including the likes of Harold Wilson and even Anthony Crosland, admired the technological advances of the Soviet Union and therefore the benefits of its programme of central planning and public ownership.[15]

Bevan praised the industrial achievements of the Soviet Union. Although his assessment was that the 'social assimilation and universal enjoyment' of the benefits of technological advance had not been obtained, he claimed that there was too much focus on its negative aspects. In 1957, he encouraged critics of the Soviet Union to acknowledge the freedom of self-expression that people were able to enjoy due to living in a technologically advanced society, possessing more liberty than they did before the revolution. Bevan also praised education in Russia, stating that in 'a society where public ownership of the means of production is the prevailing mode, working and teaching are reciprocal activities'. He argued that where private enterprise is dominant, the result is a duality between teaching and working where teaching is the function of the state and working is the function of private enterprise.[16] Bevan contended that the abolition of private property had created an educated population, emphasising the importance of changing property relations in society. Further, as the Soviet Union developed industrially, Bevan hoped that political liberty would result. He insisted that 'it must be accepted that the vast mass of workers are conscious of emancipation and not of slavery'.[17] He wrote that a workers' support of the Soviet regime 'rests on his knowledge that all around him the framework of a modern industrial community is being built, that he is helping to build it, and that in the meantime his life is substantially, if slowly, improving' (p. 139).

Bevan stressed that he was not apologising for aspects of the Soviet regime that he considered oppressive; he did, however, predict that as the material conditions of Russia developed, its political system would become more democratic, creating greater levels of political and economic enfranchisement. He argued that it was 'reasonable to suppose that Russian political institutions, must ultimately yield to the pressure of economic and social changes':[18]

> I believe it can be taken for granted that as the pressure of material privations is lightened, some benign consequences will be felt right throughout the Soviet system ... In the course of time, perhaps shorter than many imagine, even those political institutions so much disliked by the Western mind will undergo such modifications that they will be stripped of their more repulsive features.[19]

Bevan predicted the same outcome for communist China.[20] He assumed that citizens in communist countries would begin to demand more political rights as their economic circumstances improved: 'Power, when it has to justify itself before reason and the bar of public opinion, is fatally breached.'[21] The state, he argued, would be forced to respond to the demands of the people.

Bevan pointed to the history of democracy in Britain as evidence of the struggle involved in achieving it. He described this history as 'a record of bloodshed, misery, oppression, accompanied by a century and a half of social dislocation'.[22] The only way in which societies could develop was if economic conditions were significantly changed: 'Poverty and liberty have always been uneasy bedfellows. It is not a coincidence that the history of mankind, for thousands of years, was the story of poverty joined to tyranny' (p. 4). Under both capitalism and communism, the task of improving society was fraught with difficulty.

Bevan's analysis of the Soviet Union again emphasises a key theme of this book: the importance of the base-superstructure relationship in Bevan's analysis. Under capitalism, where private enterprise was dominant, the principles of competitiveness and individualism inflicted society. Whereas under communism, Bevan argued, the dominance of public ownership gave workers increased liberty and a better standard of education. Different economic conditions existed in capitalist and communist states, but in both instances, Bevan theorised that these conditions affected the political structures of society, the extent of liberty in that society and the attitudes and psychology of individuals. Ultimately, however, Bevan saw both capitalism and communism as incapable of creating a society based on co-operative values. He argued that capitalist society was characterised by competition, individual self-interest and poverty, while the communist states did not allow enough freedom and were too authoritarian and undemocratic. Bevan envisioned a path between the two ideologies: democratic socialism.

DEMOCRATIC SOCIALISM

In 1952 Bevan stated that there were 'three conceptions of society now competing for the attention of mankind: the Competitive, the Monolithic, and the Democratic Socialist'.[23] Democratic socialism was the choice that Bevan championed. Rather than rejecting communism and capitalism outright, a combination of the two could be beneficial in establishing a new society. Writing in 1941, Bevan stated:

> The Soviet Union has been brought into the main stream of western democratic history. She will inevitably make her contribution towards the shape of future society. Her experience of economic planning, the conscious organisation of her productive life, the subordination of economic activity to wider social purposes, which have been essential characteristics of her economy, all are bound to have the most profound repercussions upon western thinking. At the same time, the way in which the ordinary people of Great Britain and America have clung fiercely to traditional liberal conceptions of personal liberty, to the more spontaneous characteristics of social organisation, will bring to the world conference of the future those urbane, and I trust somewhat more civilised conceptions, which will help to modify the more austere contributions of the Soviet Union.[24]

His analysis of both led him to formulate the question which was fundamental to his political thought:

> how can we reconcile the subordination of economic activities, to central state direction, without at the same time sacrificing those

> principles of personal choice, of personal liberty, and sanctities of private judgement, which are the most cherished contributions of the last 200 years of progress? (p. 13)

Bevan argued that a gradual 'coming together, growing ever more broader and more intimate, would enable each to adjust itself to the other and come to appreciate that differences of mental outlook and ways of life do not necessarily express levels of inferiority or superiority'.[25] He foresaw that combining economic planning with political liberty could help create a better society.

By 1957, Bevan was still praising both ideologies and arguing for a combination of the two:

> Capitalism has proved that it is capable of harnessing the productive energies of mankind in the creation of material wealth. The Communists have proved they can do the same thing ... The economic achievements of the Soviet Union, especially when considered against the horrors of two world wars, foreign intervention and civil wars, are remarkable ... But have either Communism or capitalism brought into being the sort of society upon which other peoples will want to model themselves, and live their lives? Are they the designs for living which are likely to inspire the young men and women in the second half of the twentieth century?[26]

Bevan's answer was 'no'. A combination of the most attractive aspects of both was still needed.

In Bevan's vision, public ownership and economic planning, combined with parliamentary democracy, could lead to the establishment of a new pattern of life. Bevan argued that in society, 'stability can be maintained when political liberty is enlarged and economic conditions improved at a pace which is acceptable to the masses'.[27] The important question for Bevan was whether 'the state [could] be given power over our work without the same power swallowing the whole of our life? That is the question millions are asking. I believe it can be done'.[28] When establishing new patterns of living, the state needed to ensure that the protection of democratic rights was balanced against the system of economic planning. Bevan argued that:

> You cannot educate a man to be a trained technician inside the factory and ask him to accept the status of a political robot outside. To read blue prints, to make and repair modern complicated machines, to perform the hundred and one activities inseparable from a modern complex civilisation is consistent with only one type of government – a complete political and industrial democracy.[29]

He asserted a belief in the changing condition of the worker under public ownership:

> It [the demand for full employment] means more profoundly that the citizen insists in the depth of his personality that he shall be re-united with his work and with the tools of his work, from which he was forcibly separated by the Industrial Revolution. Only those who have passed through the experience of idle hands surrounded by idle tools can begin to appreciate the deep serenity which will flow in time from the re-uniting of man with the tools of his craft and the sources of his wealth. (p. 3)

Bevan set out what he saw as important in socialist states:

> In the first place there is an insistence on full political and industrial democracy as the only condition consistent with the manifold and subtle requirements of modern industrial and social techniques. The background and pre-requisite of this personal liberty implies that the serenities of private life shall not be invaded and disturbed by disharmonies arising from maladjustments in the economic machine. In short the main economic structure must be planned, purposive and reasonably predictable. (p. 4)

It can be seen that Bevan's vision for society rested heavily on the impact that state involvement in the economy could have in changing patterns of life.

Eventually, public ownership would allow democratic socialists to prioritise certain values in society, including equality and the cultivation of individual life. Bevan insisted that the solutions to the problems of capitalism could not be arrived at until it became 'possible to create a purposive and intelligible design for society'. This would only materialise once 'effective social and economic power passes from one order of society to another'.[30] He declared that one of the most important questions of modern society was: 'What is most essential and who is to decide it?' (p. 58). Bevan, however, insisted that the 'victory of Socialism need not be universal to be decisive'. He had 'no patience with those Socialists, so-called, who in practice would socialise nothing, whilst in theory they threaten the whole of private property'. He insisted that different forms of property could co-exist. Nonetheless, he maintained that it was a:

> requisite of social stability that one type of property ownership should dominate. In the society of the future it should be public property. Private property should yield to the point where social purposes and a decent order of priorities form an easily discernible pattern of life. Only when this is accomplished will a tranquil and serene attitude take the place of the all-pervading restlessness that is the normal climate of competitive society. (pp. 118–19)

Bevan highlighted the importance of changing property relations in order to create a new society. This again emphasised his view that by using the democratic and representative institutions of the state, the material conditions of economic life could be drastically altered for the benefit of the people, eventually leading to the development of new values.

Bevan warned that if decisions over what to do with economic surplus were left in private hands, then the surplus would be invested 'in the goods for which he [the individual possessor of the surplus] thinks there will be a profitable sale'. This would mean that 'those who have been most successful for the time being, that is the money owners, will in the sum of their individual decisions determine the character of the economy of the future' (p. 118). Bevan argued that the persistent attitude that regarded 'the principles of economic individualism as characteristic of modern man in modern society' prevented the 'working out [of] a system of social priorities' (p. 150).

We saw an example of this in Chapter 2, which identified the importance Bevan placed on fixing prices for different forms of consumption. He contended that consumption needed to be arranged 'in an order of priority' so that neither supply and demand nor the profit motive was 'the sole arbiter of the employment of capital'. He predicted that once:

> the Competitive Society is compelled to serve a general social aim the automatism of the market is interfered with at every point and we are no longer in the capitalist system at all. We shall have abandoned selection by competition for selection by deliberation. (p. 153)

From this point, 'moral considerations [would] take precedence over economic motives' (p. 153). The importance of public ownership for changing society is summarised by the popular Bevan phrase, cited on numerous occasions in this book: 'Freedom is the by-product of economic surplus.' By creating economic surplus and distributing it in the interests of all in society, freedom can be obtained (p. 39). This would achieve Bevan's aim of respecting personal liberty while simultaneously developing the economy.

Bevan stressed the importance of technological development for the creation of new values in society. He was, however, keenly aware of the issues regarding automation. 'The impact of its arrival', he wrote in 1955, 'is in society and in the homes of the workers. The question for us is whether our society will be able to digest its impact without causing unnecessary suffering and dislocation'. Bevan tried to be positive about the possible implications of automation, seeing it as 'the product of scientific and technical brilliance' and suggesting that whether 'it becomes a benefit or a curse will depend on our collective intelligence. There is no need for alarm but there is every need for forethought and preparation'.[31] Although he saw automation producing considerable benefits, Bevan also warned that it had the potential to cause ruin for society if an intelligent design was not developed. Without an intelligent design, principles of democratic socialism could not be achieved.

Bevan emphasised the destructive nature of industrial development, particularly on the environment:

> The ugly, dreary, squalid, endless miles of back-to-back cottages and tenements, the careless dumps of industrial waste, the poisoned rivers, the senseless slaughter on our inadequate highways, the silted canals, and innumerable other appalling legacies of a failure of social and political adaptation to swift technical change – these all point to a breakdown of collective intelligence and will. (p. 2)

Bevan was therefore concerned that any advances in technology needed to be controlled in order to mitigate against the negative consequences on society.

Recognising this need, Bevan argued that the only way automation could be controlled was by asserting the importance of public ownership: 'The real answer is not to attempt to restore the authority of the market where this is manifestly at variance with the needs of capital expansion but to restate, in modern terms, the proper relationship between public and private enterprise.' Where capital investment was vast, 'as for instance in steel, oil and chemicals', Bevan asserted that the remedy was not increased private enterprise but 'an extension of public responsibility by taking them into public ownership' (p. 2). He predicted that by redrawing the lines between public and private property, 'the relationship of both would be more intelligible and a new social synthesis made possible'. This was the path of 'democratic socialism as it is also the way to the smooth assimilation of automation into the national life'. The secret for dealing with the problems arising from automation, Bevan argued, was 'the pace of economic and political adaptation' (p. 2).

A retreat from socialism in this scenario would be the wrong path – socialism was required to deal with the issues of automation:

> The retreat from Socialism, in places where it should be least expected, is therefore the abandonment of collective intelligence at the moment when it is most needed. It results in political indifference and social anarchy under conditions where automation demands sustained communal action. (p. 2)

Bevan concluded that: 'Automation can be turned from a threat into a challenge and opportunity. What we dare not do is to wait until it is upon us and then hope to muddle through' (p. 2). Public ownership could change the course of economic development, managing automation and integrating it more positively into society.

The relationship between economic and political power in Bevan's thought was clear: by using political institutions to reverse property relations, certain values in society could be prioritised and thus flourish. Bevan praised the economic planning of the Soviet Union and wanted to combine this with democratic institutions and political liberty. This combination was central to creating a new order of values through democratic socialism. There was a risk, however, that this development could be seriously impeded by the actions of the ruling class. Not only did Bevan set out his vision for democratic socialism, but he also engaged in a critique of ideological power.

Hegemony and Consent

RULING-CLASS POWER

Bevan predicted a difficult task in establishing the values of democratic socialism in the face of opposition from the ruling class. Bevan argued that the ruling class would attempt to maintain its power and prevent this evolution – in its extreme, this would arrive under the guise of fascism, which Bevan described as 'the future refusing to be born' (see Chapter 1).[32] Chapter 1 presented Bevan's argument that the ruling class had given concessions to the masses due to the fear of unrest, and the need to educate society on the modes of production.[33] It is worth returning to this discussion due to the ideological elements of the ruling class's activity.

Bevan outlined the methods that the ruling class utilised to maintain its power. He identified a new question facing the ruling class in response to the establishment of democracy and the extension of the franchise: 'How can wealth persuade poverty to use its political freedom to keep wealth in power?'[34] The ruling class would change its behaviour when it wanted to defend its interests. Bevan demonstrated how it would even turn its back on democracy to achieve this:

> When the people look like turning them down they begin to see the 'defects of democracy as a permanent system of government', and warn us that 'we must distinguish between freedom and licence'. When we do as they want us to do, it is freedom. When we suit ourselves, it is licence.[35]

Bevan argued that the main objective of the Conservatives was to 'preserve the status quo in society. Its main strategy is to make concessions as belatedly and as grudgingly as possible, but with such dexterity as to preserve the reality of continuing power'.[36] In this interpretation, the ruling class needed to maintain the support of the people to defend against the challenge of democracy.

Bevan argued that the ruling class could not maintain its power unless it gained the consent of the nation. 'No society', he wrote, 'can long endure which fails to secure the assent of the people'. Reflecting on previous societies, Bevan wrote that it was 'difficult for us to understand how it was that men and women came not only to tolerate, but cheerfully to acquiesce in, conditions and practices which seem to us at this distance to be revolting'. He did not attribute it to the masses being 'held down by sheer physical force'; that was only possible for a short period. The rulers required the active consent of the people:

> The institutions and modes of behaviour of these societies must have, in part at least, commended themselves to ordinary men and women or they would have been undermined by sheer disapproval. Ultimately, rulers, however harsh, must share the same values as the ruled if their empire is to persist. Obedience is rendered in the last resort, and for any considerable length of time, by accepting the moral and intellectual sanctions that lie behind social compulsions.[37]

Therefore, there always needed to be 'compensations and amenities, pleasures and common rituals, making life seem worthwhile and forming the cement that bound ancient societies together in a continual reaffirmation of willing consent' (p. 5). Bevan argued that the British ruling class was the master in 'the art of avoiding sharp conflict, of muting and smothering the struggle, of encouraging the obscurity which makes the frontiers separating the two parties appear to merge into each other in a sort of grey mist'.[38] He stressed that the ruling class could not continue to exploit but had to make concessions to the people in order to maintain its dominance.

Bevan's writings echo a Gramscian understanding of the nature of hegemony and consent, both arguing that coercive power was not enough for the state to maintain its dominance.[39] Gwyn Alf Williams, analysing this concept in the work of Antonio Gramsci, wrote that by hegemony:

> Gramsci seems to mean a socio-political situation, in his terminology a 'moment,' in which the philosophy and practice of a society fuse or are in equilibrium; an order in which a certain way of life and thought is dominant, in which one concept of reality is diffused throughout society in all its institutional and private

> manifestations, informing with its spirit all taste, morality, customs, religious and political principles, and all social relations, particularly in their intellectual and moral connotation. An element of direction and control, not necessarily conscious, is implied. This hegemony corresponds to a state power conceived in stock Marxist terms as the dictatorship of a class.[40]

Bevan's writings on the ruling class also emphasise a 'certain way of life and thought' that is dominant (capitalism), its values diffused throughout society. Williams even described Gramsci as the 'Aneurin Bevan of Italian communism'.[41]

Williams wrote that hegemony 'is always associated with equilibrium, persuasion, consent, and consolidation' (p. 591). The acts of persuasion and consent were evident in Bevan's writing, such as when he critiqued attempts by the ruling class to align its interests with patriotic symbols. Towards the end of the 1930s when Bevan considered the working class to be under threat, he argued that 'the class struggle is the underlying motif of politics'. Bevan argued that the Union Jack was a central symbol being co-opted by the ruling class. 'The Union Jack', he wrote, 'is regarded by [the British ruling class] as a national flag only when their class interests and the nation's coincide'. He asserted that there 'is no protection for a British subject under the Union Jack unless he is promoting the interests of the British ruling class'. Bevan even suspected that the 'ruling class of England [was] ready at any time to exchange the Union Jack for the Swastika should the change over be necessary to preserve their class privileges'.[42] The attempt to maintain power by co-opting prevailing symbols in society demonstrates the importance in Bevan's thought of ideological apparatus being used to establish and maintain ruling-class domination.

The strategy of the ruling class was to associate its interests with those of the masses. This was evident to Bevan during the Second World War. For instance, he believed that after the war there would exist a 'universal desire for privacy and freedom of personal choice'. Bevan warned that this desire might be an advantage to the Conservatives in a post-war election. He wrote that human beings:

> possess the attributes of the cat and the dog. They want to hunt in packs at one time, and to hunt alone at others … When the war is

> over the cat nature demands satisfaction, and this takes the form of a romantic nostalgia for a life of freedom from the disciplines of State interference.[43]

Bevan predicted that this could result in 'a general lethargy of the collective will. A call to continued state action is irrationally resented, and anyone who resists it easily becomes a champion of personal liberty'. He issued a warning, however, that the interests of the worker did not align with those of the ruling class: 'The worker, engulfed in the full spate of his revulsion against hateful disciplines, mistakes the demands of the ruling class for what he himself feels he needs.' To combat this, the Labour Party needed to mobilise a campaign of 'We' against 'They' to show the working class that the ruling class did not have their interests at heart. Otherwise, by aligning its interests with the general interest, the ruling class could defend its dominant and exploitative economic position.

Bevan's writings outlined the ways in which he suspected capitalism was maintained and extended in society. As Chapter 3 demonstrated, Bevan considered adherents of capitalism to be responsible for the conflict taking place in international society. The attempt of the British ruling class to maintain its power was reflective of a battle over competing conceptions of society. Bevan urged the working class to engage with it in an ideological struggle.

WORKING-CLASS POWER

Bevan wanted the working class to compete over prevailing symbols and institutions, using collective action to challenge the hegemony of the ruling class. 'A ruling class', Bevan wrote in 1938:

> succeeds by appearing to identify its class interests with the general interest, so that the people are involved in the defence of both at the same time. They are able to represent their sectional interests in terms of the national symbols, and the emotional and traditional associations with which these latter are seeped are an immense source of strength to the ruling class.[44]

Therefore, by opposing the ruling class and the British state, the working class 'appears to be in opposition to these sacred symbols of the State, and class feeling alone provides an insufficient source of emotional drive'. Bevan predicted, however, that a:

> moment is reached in the life of the ruling class when it can no longer afford the maintenance of the very traditions for which it formerly appeared to stand. These are the conceptions of liberty and progress, which it waved like flags in its own early battles. (p. 7)

He predicted that the 'growing economic necessities of the ruling class cause it to attempt to swallow its own social progeny, and to destroy those liberal institutions which were its early pride' (p. 7). Or, to use Bevan's own language, property would attempt to destroy democracy in order to cling to its power.

Bevan urged the working class to take charge of national symbols and institutions when the correct moment arrived: 'At this moment the working class steps forward in the defence of these liberal institutions and conceptions of liberty, for they are necessary to its own progress and ultimate victory' (p. 7). Following this, the working class would use these symbols and establish a new hegemony:

> Then begins the struggle for the symbols. In this struggle the working class reverses the position ... By defending the symbols which are universally revered, it identifies its own class interest with the general interest and begins to draw strength from both sources. (p. 7)

These liberal institutions, analysed in Chapters 1 and 2, were important in the ideological battle between the working class and the ruling class. Therefore, Bevan argued that the:

> interests of the ruling class emerge more and more as a naked opposition to the general interest, and members of the ruling class begin to think more and more of their defence in military terms, and less and less in terms of constitutional action. (p. 7)

Bevan predicted that once this situation occurred, it was then the:

> supreme moment for it is at this point that Fascism appears, having for its purpose the destruction of the constitution which

> hampers the maintenance of the ruling class. We saw this happen in Germany and in Spain, and we see the beginnings of it in Britain. (p. 7)

By controlling the ideological superstructure, the working class could fracture the dominance of property over poverty. In the 1930s, during a period when Bevan argued that the ruling class was clearly attempting to maintain its power, Bevan was theorising on strategies to reverse this domination.

Despite acknowledging the achievements of the 1945–51 Labour government, during the 1950s Bevan conceded that this reversal had not been achieved. He still argued that the working class would not be content with their situation:

> Mankind has never believed that respect for a principle, enshrined in the most sanctified law, should be carried to the point of personal or national extinction ... Ask that question of any man starving to death in front of a shop window full of food. Respect for the policeman is apt to diminish in such a situation.[45]

By actively seeking power, the working class would be able to transform the economic base of society, thus establishing new values and ideas essential to democratic socialism. The importance of this struggle reiterates the centrality of working-class power to Bevan's thought, analysed in Chapter 1. It also emphasises the materialism in Bevan's thought. He was interested in political and ideological structures, but these were based on a relationship with the economic base. Between 1945 and 1951, the Labour Party had an opportunity to take control of the levers of political power and bring about a new vision for British society. However, considering the nature of labourism, Bevan's own vision for society might appear as unachievable. This vision is now considered.

Values in Society

DEMOCRATIC VALUES

Bevan asserted that the working class needed to articulate a new vision for society that challenged the dominance of competitive values. He stressed that if 'individual man is to make a home for himself in the Great Society, he must also seek to make the behaviour of social forces reasonably predictable'.[46] Bevan wrote that the:

> digging for coal, the making of steel, the provision of finance, the generation and distribution of electricity, the building and siting of factories and houses, the whole complete structure of the Great Society is, for the anti-Socialist, a great arena for private economic adventure. (pp. 36–7)

To the extent that the great mass of people were no longer 'stalked and waylaid, harried and tormented, their lives made a nightmare of uncertainty', this was because 'the economic adventurers [had] been curbed and controlled in one sphere of social activity after another' (p. 37). Bevan maintained that the application of democratic socialist values had already had an impact in changing people's lives.

The cultivation of individual life was a central priority for Bevan in any society. He rejected the utilitarian principle of 'the greatest good for the greatest number', arguing that this cannot:

> excuse indifference to individual suffering. There is no test for progress other than its impact on the individual. If the policies of statesmen, the enactments of legislatures, the impulses of group activity, do not have for their object the enlargement and cultivation of the individual life, they do not deserve to be called civilised. (pp. 167–8)

Bevan acknowledged that the preoccupation with the individual led critics to call democratic socialism dull. He detailed complaints made during the period of Labour government between 1945 and 1951 that there was too much rationing, a scarcity of 'porterhouse steaks in the fashionable restaurants' and a 'lack of colour' in the cities. Bevan disputed this, however, arguing that if critics had:

> looked closer they would have seen the roses in the cheeks of the children, and the pride and self-confidence of the young mothers. They would have found that more was being done for working people than in any other part of the world at that time. (p. 168)

Bevan declared that democratic socialism was a philosophy that 'sees the individual in his context with society and is therefore compassionate and tolerant' (p. 169). Far from being dull and colourless, Bevan pointed to improvements made to the lives of individuals.

The way to cultivate individual life and to create conditions of equality was for collective values to be at the heart of politics, emphasising the interdependence of individuals in society. The technological advancements of the preceding 100 years meant that for the individual, the 'vicissitudes that now afflict him come from what he has done in association with other men, and not from a physical relationship with the forces of nature' (p. 46). The development of society, and the resultant division of labour, wove the individual's life 'into a series of interdependencies involving not only his own personal surroundings, but moving in ever-widening circles until they encompass most parts of the earth' (pp. 46–7). Each social grouping had become connected.

Contrasting contemporary society to societies that came before, Bevan argued that 'various forms of collective action' had been developed 'as mechanisms evolved to enable the individual to struggle successfully with his social environment'. He put this impulse for collective action down to human nature, rejecting the view that private enterprise and universal competition were compatible with it. He wrote:

> When we are told that these [virtues of private enterprise and universal competition] correspond with the basic impulses of 'human nature' we reply that the facts of human behaviour contradict this contention at every turn. Human nature is as much co-operative as it is competitive. Indeed the complicated texture of modern society emphasises over and over again the greater survival value of collective action. (p. 150)

While the 'grand priority that subordinated almost everything to individual success [had] come to be insensibly qualified by our obligations to the associations of which we are members, occupational and otherwise', Bevan referred back to the problems associated with capitalist ideology, arguing that 'in spite of all this, "official" thinking still persists in regarding the principles of economic individualism as characteristic of modern man in modern society' (p. 150). Rather than individualism, modern society had connected workers and created an important interdependence.

SOCIALIST ADVANCE

Bevan admitted that the task of changing attitudes to create a new order of social priorities in capitalist society was a challenging one. He wrote that the 'climate of opinion in capitalist society is wholly opposed to this exercise' (p. 150). This was not a surprise to Bevan, as he believed that it was:

> one of the tragedies of history that the application of social purposes or priorities, or whatever you like to call them, first occurred in economically backward countries. It has therefore been accompanied by excesses that have produced a revulsion against further experiments in the same direction. (p. 150)

Bevan insisted, however, that 'a number of central aims must be worked out as guiding principles for our social and political activities, and to these all else must be related' (p. 151). Although the task was difficult, Bevan urged for it to be carried out forcefully.

'Free men using free institutions', Bevan claimed, 'have never tried this before in the long history of mankind'. He responded, however, that this fact 'should not frighten us':

> Each social circumstance is new not only in itself but in our disposition towards it. We must not allow ourselves to be deterred from the effort to introduce rational principles into social relations simply because it has never been done before; tradition, habit and authority having been made to suffice. (p. 151)

Bevan demanded that the underlying assumptions and values in capitalist society needed to be challenged: 'Children are taught in our schools to respect Bruno and Galileo and other martyrs of science, and at the same time they are encouraged to close their minds against those who question the assumptions underlying contemporary society' (p. 151). Bevan therefore saw that a project of radical change in the underlying values in society needed to be undertaken.

Many of the values that Bevan wished to establish can be identified in his reflection on the Labour government of 1945–51 and his role as a minister in that government. Being interviewed in *Tribune* in 1948, Bevan expressed the view that significant steps had been taken by the Labour government to transform society. Socialism had advanced on three fronts: first, through increasing 'the share of the available social product by way of higher wages and salaries'; second, through 'the transference of power by the transition from private to public ownership of the forces of production'; and finally, what Bevan described as the front 'which has its roots more deeply in Socialist philosophy than any other', the 'distributive front, that is, the slow destruction of the inequalities and disadvantages arising from the unequal possession of property and the unequal possession of individual strengths and opportunities'.[47] Bevan proudly reflected on these advancements in changing the structure of society.

Bevan argued that the new direct social services being put in place would lead to a reduction of inequality. The unjust inequalities that he objected to were being rectified as Labour's measures had begun to 'iron out the differences between one citizen and another which arise as a consequence of the anomalies of the wages system'. These anomalies, he argued, would be reduced as 'social services give people a share of the national product in accordance with their need', therefore emphasising the 'distributivist aspect of the Socialist advance'. Bevan admitted that the 'wages system is maintained as a stimulus to production, a traditional relationship between the worker and his industry; but distributivist activities undermine the worst consequences of the inequality' (p. 7).

The service with the greatest distributive effect according to Bevan was the NHS, for which he was of course directly responsible. 'On the active and administrative side', he wrote, 'it brings to the individual citizen all the battery of modern medicine, irrespective of the individual's means' (p. 7). Bevan proudly declared that the NHS is 'what a socialist really means by socialism'. He viewed it as a 'practical illustration of, "From each according to his capacity; to each according to his need"'.[48] He argued that 'the more and more of the world's goods that reach the individual in some other, more civilised way than by the haggling of the market, the more progress that society is making towards a civilised standard' (p. 14). Bevan identified that historically health was the area where 'the claims of individual commercialism come into most immediate conflict with reputable notions of social values'.[49] In modern societies, Bevan argued, 'the claims of the individual shall subordinate themselves to social codes that have the collective well-being for their aim, irrespective of the extent to which this frustrates individual greed' (p. 73). In the field of curative medicine, Bevan understood that 'individual and collective action are joined in a series of dramatic battles':

> The collective principle asserts that the resources of medical skill and the apparatus of healing shall be placed at the disposal of the patient, without charge, when he or she needs them; that medical treatment and care should be a communal responsibility; that they should be made available to rich and poor alike in accordance with medical need and by no other criteria. It claims that financial anxiety in time of sickness is a serious hindrance to recovery, apart from its unnecessary cruelty. It insists that no society can legitimately call itself civilised if a sick person is denied medical aid because of lack of means. (p. 75)

Collective action could ensure that the individual had access to healthcare, with this not being dependent on considerations of commercialism.

Bevan predicted that society would flourish when people knew their illnesses would be taken care of when they needed help. He argued that:

> Society becomes more wholesome, more serene, and spiritually healthier, if it knows that its citizens have at the back of their consciousness the knowledge that not only themselves, but all their fellows, have access, when ill, to the best that medical skill can provide. (p. 75)

The NHS was so successful an institution in Bevan's eyes that he was confident 'that no Government that attempts to destroy the Health Service can hope to command the support of the British people' – the current invocations of Bevan's role in establishing the NHS, even by Conservative politicians, support Bevan's claim. He concluded his chapter in *In Place of Fear* on the health service by insisting that the 'great argument about priorities is joined and from it a Free Health Service is bound to emerge triumphant' (p. 92). Thus, Bevan concluded that asserting social priorities had delivered benefits for society.

On the eve of its establishment in 1948, Bevan outlined the challenge that he faced regarding society's attitude to the service. He described the NHS as:

> an attempt at the introduction of egalitarianism through the medium of a society which is certainly not egalitarian, either in its structure or in its inspiration, and further through the medium of a profession, highly conservative, deeply traditional, and in many sections of it, hostile.[50]

Nonetheless, eight years after its establishment, Bevan argued that a report into the NHS proved that it was one of the greatest social experiments of the twentieth century and he urged other nations to follow the same path.[51] Bevan reflected that state action had changed British society fundamentally.

Despite these successes, Bevan argued that Labour had not done enough to completely establish socialism in Britain, insisting throughout the 1950s that the party needed to maintain a radical agenda. Writing in 1955, he argued that 'The need for further social experiment is certainly present in Britain. Although she has recovered from the worst consequences of the war there is yet a long way to go before she can afford to relax. But, though the need is there, the mood is not'.[52] Bevan maintained that the character of society needed to be continually reshaped to achieve progress, as it 'is the essence of power that it strives to perpetuate the mould most congenial to it'. Bevan was not satisfied with Labour's pushing for only minor changes to the economic situation in Britain.[53] The 1945–51 Labour government had not done enough, Bevan asserted, to completely transform society.

Bevan had outlined the difficulty facing the Labour Party two years into the life of the government. He referenced Marx to make his case: 'As Marx said, the weight of the traditions of the past lies like an alp on the present, and it will be time enough to go on the defensive when we have stamped our mark on the bulk of the social economy.' A couple of years of Labour advances had meant that 'We have political power, as we did not have in 1924 and 1929, but', he cautioned, 'we have not yet full economic responsibility, nor shall we have, until the main streams of economic activity are publicly canalised'. Bevan promised that after 1948 'the harvest will be as rich as we care to make it'.[54] Although he would later state his pride at the achievements of the Labour government, he would claim throughout the 1950s that further change was required.

Since the Second World War, people in Britain had experienced substantial change, which Bevan argued could actually explain Labour's defeat in the 1955 General Election. Unemployment no longer stood as high as it did, therefore Bevan suggested that the discontent with the capitalist system and the attacks on it had been allayed by the Conservative's management of the economy:

> But the consequences of this meditative attitude is that the Government has parliamentary power but lacks the moral reserves that are the main asset of great popular movements. A generation has grown up in Britain that has not experienced the frustration and privation of unemployment. The old keen edge of attack on capitalist society was therefore blunted.[55]

Nonetheless, Bevan did not consider the aims of socialism to be fully achieved.

In 1959, he was arguing for socialist policies to be pushed through more forcefully. Again calling on Marx and reflecting his conception of the base-superstructure relationship, Bevan wrote that 'The old Marxist argument that the relations of private property and the social stratifications that come within them tend to stultify and even inhibit technical progress and maximum production of wealth, is receiving fresh reinforcement'. Despite the technical advances of the Soviet Union (such as the launching of Sputnik in 1957), Bevan thought that 'the weight of the argument still lies with the defenders of Western democracy'. He admitted, however, that it was 'inevitable for doubts to arise about the possible lines of future advance'. He continued, 'It is the socialist case that a certain order of priorities should be voluntarily accepted by a democratic nation. Having been accepted, it should be driven through against all opposition and private vested interest'.[56] Right up until his death in 1960, Bevan was arguing for the need to alter social relations and for an order of priorities to be established.

FUTURE STRUGGLE

Although Bevan expressed a desire to see key principles guide social life, he argued that universality should not be sought – instead, he asserted that values and norms were in constant flux and were dependent on history and on particular circumstances. The student of politics, he insisted:

> must therefore seek neither universality nor immortality for his ideas and for the institutions through which he hopes to express them. What he must seek is integrity and vitality. His Holy Grail is the living truth, knowing that being alive the truth must change. If he does not cherish integrity then he will see in the change an excuse for opportunism, and so will exchange the inspiration of the pioneer for the reward of the lackey.[57]

Bevan argued that nations were made up of various points of view and were constantly adapting. He wrote that nations, 'as contrasted with any small governing circle, are the centre of interests, pressures and tendencies, social alignments that grow and wane in strength. The shifting balance of social forces within the nation compels endless adaptations'.[58] Therefore, he described politics as a 'conflict between opposing conceptions of society'.[59]

Bevan stressed that democratic socialism needed to protect principles of private judgement. It was outlined in Chapter 2 that Bevan accepted that there was a role for private enterprise, and this meant that the principle of choice needed to be respected. He wrote that because democratic socialism 'knows that all political action must be a choice between a number of possible alternatives it eschews all absolute proscriptions and final decisions'. Bevan did not want to see a regimented society, arguing instead for a move towards 'an eclectic society' – 'we are not going to have a monolithic society, we are not going to have a society in which every barber's shop is nationalised'.[60] He conceded that democratic socialism was 'not able to offer the thrill of the complete abandonment of private judgement, which is the allure of modern Soviet Communism and of Fascism, its running mate'.[61] Instead, it offered what Bevan considered to be principles of choice, individual liberty and freedom.

The redistributive effects of public ownership on people's lives were emphasised by Bevan, particularly in relation to inequality. He considered there to be 'a sense of injustice arising from gross inequalities', which public ownership could rectify. He did not, however, consider the discontent arising from inequality to be by itself 'fatal to the existing order'. He highlighted that there had been 'inequalities throughout the history of mankind, but they have not always proved incompatible with a certain degree of social stability'. He argued that 'Complete equality is a motive that has never moved large masses for any decisive length of time' (p. 60). He claimed that a 'sense of injustice does not derive solely from the existence of inequality. It arises from the belief that the inequality is capricious, unsanctioned by usage and, most important of all, senseless' (pp. 60–1). Bevan therefore accepted a certain level of inequality in society, as long as it did not emerge from injustice imposed on individuals.

Accepting that people were different, Bevan argued that it was wrong to say that people were born unequal; rather, 'we are born with different potential aptitudes'. He contended that whether different aptitudes or qualities 'turn out to be of later advantage, and place us higher in the social scale than others, will turn upon whether they are sufficiently cultivated, and ... whether they happen to be the sort our particular society finds valuable' (p. 61). Bevan did not find that workers 'resent higher rewards where they manifestly flow from personal exertion and superior qualities'. Instead, 'proper recognition' should be given to scientists, artists and inventors, and there was not 'a disposition to object to the higher incomes awarded certain of the professional classes' (p. 61). Bevan did accept, however, that people were beginning to express unhappiness with the benefits that some professionals were receiving, particularly in education, which working-class families did not necessarily have access to (p. 62). Tensions were beginning to arise when the 'standard of life of the student is higher than that of the industrial worker who maintains him' (p. 63). Bevan asserted that 'Resentment against inequality occurs when it quite clearly flows from social accident, such as inherited wealth or occupations of no superior social value' (p. 64). He appeared to be arguing that there would exist some inequality in society, but that this needed to be based on different aptitudes at birth. It was important, however, for everyone to be given the chance to be the best person they could be. Equality of opportunity was vital.

Bevan's analysis of equality reflects the position of José Enrique Rodó, the Uruguayan philosopher who Bevan considered to be a major influence. Rodó argued that:

> it is the duty of the state to provide all members of the society with the unspecified conditions that will lead to their perfection ... [and] human superiorities where they exist. In this way, if all are granted initial equality, subsequent inequality will be justified.[62]

In a 1950 Fabian Society lecture, Bevan quoted Havelock Ellis, writing in the introduction to Rodó's *The Motives of Proteus*, asserting that 'Democracy alone can conciliate equality at the outset with an inequality at the end, which gives full scope for the best and is most apt to work towards the good of the whole'.[63] Bevan's writing reflects a similar understanding and acceptance of inequalities in society.

As for the future, Bevan maintained that even in a democratic socialist society there would still be conflict over values and ideas. This conflict, he stated, would be over new values, standards and goals. Progress, he argued, 'is not the elimination of struggle but a change in its objectives and we all hope a more civilised way of carrying it on'. Even if differences in the future were trivial, they would still be differences and would need to be resolved. 'If a Socialist society proves to be so satisfactory', Bevan wrote in 1954, 'that only unimportant differences survive, then people should still be free to express them after their own fashion'. He stated that there 'is no last question so there is no last answer'. He proclaimed that 'We have two duties; to win our own battles and to keep the arena open for others. A closed arena is a closed mind. It is not by accident that these arise together'.[64]

In 1953, on a radio programme titled 'This I Believe', Bevan expressed his view that because society meant deciding between competing claims, 'then the mood in which we approach our fellow human beings should be one of tolerance' (a far cry from his infamous outburst that the Conservative Party was 'lower than vermin', perhaps demonstrating the difference between Bevan as a thinker and as a partisan, active politician). He continued:

> If, furthermore, I am right in saying that the search for the truth will result in a number of different answers to the extent that the circumstances are different, then to tolerance we must add imagination so that we can understand why the other truth differs from ours. We should 'learn to sit where they sit'.[65]

He concluded, 'I believe imaginative tolerance to be among the foremost virtues of a civilized mind'. Competing claims needed to be treated with equal dignity, merit and care. Bevan insisted that only when democratic plans are outlined with the contribution of the people can a society be called civilised. He argued that when:

> you have democratic plans, and when you have assumed the power that should accompany political responsibility … the ordinary man and woman is called into the general conference for the purpose of determining what he considers to be the right way in which the national resources should be spent. When that happens, then the ordinary man and woman has reached full stature.[66]

He asserted that what must be done was to 'arrange all your plans in a hierarchical order of values, some above the others'. Therefore, the result is the 'reaching of a new kind of authoritarian society, but it is the authority of moral purpose freely undertaken' (p. 12). Bevan emphasised that democratic socialism is:

> a child of modern society and so of relativist philosophy. It seeks the truth in any given situation, knowing all the time that if this be pushed too far it falls into error. It struggles against the evils that flow from private property, yet realises that all forms of private property are not necessarily evil. Its chief enemy is vacillation, for it must achieve passion in action in the pursuit of qualified judgements. It must know how to enjoy the struggle, whilst recognising that progress is not the elimination of struggle but rather a change in its terms.[67]

Bevan maintained that the values that democratic socialism emphasised needed to be constantly renewed in the struggle for a better world.

In the same 1950 Fabian Society lecture detailed above, Bevan outlined his vision of society based on public ownership and the purpose of collective action. He declared:

> That is why, when eventually the story that we have only just began to see has unfolded itself, and when democratically elected institutions have armed themselves with the full panoply of economic power; when all the members of the community share an equal responsibility for determining the use to which social resources are put; when we have begun to create a type of society in which everyone will regard himself as the ruler, and having regarded himself as a ruler, will realise that he can rule only by

> putting the social service first and himself last, only then can we really achieve the best results of all that we are planning to do.[68]

Bevan's reflections on democratic socialism being a 'relativist philosophy' correspond with his attitude towards society as being dynamic and constantly changing. The nature of ideas and values may change, but they had their foundation in the real experiences of the people. The teachings of Dietzgen, identified by authors as an influence on Bevan's understanding of the materialist conception of history, may have affected Bevan in this regard. Macintyre quotes a H. Wynn-Cuthbert as declaring, 'The Materialist Conception of History shows how changes in ideas result from changes in social conditions, and these from changes in economic conditions. Dietzgen explains *how* our conditions determine our thoughts'.[69] While Bevan avoided an economic deterministic view, this chapter has demonstrated that this relationship is a central component of his political thought and his desire to give order and a plan to the development of society.

Conclusion

This chapter has analysed the importance of ideas, values and morals in Bevan's political thought and their relationship to economic development. He argued that the modes of thought resulting from capitalist and communist ideologies, while different, were both informed by the underlying economic structure: the dominance of private property created an individualistic society, while communism created a society based on shared ownership, although it demonstrated features that Bevan thought to be authoritarian. The economic base, therefore, shaped the dominant modes of thought in society. This is not to suggest a wholly economic determinist conception of societal development. Bevan also emphasised the role that ideology plays in shaping, determining and maintaining property relations and the dominance of a certain class. Bevan's analysis hints at an understanding of the nature of hegemony in class conflict.

Bevan also understood that in a democratic society there would always be conflicting claims over what form society should take and what values should be dominant. The different classes in society were battling over control of production, while also competing over different values. This battle involved capturing national symbols and associating a group's interests with that of the general interest. Ultimately, Bevan felt that to create a civilised society people needed to be engaged in deciding on an order of priorities. This required the functions of economic planning to transform society, and the assertion of working-class interests to correspond to the general interest.

Chapters 1 and 2 emphasised the importance in Bevan's thought of the role of economic conditions in the development of society, particularly political structures. Economic conditions also informed the way values were created and shaped. A society based on the dominance of private enterprise would lead to values of individualism and competitiveness. But a society based on the dominance of public ownership combined with democracy could transform people's lives and include them in the ordering of society's values. Similar arguments can be seen in Bevan's analysis of societies that were experiencing their own industrial revolutions, discussed in Chapter 3. Thomas-Symonds argued that Bevan derived more from Rodó than Marx in his critique of capitalism.[70] Bevan's criticisms of the vulgarities of capitalism certainly echo Rodó's, who protested against the Americanisation of Latin American society, arguing instead for the recognition of arts, culture, aesthetics and individuality within the collective effort.[71] Yet, we can see that Bevan's interpretations of the nature of values and ideas were rooted in his materialist conception of development.

However, Bevan was to be frustrated with the lack of progress after 1951. While society had indeed changed, Bevan was insisting that property relations needed to be further challenged in order to create a flourishing democratic socialist society. While Labour was successful in many areas in terms of building socialism,[72] it can be argued that the party did not do enough to achieve a socialist transformation of society, certainly along Bevanite lines. Both Bevan and the revisionists within the party accepted the importance of equality. For Bevan, capitalism was the biggest barrier to equality as private ownership prevented redistribution.[73] The revisionists, on the other hand, stressed equality as the main goal of the Labour Party and saw nationalisation merely as a (poor) means to an end.[74] While revisionists felt that the changes brought about by the 1945 Labour government had created an affluent society, and thus managing capitalism should be the aim (pp. 35–7), Bevan clearly did not believe that public ownership should be abandoned. The ideology of labourism, as we shall explore in more detail in the final chapter, prevented a radical transformation of society in the way that Bevan had envisioned. Rather than consolidation, Bevan maintained that further advance was needed.

Achieving hegemony in this way has proven to be extremely difficult for the left. Saville, utilising Gwyn Alf Williams' understanding of hegemony detailed in this chapter, explained that the British working class accepted its subordinate position in the existing framework of society as a way to achieve its goals.[75] Workers, he argued, were radical in economic terms but collaboration took place within political affairs (p. 217). British politics in general has been hostile to grand theories and large upheaval (p. 220), which Bevan was arguing for in the transformation of property relations. Saville argued that British politics was about piecemeal reform, and this was central to the ideology of labourism. He recognised all the groups and societies that helped to create class consciousness and class independence, but he argued that these were purely defensive: they did nothing to fundamentally change society. The working class, Saville argued, accepted a 'subordinate role' (p. 222), instead of challenging ruling-class hegemony. The role of intellectuals was also important in providing a directive function – intellectuals must provide historic blocs with theory and strategy.[76] Yet, in Britain, the intellectual function in socialist politics was largely carried out by 'traditional' intellectuals, rather than organic ones (p. 3). The Webbs and the Fabians argued for a small, educated elite to lead the way and provide ideas to each of the political parties. Socialist *ideology* was therefore not necessarily based on a mass movement (p. 48).

Saville insisted that this intellectual torpor was not inevitable in Britain. In fact, despite the moderate nature of the Labour Party leadership, socialist ideas were always being disseminated throughout the labour movement.[77] Yet, referencing Lenin, Gramsci and the role of organic and traditional intellectuals, Saville argued that British intellectuals did not question bourgeois society.[78] Bevan, however, could be considered as an organic intellectual, someone who emerged from the working class and attempted to articulate a strategy for it to achieve power (perhaps this is why his politics differed from the likes of Gaitskell, an Oxford-educated economist). The labourist tradition, however, was based on a blueprint for gradual and evolutionary politics. Marxism failed to take hold and British socialism failed to develop a reinterpretation of history in Marxist terms.[79] Bevan's own ideology and his outline of democratic socialism also failed win popular support within the Labour Party.

Taken together, these four chapters emphasise common themes in Bevan's political thought. Importantly, the chapters reveal the connections between these themes. It has been demonstrated that concepts such as class conflict, public ownership, parliamentary democracy, international power politics and competing ideologies and values were inter-connected. The primary feature that these concepts had in common was the relationship between economic conditions and the political-ideological superstructure. Bevan's own articulation of the materialist conception of history is apparent throughout.

NOTES

1 Bevan, *In Place of Fear*, p. 12.
2 Jones, *The Russia Complex*, p. 91.
3 Aneurin Bevan, 'The slump and the summit', *Tribune* (7 March 1958), p. 5.
4 Bevan, *In Place of Fear*, p. 47.
5 Jones, *The Russia Complex*, p. 9.
6 Callaghan, *The Labour Party and Foreign Policy*, pp. 154–5.
7 Bevan, *In Place of Fear*, p. 125.
8 Aneurin Bevan, in *Denis Healey, The Curtain Falls: The Story of the Socialists in Eastern Europe* (London: Lincolns-Prager, 1951), p. 6.
9 Aneurin Bevan, 'After Stalin: the big test for communists', *Tribune* (23 March 1956), p. 1.
10 Aneurin Bevan, 'A very dangerous game', *Tribune* (16 August 1957), p. 12.
11 Aneurin Bevan, 'The Communist failure in the West', *Tribune* (28 November 1958), p. 8.
12 Aneurin Bevan, 'The real arguments behind the Tito-Khrushchev row', *Tribune* (11 July 1958), p. 6.
13 Editorial, 'What about Russia?', *Tribune* (7 August 1942), p. 1.
14 Bevan, 'In place of the Cold War', p. 4.
15 Callaghan, *The Labour Party and Foreign Policy*, pp. 199–200.
16 Aneurin Bevan, 'Why Russia wins space race', *Tribune* (11 October 1957), p. 5.
17 Bevan, *In Place of Fear*, pp. 138–9.

18 Aneurin Bevan, 'Kremlin personalities', *Tribune* (1 October 1954), p. 1.
19 Bevan, 'Communism or suicide? That's not the real choice', p. 5.
20 Aneurin Bevan, 'How much freedom in the new China?', *Tribune* (22 October 1954), p. 4.
21 Aneurin Bevan, 'The world of Gomulka, Tito – and Djilas', *Tribune* (27 September 1957), p. 6.
22 Bevan, 'Give China the help she needs', p. 4.
23 Bevan, *In Place of Fear*, p. 43.
24 Aneurin Bevan, 'Meaning of the alliance', *Tribune* (18 July 1941), p. 13.
25 Aneurin Bevan, 'Russia must take her share of the blame', *Tribune* (25 November 1955), p. 4.
26 Aneurin Bevan, 'At last the Socialist International wakes up!', *Tribune* (12 July 1957), p. 12.
27 Bevan, *In Place of Fear*, p. 22.
28 Bevan, 'Blind men are leading us!', p. 11.
29 Aneurin Bevan, 'The people's coming of age', *Tribune* (3 February 1950), p. 3.
30 Bevan, *In Place of Fear*, p. 118.
31 Aneurin Bevan, 'Automation: the socialist answer', *Tribune* (8 July 1955), p. 2.
32 Bevan, 'Freedom is not enough', p. 13.
33 Bevan, *In Place of Fear*, p. 22.
34 Bevan, *In Place of Fear*, pp. 3–4; Aneurin Bevan, 'The budget and the unions', *Tribune* (17 April 1959), p. 1.
35 Bevan, *In Place of Fear*, p. 5.
36 Bevan, 'Bevan on Parliament', p. 12.
37 Bevan, *In Place of Fear*, p. 55.
38 Bevan, 'Bevan on Parliament', p. 12.
39 Antonio Gramsci, *Selections from the Prison Notebooks* (New York: International Publishers, 1992).
40 Gwyn Alf Williams, '"The Concept of 'Egemonia" in the Thought of Antonio Gramsci: Some Notes on Interpretation', *Journal of the History of Ideas*, 21/4 (1960), 587.
41 Gwyn Alf Williams, *The Welsh in their history* (London: Croom Helm, 1982), p. 200.
42 Aneurin Bevan, 'A swastika nailed to England's mast', *Tribune* (24 June 1938), p. 7.
43 Aneurin Bevan, 'The parties' line-up in Parliament', *Tribune* (1 December 1944), p. 6.

44 Aneurin Bevan, 'This is how fascism is born', *Tribune* (1 July 1938), p. 7.
45 Bevan, 'Crisis time for United Nations', p. 5.
46 Bevan, *In Place of Fear*, p. 36.
47 Bevan, 'July 5th and the socialist advance', p. 7.
48 Aneurin Bevan, *Democratic Values: First in the series of Fabian Autumn Lectures* (Fabian Tracts, 1950), p. 14.
49 Bevan, *In Place of Fear*, p. 73.
50 Bevan, 'July 5th and the socialist advance', p. 7.
51 Aneurin Bevan, 'This famous victory', *Tribune* (3 February 1956), pp. 1 and 12.
52 Aneurin Bevan, 'Why Winston Churchill has been gagged', *Tribune* (20 May 1955), p. 2.
53 Aneurin Bevan, 'Now – let's give a socialist lead', *Tribune* (12 October 1956), p. 5.
54 Bevan, 'Ten years – *Tribune*, 1937–1947', p. 7.
55 Aneurin Bevan, 'Aneurin Bevan gives his verdict', *Tribune* (3 June 1955), p. 1.
56 Bevan, 'Private enterprise vs public ownership: the moon and the £', p. 5.
57 Bevan, *In Place of Fear*, p. 13.
58 Aneurin Bevan, 'My private talk with Malenkov', *Tribune* (24 September 1954), p. 1.
59 Aneurin Bevan, 'This minor Caesar', *Tribune* (28 September 1956), p. 4.
60 Bevan, *Democratic Values*, p. 8.
61 Bevan, *In Place of Fear*, p. 169.
62 José Enrique Rodó, *Ariel* (Austin TX: Texas University Press, 1988), p. 66.
63 Ellis 1918, cited in Bevan, *Democratic Values*, p. 13.
64 Aneurin Bevan, 'Freedom and socialism', *Tribune* (5 November 1954), p. 1.
65 Aneurin Bevan, 'Traitors or Heroes?', in *This I Believe* (CBS, 14/12/22 1953).
66 Bevan, *Democratic Values*, p. 11.
67 Bevan, *In Place of Fear*, p. 170.
68 Bevan, *Democratic Values*, p. 14.
69 Macintyre, *A Proletarian Science*, p. 131.
70 Thomas-Symonds, *Nye*, p. 228.
71 José Enrique Rodó, *The Motives of Proteus* (Delhi: Facsimile Publisher, 1928); Rodó, *Ariel*.
72 Francis, *Ideas and Policies under Labour 1945–1951*, pp. 225–6.
73 Jackson, *Equality and the British Left*, p. 159.
74 Callaghan, 'The Left', p. 33.

75 Saville, 'The ideology of labourism', pp. 215–16.
76 Desai, *Intellectuals and Socialism*, p. 2.
77 Saville, *The Labour Movement in Britain*, p. 80.
78 Saville, 'The ideology of labourism', pp. 222–4.
79 Saville, 'The ideology of labourism', pp. 224–6.

5
BEVAN AS A POLITICAL THINKER

This book has drawn on Bevan's extensive writing to develop an interpretation of his political thought, laying out, in detail, its core ideas. This chapter now uses the insights generated by this detailed engagement to reconsider the debates surrounding Bevan and the Labour Party. It begins by reiterating the core findings of the research, reflecting on how Bevan's economic analysis informed his outlook on class struggle, Parliament and political power, international development and ideological conflict. Not only does this chapter explore these themes, it also considers Bevan's location within Labour's intellectual traditions. It is argued here that considering Bevan as a political thinker has led to an improved understanding of his politics. An understanding that is more securely based in the text of his writings. As a result, we are armed to respond more clearly to the ongoing debates concerning his political thought than has previously been possible.

Bevan's Political Thought

Studying Bevan as a political thinker has been challenging due the unsystematic nature of his writing. *In Place of Fear* was his only concerted effort at systematising his ideas. Therefore, the fundamental task of this book has been to reconstruct and organise Bevan's voluminous writing and present it on its own merits. The variety of topics analysed by Bevan has also made it more difficult to achieve this task. Nonetheless, despite these challenges, a study of Bevan as a political thinker has been possible. Although they were often journalistic in style, Bevan's writings in *Tribune* and elsewhere demonstrated his concerted attempt to reveal the forces that shaped political events. In this sense, it can be argued that studying Bevan as a political thinker is rewarding: it has been shown that there was a core set of ideas underpinning the bulk of his writing.

Bevan thought deeply about the underlying processes and patterns of politics. In Chapter 1 we saw that he emphasised the importance of political theory in clarifying and explaining experience. So, although bringing together Bevan's writing and giving structure to his political thought has been a challenging task, the persistent focal themes of his analytical reflections encourage consideration of Bevan as a political thinker rather than just as a politician or institution builder. The book has sought to lend structure to Bevan's writings by taking its lead from Bevan himself, and thus analysing them through the prism of power. Specifically, Michael Mann's theory of the four sources of social power has been adapted as an organisational framework within which to analyse Bevan's writing. Organising the analysis in this way has allowed for a variety of concepts, themes and ideas in Bevan's thought to be more systematically drawn out, also highlighting how these themes and ideas relate to each other. We start with an evaluation of what has emerged as the two core features of Bevan's thought, which are also two prominent sources of debate over Bevan's legacy: his Marxist-influenced economic analysis and his reverence for Parliament.

MARXISM

As shown in the Introduction, a common, though contested, theme in the literature is the extent to which Marxism was a consistently important aspect of Bevan's thought. The disagreement centres on those who criticise Bevan for sticking dogmatically to a Marxist interpretation of society and those who argue that while he acknowledged the importance of Marxist thought, Bevan was a pragmatist who sacrificed his Marxist principles when he needed to. John Campbell, for instance, argued that Bevan's theoretical education never went beyond Marx and that he clung too closely to a Marxist analysis through most of his career. Other authors, however, such as Michael Foot, Nick Thomas-Symonds and Dai Smith denied that Bevan was dogmatic in his beliefs.

This book has found that a Marxist interpretation was central to Bevan's analysis of capitalism. His understanding of the materialist conception of history and the relationship between the base and superstructure were continuing themes throughout his writings. Whether by referencing Marx explicitly or implicitly, Bevan's writings demonstrate that this core analysis underpinned his understanding of politics and society. Bevan viewed the changes in the development of society primarily from an economic perspective and emphasised the role that economic conditions played in shaping its structure. The way in which Bevan analysed the development of Britain and other nations heavily reflected a materialist interpretation of society and historical development. This became a guide for Bevan to understand the world and consistently informed his political outlook.

This conception of history is evidenced in Bevan's critique of capitalist society through the lens of class conflict. The clash between the working class and the ruling class was central to his argument that the dominance of private property characterised capitalism and was responsible for its negative features; namely, the creation of poverty, greed and the rejection of collectivist principles. He derived this view from his reading of the *Communist Manifesto*, emphasising throughout his career the importance of radically changing the economic base of society and altering property relations. Bevan anticipated that once property relations were altered then this would have a profound effect on the political-ideological superstructure of society. Permeating Bevan's writings was the idea that once the dominance of private property had been restricted, making public property the dominant property form, then principles of economic planning could be followed. Therefore, a new order of values could be established. Again, implicit in this analysis is a view of property relations centred on the economic base shaping the political-ideological superstructure.

While supporting the conclusions of those writers who emphasise the significance of Marxism in Bevan's thought, this book has gone into more detail in highlighting the precise nature of Bevan's engagement with Marxism and how he applied it to his analysis. This book has also shown moments where Bevan presented a more complicated relationship between the economy and the structure of society than is evident in the majority of his writing. Bevan's writings demonstrate that he also understood the role that ideas played in shaping attitudes, values and politics in a society. Perhaps echoing Dietzgen's focus on both the material and the metaphysical in historical materialism, Bevan highlighted the dynamic nature of societal development resulting from the conflicting nature of ideas. He asserted that ideas in society were not fixed, with values and principles changing depending on cultures and time.

Bevan was also interested in the relationship between the economic base, ideas, values and political culture, expounding his theory on how the ruling class maintained its power. He pointed to conflict over values and symbols in society between the different classes, similar to a Gramscian understanding of hegemony (although it is unlikely that Bevan would have had knowledge of Gramsci's ideas). For example, this study has highlighted instances where Bevan wrote of the struggle over national symbols[1] and how the ruling class associated its interests with those of the masses.[2] His thought was not completely economically deterministic, contrary to Campbell's argument;[3] it also revealed the way that conflict over ideas shaped economic and social conditions. These features of his analysis were not developed extensively, although they do demonstrate a more sophisticated and nuanced understanding of the relationship between ideas and economic conditions than generally identified. This represents an aspect of Bevan's thinking that is often understated because of the literature's predominant focus on public ownership and Parliament in Bevan's thought.

Although Bevan's recognition of the ideological nature of class struggle is an often-overlooked aspect of his thought, it is apparent that his writing was nonetheless still grounded in the theory of class struggle and a materialist conception of history. In terms of providing coherence to his political thought, this outlook equipped Bevan with a clear view and understanding of political conflict. Campbell was quite dismissive and critical of Bevan's continuing to base much of his understanding of the economy on Marxism, whereas authors such as Foot and Thomas-Symonds praised Bevan for not being dogmatic in his politics.[4] The underlying theories in Bevan's thought were more complex than Campbell allowed, while it is also apparent that – although often only implicitly – this understanding of the economy consistently informed Bevan's political thought. Further, rather than Bevan's appearing to discard his Marxism by the end of the 1950s, as argued by Campbell,[5] it was a persistent theme in his work. By analysing

Bevan's diverse writings from the 1920s to the 1950s, the prominence and continuity of Bevan's economic analysis and his debt to Marxism has been shown to exist throughout his career.

DEMOCRACY, PARLIAMENT AND THE STATE

Nonetheless, despite the evident foundation in Marxism, Bevan deviated from it in important ways, most notably in his advocacy of liberal democratic political institutions. The biographical and academic literature on Bevan firmly establishes him as a parliamentarian who argued that, at least after the 1920s, Parliament, particularly the House of Commons, was the weapon through which to agitate on behalf of the working class. This has certainly been the way that Bevan is invoked by 'pragmatic' Labour politicians. Bevan rejected the traditional Marxist view of the state as an instrument of the ruling class, arguing that representative institutions could be used by socialists as a weapon in the class struggle. A vital force in the conflict between poverty and property outlined by Bevan was democracy. This formulation defined his strategy for using political power. Bevan envisioned representative institutions as potentially reflecting the voice of the masses against the interests of property. His rejection of the classical Marxist understanding of the state demonstrates that he was not a conventional Marxist. In essence, he was a Marxist in terms of his economic analysis. His rejection of what he saw as 'Marxist dogma' meant that he would never join the Communist Party or any other party that would not advocate reform through Parliament. He accepted the Marxist argument of social change yet rejected its analysis of the state.

Here, Bevan's British radicalism interacts with his Marxism. Some writers such as David Marquand and Roger Spalding have argued that Bevan's politics were rooted in the traditions of British radicalism and that his reading of the history of democracy centred on the reforms won by the British working-class movement. While such views are accurate (Bevan's conception of political liberty being based on British parliamentary democracy), Bevan's reflections on the development of democracy, whether in Britain or in other nations, can be understood through focusing on his understanding of the materialist conception of history. He declared a belief that as the economic base of society was developed, for example in the Soviet Union as a result of central planning, then political liberty would eventually materialise for the people in that country. Thus, Bevan's economic analysis merged with his admiration for the advancements won by the working class throughout history.

This understanding can be seen clearly in Bevan's writings on developing countries and particularly in his analysis of communist societies. The literature contains discussion of Bevan's reflections on the need to support the economic development of other nations, but understanding Bevan's political thought more deeply reveals the way in which his writings on this issue emphasise the importance of the material economic base in his political thought. Bevan argued that as the economic base of communist societies developed, there would be a resultant change in their political-ideological super-structures. His writings in *Tribune* throughout his career on the Soviet Union[6] and communist nations such as Yugoslavia[7] and China[8] demonstrated his belief that greater political liberty and freedoms are granted in nations as a result of the changing position of the worker in society, a theory in Bevan's thought identified most explicitly by John Callaghan in his analysis of the Bevanites and the Soviet Union.[9]

This aspect of Bevan's political thought is also echoed through his analysis of the development of poorer nations and the need to establish the principles of global justice. Whereas historically the larger nations had exploited poorer countries, Bevan argued that in the future, that relationship needed to change. The interests of large nations needed to be set aside for the benefit of developing countries. Throughout Bevan's writings on this subject, he stressed the importance of fostering economic development in these countries, which would result in the creation of political institutions enshrined with the democratic values seen by Bevan as imperative to the functioning of society. The importance of changing property relations was wedded to Bevan's analysis of the development of democracy, underlining the influence of the materialist conception of history on Bevan's thought.

Bevan's writings on the phenomenon of nationalism were also underpinned by this materialist conception of history. In particular, his writings in *Tribune* during the Suez crisis focused heavily on the tensions between social revolution, national sovereignty, nationalism and the international community. The emphasis he placed on economic conditions in social revolutions can be most clearly identified by studying his articles on Egypt.[10] His articles analysing imperialism also demonstrate the connections he made between nationalism, social revolutions and economic conditions.[11]

Bevan's economic analysis, combined with his advocacy of democracy, also drives his reflections on international organisation. He emphasised the role of democracy in international affairs, placing central importance on international institutions, specifically the UN, in directing wealth to different countries. Just as state-action could change the economic conditions of a country, Bevan argued that collective action through the UN could change property relations in developing nations. This would allow democratic principles to become embedded in these countries. History has shown Bevan to have been quite idealistic in his vision for the future of international co-operation. Nevertheless, his writing on international politics demonstrates his attempting to understand ideas of nationalism, sovereignties and relations between states.

The introduction identified a clear disagreement among Bevan commentators concerning these two important features of his thought: his Marxism and his parliamentarianism. For example, as noted above, Marquand saw Bevan as a radical dissenter rather than a Marxist. He argued that the way to understand Bevan is through stressing the radical side of his politics, a conclusion also arrived at by Spalding. Foot saw Bevan – on becoming an MP in 1929 – as placing more emphasis on liberal and democratic virtues than on a Marxist interpretation of political events, with these views being reinforced during the Second World War. Francis also argued that Bevan's 'crude Marxism ... needs to be balanced against his essential radicalism and libertarianism'.[12] Foote's consideration of Bevan's politics as a restatement of Labour Marxism includes the caveat that it was presented in a way that appealed to labourism.[13]

It is true that Bevan added to his understanding of Marxist economics to include an appreciation of the development of democracy in Britain and the importance of parliamentary institutions. He understood democracy through an appreciation of British radical history, particularly the Chartist movement and the Tolpuddle martyrs. He saw British history as being a 'continuous struggle against [oppression]',[14] his liberalism also forming part of his understanding of historical development, which derived from his reflections on the development of productive forces and of working-class agitation in society.

However, studying Bevan as a political thinker has identified that these two themes in Bevan's thought are inextricably connected. Marquand and Spalding are incorrect, therefore, to dismiss the Marxism of Bevan's thought as simply rhetoric or a 'nostalgic attachment to the rhetoric of class struggle'.[15] This is to ignore Bevan's emphasis on the centrality of property relations and the relationship between the state and the economy. Bevan envisioned that in Britain the economic conditions of society would be radically altered as a result of the state's intervening in the economy. He had faith in Parliament, as a tool in the right hands, to alter the economic base and therefore change people's lives through the processes of public ownership and economic planning. Spalding, in particular, fails to sufficiently acknowledge this crucial aspect of Bevan's thought, despite conducting an analysis of Bevan's writings in *Tribune* between 1937 and 1945. For instance, Spalding referenced Bevan's 1940 article on the planned economy,[16] which formed the basis for his 1943 Fabian essay 'Plan for Work'.[17] However, the limited discussion of it is not included in his chapter on Bevan, thus disconnecting it from Bevan's broader thought.[18] When assessing why Bevan saw Parliament as being so vital to the working class, his logic for promoting public ownership cannot be ignored, being predicated on his interpretation of the materialist conception of history.

Bevan fused his belief that property relations needed to be altered with his conception of state power. Rejecting the Marxist theory of the state as necessarily an instrument of class oppression, Bevan combined his belief in Parliament with his analysis of the economy. This analysis was then transported to the international stage and to countries around the world. This was to prove problematic, as Bevan's analysis of economics and his belief in parliamentary democracy appeared to confront each other. As Campbell argued, while Bevan's Marxism was a strength, it also became a source of weakness for him, as the next section demonstrates.[19]

Bevan and the Labour Party

The analysis undertaken in this book advances our understanding of Bevan's thought by comprehensively reconstructing and evaluating its core ideas. It therefore contributes to the at least partial resolution of interpretive disputes in Bevan scholarship. This section now turns to consider Bevan's thought within the Labour Party, particularly the prevailing view put forward that Bevan's ideas failed to achieve dominant status in comparison with those of the revisionists. It begins by detailing the findings of the book as they relate to discussions of Bevan and the revisionists, critically analysing Bevan's arguments for public ownership and state power. Potential reasons explaining the failure of Bevan's ideas to achieve ascendancy are identified, focusing on the limits of the political traditions in which Bevan was situated. Finally, in agreement with New Left critics of the Labour Party, it is demonstrated that Bevan's thought did not transcend the ideology of labourism, which was central to Labour's thought.

BEVAN, PUBLIC OWNERSHIP AND THE REVISIONISTS

Studies of Labour's political thought often characterise the 1950s as a battle between the Bevanites and the revisionists (or Gaitskellites) within the party. Bevan is often dismissed as having failed to develop a theory that challenged the revisionists and the prevailing thought of the Labour Party, resulting in his losing out in the battle for theoretical ascendancy. The dominant view in the literature focuses on the divide between those on the left of the party who wanted to see it reaffirm and extend its commitment to nationalisation and those on the right who expressed concern about public ownership, instead placing an emphasis on ensuring equality, redistribution and managing capitalism.[20] This literature identifies the failure of the Bevanites to develop a plan that challenged the scepticism towards public ownership that was expressed by the revisionists. They are accused of being intellectually limited and developing only vague and broad principles of socialism. This judgement is also made of Bevan himself.

Marquand and Thomas-Symonds both downplayed the difference between Bevan and the revisionists on this point. Marquand argued that it was the moral character of the revisionists' plans for a mixed economy that Bevan was against,[21] while Thomas-Symonds contended that the differences on the mixed economy were theoretical rather than practical, arguing that Bevan was more in favour of the revisionist position of consolidation (the idea that further nationalisation was not necessarily needed) than at first appears.[22] Although both sides acknowledged the importance of the mixed economy, there was a significant difference between Bevan's and the revisionist's visions for how it was to be implemented. Bevan remained committed to a radical transformation of the economic base of society, emphasising the effect that this would have on shaping values and politics. The materialist conception of history that underpinned Bevan's economic analysis represented a significant difference from the revisionists who dismissed Marxist theories of social change.[23]

As Ben Jackson has noted, Bevan disagreed with the revisionists' focus on redistribution instead of public ownership, arguing that the structure of the economy needed to be significantly altered before that could occur.[24] Foote stated that while there was agreement on the mixed economy, Bevan placed significant emphasis on the dominance of public over private property.[25] The analysis of Bevan's political thought in Chapter 2 supports these arguments concerning theoretical differences between Bevan and the revisionists.

While the findings of this book generally do not contradict the arguments in the literature that Bevan did not seriously develop coherent plans for public ownership,[26] by considering and analysing Bevan's writing on the state and public ownership throughout his career, it has been shown that there were instances where Bevan attempted to provide more detailed plans. As demonstrated in Chapter 2, Bevan's article for *Tribune* in 1940 as well as his 1943 Fabian essay were examples of his attempt to develop a theory of public ownership and economic planning that accounted for the relationship between the economy and representative institutions. These writings demonstrated a much more detailed attempt to outline plans for nationalisation, which are generally, and undeservedly, overlooked in evaluations of Bevan's political thought.

Regrettably for Bevan's supporters, he did not sufficiently reformulate or reassess his ideas during the 1950s. He did not offer a stronger challenge to the revisionists, failing to develop an alternative model for the Labour Party that would have advocated for the transformation of the economy that Bevan argued was necessary. Jackson argued that there was a failure on behalf of the Bevanites to develop 'policies that followed their ideological commitments'.[27] Campbell and Thomas-Symonds both also agreed that Bevan did not develop detailed plans for public ownership.[28] The nationalisation measures undertaken by the 1945–51 Labour government took some industries out of private property, but Bevan argued throughout the 1950s for further public ownership and for the principles of economic planning to be applied more vigorously. He did not, however, attempt to significantly revise his plans for public ownership in response to the economic situation that had emerged after the measures of the 1945–51 Labour government. The revisionists, in contrast, did produce updated proposals for nationalisation, with figures such as Anthony Crosland helping to shape the political direction of the party.

There is a distinction to be made, however, between *plans* for public ownership and a *theory* of public ownership. Bevan did have a strong theory of public ownership, contrary to arguments in the literature. It was a theory that was inherently progressive because it undermined capitalist property relations and put the means of production into the hands of the working class (at least, indirectly) via its potential control of Parliament. It was also underpinned by his materialist conception of economic development. While critics have argued that Bevan failed to respond to societal changes in the 1950s, Bevan was insisting that his theory of public ownership and economic planning was still relevant. The mixed economy established post-war had still not transformed property relations, which Bevan argued was vital.

The problem, however, is that his understanding of what public ownership could look like was very narrow. Bevan essentially equated public ownership with state control. Alternative ideas that might have involved co-operative ownership or more workers' involvement/control appeared of little interest to him. Bevan's preoccupation with the capacity of the state – and the Labour Party for that matter – to achieve significant economic change resulted in his failing to recognise the limits of state action in carrying out public ownership, leading him to ignore other avenues of collective action. His political education was rooted in the local community, trade unions and in organised working-class activity, yet his preoccupation with the state led him to discard or not think about options for collective action that were rooted in other institutions. For instance, in discussing the NHS, the anarchist academic Colin Ward argued that Bevan ignored the potential for people to organise themselves for medical means through organisations such as the Tredegar Medical Aid Society. Ward asked, 'Why didn't the whole country become, not one big Tredegar, but a network of Tredegars?'[29] He answered that the reason for this was that political parties began to advocate for the state over society. He asserted that the state assumed a monopoly over revenue-gathering:

> When every employed worker in Tredegar paid a voluntary levy of three old pence in the pound, the earnings of even high-skilled industrial workers were below the liability to income tax. But ever

> since PAYE was introduced in the second world war, the Treasury has creamed off the cash which once supported local initiatives. (p. 16)

Ward's argument was that the NHS cannot be described as 'user-controlled', insisting that:

> There once was the option of universal health provision 'at the point of service' if only Fabians, Marxists and Aneurin Bevan had trusted the state and centralised revenue-gathering and policy-making less, and our capacity for self-help and mutual aid more. (p. 16)

Ward bemoaned that in Britain 'we have stifled the localist and voluntarist approach in favour of conquest of the power of the state. We took the wrong road to welfare' (p. 17). Bevan did not necessarily 'Tredegarise' Britain, a quote often attributed to Bevan but not traceable.[30] Rather, it could be argued that he took power away from people and placed it in the hands of the state. Foot noted that a common phrase of Bevan's was 'the purpose of getting power is to be able to give it away'.[31] This notion was not necessarily reflected in Bevan's writings, however, which paid little attention to the potential avenues for taking power away from the state. Bevan's failure to develop a plan for workers' participation in industry, despite declaring the need for workers to have an elevated status within it, is an example of the limits to his conception of the state's role in managing industries. Ralph Miliband, in *The State in Capitalist Society* written in 1969, highlighted the limits of nationalisation when it is not extended beyond a minimal programme.[32] Bevan can be criticised for insisting on the importance of public ownership without developing a significant critique of the state and its functions.

Beyond emphasising the importance of economic planning and the state, Bevan's plans for public ownership, as noted above, were limited. Although the Labour Party in Parliament had achieved many reforms, there was perhaps an opportunity to move beyond Parliament and the state to further consider extending the scope and form of public ownership and the state's relationship with the economy and society. This gave the revisionists in the Labour Party the opportunity to argue that the state had gone far enough and could not go any further. In Bevan's defence, it must be recognised that he had himself acknowledged in the 1950s that people were tired of reform and unhappy with intrusive actions on individual liberty such as taxation.[33] There were signs here that Bevan understood that society had changed, and that the British people were not eager to see further modifications being made to the economy. His response, however, did not contain much substance beyond arguing for further measures of nationalisation, despite it being rooted in progressive principles. Bevan was fighting a battle within his own party and with a British public sceptical of further state involvement.

As with his plans for nationalisation, Bevan's writings on the state were occasionally more sophisticated pre-1945 but were not developed further in the 1950s. The former writings contained greater critical scrutiny of the state's functions and its institutions – such as the Civil Service – as well as its relationship with the economy, demonstrating a more nuanced analysis than appeared in his writings post-1945. For example, Bevan's reflections on the relationship between capitalism and the state, the development of fascism and its relationship to capitalist development and his blueprints for future public ownership are evidence of his attempts to outline the challenges facing socialists and to develop proposals for the future of society. Articles written in 1938 and 1944 showcase Bevan engaging in a more sophisticated analysis of the limits of state power, the different institutions within the state and their functions, and the state's relationship with the economy.

Quite often, however, Bevan would pull back to more prosaic concerns just as he appeared to be engaging more critically and creatively with a certain issue (see Chapter 2). His failure to develop the analysis presented in these articles, as well as those on nationalisation, might be reason enough for the literature to dismiss them. Indeed, these are rare examples of Bevan's thinking through these issues. Although some of the themes are touched on in later writing after 1945, Bevan did not go further in developing these ideas. *In Place of Fear* returned to asserting the notion that Parliament is supreme and can be utilised to change society, with Bevan's reflections on the limits of the state not featuring prominently. *In Place of Fear* also did not contain a blueprint for public ownership that matched the detail of his 1943 Fabian essay and other writings pre-1945. It is understandable, therefore, that this analysis failed to be taken seriously by the party leadership into the 1950s. However, it is imperative to note that when the wider scope of his writings is analysed, it is apparent that Bevan did attempt to develop plans for nationalisation and reconsider the role of the state.

THE LIMITATIONS OF BEVAN'S INTELLECTUAL INHERITANCE

Why then did Bevan fail, post-1945, to develop his more critical analysis of the state and the more detailed plans for public ownership? One possible explanation is that he was unable to commit time to his theoretical writings due to the responsibility placed on his shoulders as a minister in government. He would not have had the time to contribute as regularly to *Tribune* as he did between 1937 and 1945 and to write and think through political questions; therefore, there is less evidence of his attempting to develop theories or plans for public ownership. In contrast, Anthony Crosland, for example, might have had more time to develop his ideas considering he lost his parliamentary seat in 1955. Therefore, it is understandable that Bevan's thought was limited in some respects. He did, however, publish *In Place of Fear* in 1952 after he had resigned from government and Labour had lost power. Arguably, without the pressures that came with a ministerial position, Bevan might have had the opportunity to carry out a more systematic analysis than he did, as well as engaging in more detailed works later in his career. It must be remembered that during a thirty-one-year parliamentary career, Bevan was in government for only six years.

Another possible explanation for Bevan's failure to develop his ideas further relates to the pragmatic nature of his politics. An argument common in the literature is that Bevan was ultimately a pragmatist who understood the importance of working with and within institutions and the need to compromise in order to get measures through. Nuttall, for instance, stated that Bevan understood the multi-faceted nature of power, leading him to seek compromise with others.[34] As noted in the Introduction, this is a common argument in contemporary invocations of Bevan. New Left writers such as Miliband and Nairn criticised the way in which he compromised with the leadership and was willing to shift his position and adapt his views towards certain policies in the name of unity.[35] This suggests that Bevan acquiesced in letting through certain proposals that he disagreed with. This argument has merit when analysing his ministerial career and his becoming closer to Gaitskell from 1955 onwards: Bevan had to compromise on some issues when he developed the NHS; he had to work within restrictions placed on his ministry when developing the government's house-building programme; and he was also willing to compromise on Labour Party policies that did not go far enough in pushing for socialism. His 1957 Brighton speech on the bomb is perhaps the most prominent example of the 'pragmatic' Bevan.

Despite this, however, in stepping back from the personal and political controversies of Bevan's career this book has demonstrated that his writings contained consistent arguments throughout the 1950s that were out of step with those of the leadership of the Labour Party. Although he was willing to compromise and adjust his position in the name of unity, Bevan was still arguing the same central points in his writings, which reflected a foundational belief in the idea of altering property relations in society and the need to move beyond capitalism to a new order of society. Campbell's argument that Bevan doubted Marxism in the late 1950s is not supported by an analysis of Bevan's writings during this period.[36] As Ellison pointed out, personal ambition and actions do not necessarily equate to the abandonment of someone's vision for society.[37] Bevan's pragmatism does not, therefore, provide a satisfactory explanation for his failure to develop his ideas further: the need to compromise did not prevent Bevan from arguing his case in the pages of *Tribune* and elsewhere.

A more satisfactory explanation might be found by considering the limitations of Bevan's intellectual traditions. Macintyre noted the competing theories of the state between Labour Party socialists and Marxists in Britain that emerged after the First World War. He asserted that 'Labour leaders regarded the state as the political expression of the community'.[38] At various points the state was misused, but, he argued, this did not mean that Labour leaders felt it needed to be discarded. The Labour socialists' argument was based on a belief that through 'the state the community would take control of economic life; it would confiscate private wealth and take industry into public ownership' (p. 178). Barry Jones and Michael Keating argued that the Labour Party 'has rarely given any sustained attention to the form of the state whose power and role it is pledged to extend'.[39] This neglect:

> stems from a sheer intellectual failure on the part of Labour leaders and policy makers ... to specify the changes in the state necessary to achieve their policy goals while preserving and extending individual and associative liberties; or to identify and frankly recognize the limits to state power. (pp. 2–3)

British Marxists, on the other hand, argued that the 'very function of the state was class coercion'. They also, Macintyre noted, 'appreciated that the capitalist state was far more complex than earlier forms of state organisation'. Macintyre also argued, however, that in other ways British Marxists in their analysis of the state 'were far more simplistic'. According to Macintyre, they saw the state simply as an organ of the capitalist class and institutions 'as mere camouflage for capitalism'. This was 'pervasive in British Marxism, and is closely related to its over-simple view of the materialist conception of history'.[40] We can identify elements of Bevan's thought within the two political traditions that he was most associated with, Marxism and labourism. Yet in both there existed serious issues with their analyses of the state.

The Marxist analysis of the economy and the radical traditions of Parliament and British democracy from which Bevan drew were both insufficient to provide sophisticated understandings of the British state and the limits of political power. It was after Bevan's death that more sustained critiques of the British state and critical interpretations of state power began to emerge (from the likes of Perry Anderson and Tom Nairn, for instance).[41] Writers such as Raymond Williams also began to develop critiques of materialism in Marxist thought.[42] Alongside this, theorists such as Ralph Miliband and Nicos Poulantzas began to engage with substantial critiques of the role and character of the state in Marxist theory.[43] Writing in 1970, Miliband argued that 'the exercise of *socialist* power remains the Achilles' heel of Marxism'.[44] Christopher Pierson in *Marxist Theory and Democratic Politics* outlined the many different attempts to overcome weaknesses in the Marxist tradition by 'building their differing accounts of state, society and democracy upon a critique of the more familiar premisses [*sic*] of conventional Marxist analysis'.[45] As detailed above, there were instances where Bevan began to question the exercise of state power in relation to his analysis of the economy. He did not, however, begin to question it systematically, or even persist with his questions.

The core foundations of Bevan's thought – class conflict, property relations, economic development, the importance of Parliament and democracy – are evident in his writings throughout his career. His thought, however, was not extensively developed beyond these initial foundations. Bevan appeared stuck in a certain period, analysing society in the terms that he understood from the 1920s onwards. Referring to the Bevanites as a movement, rather than Bevan himself, Raymond Williams questioned the relevance of their politics to the 1950s. He argued that 'they did not understand at all the changes of post-war Britain. The capitalism they were describing was the capitalism of the thirties which led inevitably to depression and dire poverty'.[46] Speaking of Bevan individually, Williams stated that he 'never thought Bevan was defining the problems of contemporary British society', Bevan seemingly being unable to identify what the problems were in Britain (p. 369). This is not to argue that Bevan should necessarily have followed the arguments of the revisionists in the party; but certain aspects of his political thought could perhaps have been developed further. As noted in this chapter, Crosland, for example, attempted to comprehensively reassess the nature of British society and British socialism. Throughout the 1950s Bevan did not try to do the same. His most insightful analysis of the state came pre-1945.

Bevan's reliance on his understanding of the economy can be considered as a reason why he never revised his analysis during the 1950s. Foote noted that Bevan had once declared that 'if private enterprise could provide security there would be no need for public ownership, yet that was precisely what private enterprise appeared to be doing, at least in Britain'.[47] He argued that Bevan's politics and stress on the struggle between poverty and wealth were not appropriate to the 'wealth and boom' of the 1950s. He asserted that Bevan gave the impression of 'a society frozen in the political and social attitudes of twenty years before', going on to argue that Bevan's 'Labour Marxism belonged to an earlier age than that of washing machines, televisions and rising living standards' (p. 281). To his critics, Bevan's evaluation of society as a clash between poverty and property, a clash between the working class and the ruling class, did not reflect the ways in which class and economic conditions had changed in Britain. They argued that capitalism no longer appeared as a threat to society as it was being effectively managed by the state. The conflict between public and private property did not seem as stark as Bevan had defined it. The failure to fully appreciate this change has been seen as a weakness in the development of Bevan's thought. It may help explain why he never reassessed his proposals for nationalisation post-1945.

Foote pointed to Richard Crossman, a prominent Bevanite in the Labour Party, as someone 'who was aware of the need to develop a new analysis more suited to conditions of prosperity' (p. 282). He argued that as early as 1952 Crossman 'was aware of the sterility of merely repeating old nostrums of Labour Marxism' (p. 283) and that the Labour left had failed to take account of 'Keynesian economic techniques [that] had made unemployment and economic crisis nightmares of a past never to return' (pp. 283–4). Although a highly presumptive argument to make – economic crises have been a regular occurrence in liberal democracies since the 1950s – Bevan's writing in the 1950s did appear to retain the hallmarks of his writing in the 1930s and 1940s. This is not to argue that Bevan should have rejected his beliefs, but rather to state that if Bevan had engaged in a process of revision, then he may have been able to offer a more convincing theory of social change. More convincing, at least, to his Labour Party colleagues.

It is appropriate at this juncture, however, to provide a defence of Bevan. This book has repeatedly emphasised that a failure to treat Bevan as a political thinker and engage more closely with his voluminous output leads to certain elements and specific arguments of his political thought being overlooked. Rather than failing to reassess ideas in the light of economic changes, it has been shown that there were instances when Bevan did reflect on the changes brought about by the post-war Labour government. As previously discussed, he noted the increased prosperity of the 1950s and how Labour's advances had made people more comfortable, leading them to resent aspects of state intervention. Bevan, however, was not satisfied with this. Probing deeper into the 'never had it so good' Britain of the 1950s, poverty was a fact of life in many communities,[48] while inequality had not shrunk significantly.[49] Maintaining a desire to see property in public hands and believing that the working class in Britain still lacked wealth and power in more profound ways, Bevan would have insisted that his arguments still held true in 1950s Britain.

It has been established that authors such as Campbell argued that Bevan was too dogmatic in sticking with outdated principles (although he also argued that Bevan abandoned his Marxism in the late 1950s). Again, in

Bevan's defence, it is perhaps understandable that in the 1950s he would have retained faith in his initial view of socialism. Although he was critical of the Labour government's not going far enough, he was still proud of the measures that it implemented between 1945 and 1951. As the minister responsible for establishing the NHS, he would have experienced first hand what could be achieved through parliamentary action. David Howell asserted that there was 'a tendency to assume that the post-war reforms provided a springboard for Socialist advance – that somehow they marked an invasion of capitalist priorities by those of a Socialist alternative'. He argued that this 'positive appraisal led to Socialists taking a relatively benign view of the British State ... Now much of the Labour Left takes a much more limited view of the record of 1945–51 and has little illusion about the role of the State'. Howell insisted that it:

> is unfair to say simply that a later generation has seen through the illusion of an earlier period – unfair because given the contrasting political experiences of the 30s and 40s, such illusions were hardly surprising ... Awareness of the limitations of post-war Labour reforms has sharpened the Left's perceptions of the complexities of capitalist power.[50]

A reading of Bevan's political thought throughout the 1950s demonstrates that he maintained a benign view of the state, although, as detailed in Chapter 2 and in this chapter, Bevan did question the extent to which Labour's post-war reforms had radically altered society, at the same time acknowledging how attitudes were shifting. His political thought reflected an adherence to an almost Marxist analysis of the economy that he did not attempt to reassess during the 1950s, as well a benign view of the state that has been the hallmark of the labourist tradition in Britain. Bevan did not appear to have the intellectual toolkit necessary to move beyond or develop these political traditions.

LABOURISM

Ultimately, adherence to these political traditions probably explains why Bevan never moved beyond the core assumptions of labourism. Nairn and Miliband, writing after Bevan's death in 1960, argued that Bevan reaffirmed the dogmatic faith that the party had in parliamentary institutions. This led Bevan to regularly compromise with the leadership.[51] It is claimed that the structure of the party placed limits on what the Left could achieve. Leach, for example, argued that due to the dialectic between evolutionary and revolutionary socialist positions, accommodation between different groups was an important feature of labourism.[52]

The analysis carried out throughout this book supports the claim that Bevan's thought fitted comfortably within the ideology of labourism. Arguably, Bevan placed too much faith in Parliament's ability to radically transform society. He rejected the thesis that the state was inherently an instrument of the ruling class and of class oppression; this was a feature of the Conservatives in government. Instead, Bevan maintained that the state could be used to transform society on behalf of the working class. New Left critics, however, have claimed that the Labour Party was led by figures who did not share Bevan's desire to see society radically transformed. Bevan appeared to recognise this, regularly arguing that leaders Attlee and Gaitskell were too moderate in advocating for socialism. As detailed in Chapter 2, Bevan wanted to guard the party against 'revisionists' and proponents of 'pragmatism' and 'compromise', arguing that the Labour Party needed to go further in its reforms than it did between 1945 and 1951. His vision was not shared by the Labour leadership.

The problems with the Labour Party identified by critics of labourism were also recognised by Bevan himself. He consistently argued for the party to push for more radical change, criticising what he saw as its conservative nature. He argued, particularly during the 1950s, against moderation and those who wanted to see the Labour Party become more 'pragmatic'.[53] He accused the leaders of the largest trade unions within the party of being too conservative and having too great an influence on party policy to the detriment of socialist aims.[54] He insisted on the need for the Labour Party to provide socialist education to the working class in order to raise class consciousness, and he also argued for a form of nationalisation that went beyond the bureaucratisation of industry. Although, as noted above, he did not detail extensively what this would entail. Therefore, it could be argued that the structures of the Labour Party and the nature of labourism would have prevented his ideas from being adopted even if they were presented more systematically or if Bevan had been more forceful in asserting them.

Nairn and Miliband did not provide a detailed analysis of Bevan's political thought. Instead, they focused on the actions of the Bevanites and the left of the Labour Party in failing to challenge the limits of labourism. The analysis developed in this book has uncovered a possible explanation for Bevan's failure to challenge Labour orthodoxy; namely, that his faith in British parliamentary politics fitted comfortably with the core assumptions of labourism. As already mentioned above, Foote described Bevan's politics as 'a restatement of Labour Marxism, but presented in a manner appealing to the emotions of labourism'.[55] This is certainly evident when Bevan's thought is analysed. Bevan appears to have been inspired by the economic analysis of Marx but dismissive of the orthodox Marxist conception of the state, instead maintaining a reverence for British Parliament. This allowed him to adapt his analysis of economics to accommodate his faith in parliamentary institutions, arguing for public ownership to reverse property relations but also insisting on the primacy of Parliament and the features of British democracy that went with it (party competition, elections, representatives, etc.) Alongside this, Bevan remained acceptable to the mainstream of the Labour Party as he argued for a mixed economy rather than complete socialisation of industry. Therefore, Bevan fitted comfortably within the Labour Party without being able to offer a fundamental challenge to its core assumptions.

Whether Bevan *wanted* to challenge these assumptions is difficult to judge. A reading of the 1959 diary entries of Geoffrey Goodman – a journalist with whom Bevan developed a good relationship – while following Bevan on the 1959 General Election campaign, point to someone who was exhausted (often physically) from the battles he was facing within the Labour Party.[56] In this account, Goodman quoted Bevan as complaining that 'No more than about fifty M.P.s [about one-fifth] are socialists' (p. 623) and describing Gaitskell as 'a complete gimmick man' (p. 626). Bevan is said to have proclaimed, 'I refuse to belong to a Party unless that Party is the vehicle of principles in which I believe – Socialist principles' (p. 627). This account of Bevan's losing faith in the Labour Party as a vehicle for socialism demonstrates his desire to see the party undergo fundamental change. He was not content with its strategy, undermining arguments that Bevan moved to the right of the party in accommodation with Gaitskell. The approach of this book confirms this reading. By identifying the basic ideological underpinnings of Bevan's thought and analysing his voluminous work, it has been demonstrated that Bevan did not depart significantly from them in the 1950s.

As noted above, throughout his career Bevan identified serious problems that would later be critiqued by the New Left – the moderate nature of the Labour Party, the conservative nature of the state, the limits of working-class consciousness in Britain, and the role of culture, civil society and the press in shaping attitudes and values. Although these aspects were evident in his thought, he did not develop them extensively, instead insisting on the centrality of public ownership and economic planning to the building of socialism in Britain. He touched on the issues identified by the New Left but did not carry out a thoroughgoing critique of the Labour Party.

Conclusion

From the outset, this book had two central aims: first, to investigate Bevan through the prism of his political thought, reconstructing his political philosophy from his written works; and, second, to use the insights generated by this approach to reconsider the debates about Bevan's ideas that can be found in the extant literature. To achieve these aims, three core interpretive decisions were made. These were, first, to focus on Aneurin Bevan primarily as a political thinker rather than a politician or institution builder; second, in doing so, to adopt power as a lens or framework through which to view and understand Bevan's political thought; and, finally, in particular, to adopt Mann's typology of power as a heuristic device that is particularly suitable for analysing Bevan's political thought.

This approach has enabled a more detailed analysis of Bevan's political thought to be developed than has previously been achieved. It has allowed the first aim to be fulfilled and for Bevan to be studied as a political thinker, his writings to be reconstructed in as coherent a way as possible and the main features of his political thought to be analysed and assessed. By studying Bevan's thought in this way, *The Political Thought of Aneurin Bevan* has provided fresh insight into many of the features identified in the literature such as his Marxism and parliamentarianism, as well as analysis of concepts and themes previously overlooked or underplayed, such as the importance of Bevan's writings on the international arena to explaining his political thought, and on the ideological nature of class struggle.

This book has identified the importance of Marxism in Bevan's thought, but it has also highlighted instances where his writing deviates from the Marxism that he appeared to adopt from his initial reading of the *Communist Manifesto*. It has been shown that although Bevan's thought was often rooted in key Marxist concepts, such as class conflict and historical materialism, he would often depart from an orthodox understanding of these concepts. Important deviations from this understanding included his faith in Parliament and liberal democracy to achieve power for the working class and his argument that property relations needed to be reversed rather than abolished. In addition, while Bevan's analysis of historical development often focused on the dominant role of the economic base, he frequently demonstrated a more nuanced understanding of the important role played by the political and ideological superstructure in society, making the case that ideas and political institutions could be used to alter the economic base. The analysis, therefore, has revealed tensions between Bevan's reliance on Marxist-derived principles and instances where he deviated from them. There is potential to further explore these nuances in future research to more fully understand Bevan's engagement with Marxism and its location among British Marxist thought during his lifetime.

Despite moments in his career when Bevan sacrificed certain principles for political expediency, core assumptions on economic and political development remained central to his political thought. He emphasised the importance of class conflict and the centrality of property relations in shaping the social structure of society and its dominant ideas, attitudes and values. Bevan also applied this philosophy to the international realm. A prominent theme in the literature, however, was that his politics was based on vague socialist principles that did not add up to a systematic and developed political thought. Francis, for example, argued that Bevan's political thought was instinctive rather than systematic, being based on a mixture of Marxism, radicalism, libertarianism and romanticism.[57] Ellison contended that Bevan was interested in only the 'broad nature of socialist ideas', meaning that there was a lack of strong foundations in his thought,[58] while Campbell emphasised the vagueness of Bevan's Marxist first principles.[59] This led some authors to argue that Bevan's ideas were not applicable to the 1950s due to their underdevelopment.

The Political Thought of Aneurin Bevan has demonstrated that rather than being based on a set of vague principles, there was an underlying argument and foundation that guided Bevan's political thought. His understanding of Marxism allowed him to analyse the internal politics of Britain and other nations, as well as international relations. This reliance on Marxism, however, while being a source of strength in Bevan's political thought, was also a source of weakness. His reliance on arguments reflecting the base-superstructure division in society and the centrality of class conflict limited the extent to which he developed his understanding of the world to reflect changes that had occurred throughout the 1950s.

Bevan's deviation from orthodox Marxist *political strategy* to argue for the potential of Parliament to radically change society never fully synthesised with his economic analysis as he failed to merge his materialist conception of economic development with his reverence for liberal democratic institutions. He noted the recognition that thinkers such as Marx, Engels and Lenin gave to parliamentary institutions, but argued that they did not develop their analysis far enough.[60] Bevan's contention that Parliament needed to be used in order to capture state power and intervene in the economy to change property relations led him to argue for public ownership. His reverence for Parliament, however, as well as his commitment to the Labour Party, meant that he was unable to sufficiently develop proposals for public ownership to the extent that he did pre-1945 when he questioned the relationship between representative institutions and state-owned companies.

Bevan's almost uncritical analysis of the state (apart from the few instances pre-1945, discussed at length) can be attributed to the limitations of his intellectual inheritance. The weaknesses of the Marxist conception of the state were identified by Bevan, but he did not recognise the limits to the conception of the state also inherent in the labourist tradition. He maintained a strong faith in the power of parliamentary institutions, enhanced by his reflections on the achievements of the 1945–51 Labour government. Yet, despite a few instances, he did not develop proposals for public ownership or an analysis of political power that was based on a reassessment of property relations in light of changes in British society that had occurred during the 1950s (largely as a result of the changes made by the Labour government). This allowed the revisionists to take the initiative. Crosland developed a significant revision of socialism and has been hailed as the dominant theoretician in the party. After Bevan's death, substantial critiques of the Marxist and labourist understandings of the state proliferated, evident in the work of thinkers such as Nairn, Anderson, Miliband and Poulantzas. Bevan was not so critical as these writers. Despite proclaiming the need for Labour to become more radical in its socialism and its commitment to public ownership and economic planning, Bevan was unable to transcend the limits of labourism.

Some of Bevan's writing, particularly during the 1940s, demonstrated a more critical analysis than his post-1945 writings, particularly concerning the role of the state and the role of ideology in affecting and shaping society. And despite claims to the contrary, there was evidence that Bevan recognised the fundamental changes to British society in the 1950s. Nevertheless, the views expressed in these articles were not developed. It is therefore interesting to ponder on what could have been. Ultimately, Bevan did not build on his early ideas. Several explanations have been offered as to why this was the case. In terms of Bevan's intellectual development, the most convincing explanation can be found in the limits of the political traditions that Bevan's thought was rooted in. He did not develop a substantive theory of the state, its functions and its relationship to the economy or adapt his theory of property relations and the development of the economy. Bevan's political thought meant that he fitted comfortably within the mainstream of labourism, despite often appearing to be a challenger to its core assumptions. His advocacy of Parliament and the British state aligned with the dominant political strategies within the party. This may also help to explain why Bevan has been appealed to by politicians across the ideological spectrum in the Labour Party today.

The approach adopted in this book has also contributed to achieving the second aim of using the insights developed in this study to reconsider the debates about Bevan found in the literature. Writers studying Bevan's political thought focus predominantly on *In Place of Fear* to explain its key features. Although it offers an accurate portrayal of his thought, representing his most systematic attempt at articulating it, this book has demonstrated the value of analysing a much wider literature. The comprehensive analysis of Bevan's writings has also allowed a temporal analysis of Bevan's thought to be undertaken. This has enabled the identification of the continuity of important themes in Bevan's thought, such as his Marxism, as well as highlighting periods, not adequately captured in the existing literature, when Bevan's writings deviated from his more general analysis (such as instances where he developed a more critical analysis of the state).

By focusing predominantly on Bevan's writings and taking them at face value, it could be argued that this analysis risks ignoring potential contradictions that emerged during his career. The disconnect between much of his writings on international relations and his speech on the bomb is an example of this. It is true that Bevan's writings did not always correspond with his actions. For instance, the argument that he became closer to Gaitskell in the late 1950s and tempered his radicalism is certainly evident when his actions within the Labour Party are considered. Nevertheless, just focusing on an event such as this does not fully appreciate Bevan's political writing during the same period. Instead, this book has attempted to get to the heart of Bevan's political ideas, and, as a result, this analysis offers a different perspective to these debates over Bevan's career. As noted in the Introduction, the study of ideas can generate fresh insights into many aspects of British politics. Engaging with Bevan's myriad writings has resulted in the production of a book Appendix that for the first time contains an accessible index of Bevan's contributions to *Tribune* between 1937 and 1960. This index will act as a valuable resource for future scholars studying Aneurin Bevan.

Quite often, this book has arrived at similar conclusions to those in parts of the literature. Nonetheless, approaching Bevan through a significant engagement with his writings has allowed for a more detailed analysis of Bevan's political thought to be carried out than is evident in the existing literature. In addition to this, studies of Bevan's political thought are quite disparate. This book has allowed for the various issues considered by Bevan to be brought together and for the connections between them to be established. There is more to unpack that is of both historical and contemporary relevance, such as Bevan's views on Welsh nationhood, the British nationalism within his politics, and how his ideas have been understood in relation to the NHS. It is hoped therefore that the analysis developed here can provide a foundation for future research into Bevan's life, career and political thought, as well as the history of the Labour Party.

Indeed, this book has also contributed to debates concerning the nature of Bevan's thought. The most prominent of these debates concerns the precise nature of Bevan's Marxism and his attitude towards Parliament. Indeed, interpretations of the 'radical' and the 'moderate' Bevan are prevalent in political discourse today. Rather than trying to characterise Bevan as either a Marxist or a British radical, this book has presented a more complex picture of the relationship between Marxism and liberal democracy in Bevan's political thought. It has reinforced explanations for the limits of Bevan's ideas that focus on the weaknesses of the political traditions in which he was situated. It has, however, contradicted attempts to define Bevan by either his Marxism or his radicalism: it is imperative to understand the interactions between these two traditions. This approach has established a greater understanding of these aspects of Bevan's political philosophy to an extent that has not been possible through a biographical approach or through the more general literature that provides a less extensive analysis of Bevan's work. Consequently, it has provided explanations for some of the limitations of Bevan's ideas that build on the arguments of other theorists. It is hoped that this approach contributes to a greater understanding of Bevan's political thought.

***

Despite the plethora of resources available to study Aneurin Bevan, he is often considered to be an enigmatic figure, his precise desires and aims difficult to interpret. He is seen by many as a deeply principled politician, refusing to budge in his desire to achieve a better world. At the same time, however, he is seen as a pragmatic politician, fully aware of the nature of power in British politics and perfectly willing to compromise with those he disagreed with, even on fundamental principles. He was willing to denounce the Conservatives as vermin and condemn the actions of many in the Conservative Party as bordering on fascism, while at the same time wining and dining with his political opponents. He enjoyed the finer things in life, insisting that nothing was too good for the working class and that it was important to discuss and engage with your enemies. He was a product of the industrial working class of south Wales, but he also increasingly enjoyed the comforts of the English countryside. He was considered by many as the leader of the Left in Britain, yet he was also considered by left-wing critics of the party as being in thrall to the moderate tendencies of labourism. These conflicting views inform many of the appeals to Bevan in contemporary politics. Establishing a definitive interpretation of Bevan is not something that is likely to be achieved.

This book has not attempted to do that. It is the nature of discussions on figures who have left such a significant legacy that there will always be disagreement. It is regrettable that Bevan never produced an analysis as systematised and as complete as those of other prominent thinkers at the time. Nevertheless, this book has demonstrated the value of considering Bevan as a political thinker and attempting a more systematic reconstruction of his voluminous writing. As a figure continuously invoked by politicians for many different reasons, it is vital to understand his political thought. In a time of heated debates between different factions of the Labour Party and the British left over its strategy, a study of this kind can shed light on what has come before and where the future road might lie. More than sixty years after his death, the challenges and issues analysed by Bevan are still being grappled with by the Left and in increasingly fractious times. In seeking answers to these crises, Bevan will almost certainly continue to be an influential figure in the Labour Party and beyond. *The Political Thought of Anuerin Bevan* has sought to enhance our understanding of such a complex figure and contribute to these discussions.

NOTES

1 Bevan, A swastika nailed to England's mast'.

2 Bevan, 'The parties' line-up in Parliament'; Bevan, 'Bevan on Parliament'.

3 Campbell, *Nye Bevan and the Mirage of British Socialism*, p. 346.

4 Foot, *Aneurin Bevan: 1897–1945*, p. 303; Thomas-Symonds, *Nye*, p. 236.

5 Campbell, *Nye Bevan and the Mirage of British Socialism*, p. 346.

6 Bevan, 'Meaning of the alliance'; Bevan, 'Kremlin personalities'; Bevan, 'At last the Socialist International wakes up!'; Bevan, 'Communism or suicide? That's not the real choice'.

7 Bevan, 'Farewell to the Trojan Horse'.

8 Bevan, 'Do not dismiss our ideas of freedom'; Bevan, 'How much freedom in the new China?'.

9 Callaghan, 'The Left and the "Unfinished Revolution"'.

10 Bevan, 'It must be world control for all the commercial waterways'; Bevan, 'Aneurin Bevan asks: do they want to wreck the United Nations?'; Bevan, 'Two crimes we can never forget'.

11 Bevan, 'America must be told: "You go it alone"'; Bevan, 'Do not dismiss our ideas of freedom'; Bevan, 'How much freedom in the new China?'; Bevan, 'Wanted: a new bold policy for peace – that will save Hungary'.

12 Francis, *Ideas and Policies under Labour 1945–1951*, pp. 24–5.

13 Foote, *The Labour Party's Political Thought*, p. 273.

14 Aneurin Bevan, 'The blackest page in Britain's history', *Tribune* (3 March 1939), p. 5.

15 Marquand, *The Progressive Dilemma*, p. 121.

16 Bevan, 'Next steps to a new society'.

17 Bevan, 'Plan for Work'.

18 Spalding, *Narratives of Delusion in the Political Practice of the Labour Left*, p. 197.

19 Campbell, *Nye Bevan and the Mirage of British Socialism*, p. xiii.

20 Foot, *Aneurin Bevan: 1945–1960*, pp. 254–5; Campbell, *Nye Bevan and the Mirage of British Socialism*, p. 245.

21 Marquand, *The Progressive Dilemma*, p. 122.

22 Thomas-Symonds, *Nye*, p. 193.

23 Crosland, *The Future of Socialism.*

24 Jackson, *Equality and the British Left*, pp. 159–60.

25 Foote, *The Labour Party's Political Thought*, p. 276.

26 For example, Campbell, *Nye Bevan and the Mirage of British Socialism*, p. 206; Miliband, *Parliamentary Socialism*, p. 327; Thomas-Symonds, *Nye*, p. 234.

27 Jackson, *Equality and the British Left*, pp. 159–60

28 Campbell, *Nye Bevan and the Mirage of British Socialism*, p. 271; Thomas-Symonds, *Nye*, p. 234.

29 Colin Ward, *Social Policy: An Anarchist Response* (London: Freedom Press, 2000), p. 15.

30 Steve Thompson, 'NHS was not solely modelled on a Welsh workmen's medical society', *The Conversation*, 3 July 2018, *https://theconversation.com/nhs-was-not-solely-modelled-on-a-welsh-workmens-medical-society-98024* (accessed 9 January 2024).

31 Aneurin Bevan, cited in Foot, *Aneurin Bevan: 1945–1960*, p. 18.

32 Miliband, *The State in Capitalist Society*, pp. 97–9.

33 Bevan, 'Facts and taxes', p. 5.

34 Nuttall, 'Equality and freedom', p. 25.

35 Miliband, *Parliamentary Socialism*; Nairn, 'The Nature of the Labour Party – 2'.

36 Campbell, *Nye Bevan and the Mirage of British Socialism*, p. 346.

37 Ellison, *Egalitarian Thought and Labour Politics*, p. xi.

38 Macintyre, *A Proletarian Science*, p. 177.

39 Barry Jones and Michael Keating, *Labour and the British State* (Oxford: Clarendon Press, 1985), p. 2.

40 Macintyre, *A Proletarian Science*, p. 179.

41 Anderson, 'Origins of the Present Crisis'; Tom Nairn, 'The Twilight of the British State', *New Left Review*, 1/101 (1977), *https://newleftreview.org/issues/I101/articles/tom-nairn-the-twilight-of-the-british-state* (accessed 9 January 2024); Tom Nairn, 'The Crisis of the British State', *New Left Review*, 1/130 (1981), *https://newleftreview.org/issues/I130/articles/tom-nairn-the-crisis-of-the-british-state* (accessed 9 January 2024).
42 Raymond Williams, 'Base and Superstructure in Marxist Cultural Theory', *New Left Review*, 1/82 (1973); Raymond Williams, 'Problems of Materialism', *New Left Review*, 1/109 (1978).
43 Miliband, 'Poulantzas and the Capitalist State'; Nicos Poulantzas, *State, Power, Socialism* (London: Verso, 2014).
44 Ralph Miliband, 'Lenin's The State and Revolution', *Socialist Register*, 7 (1970), 309, *https://socialistregister.com/index.php/srv/article/view/5303* (accessed 10 January 2024).
45 Pierson, *Marxist Theory and Democratic Politics*, p. 133.
46 Raymond Williams, *Politics and Letters: Interview with* New Left Review (London: Verso, 1981), p. 368.
47 Foote, *The Labour Party's Political Thought*, p. 282.
48 Selina Todd, 'Affluence, Class and Crown Street: Reinvestigating the Post-War Working Class', *Contemporary British History*, 22/4 (2008), *https://doi.org/10.1080/13619460802439382* (accessed 10 January 2024).
49 Pat Thane, *Divided Kingdom: A History of Britain, 1900 to the Present* (Cambridge: Cambridge University Press, 2018), p. 261.
50 Howell, *The Rise and Fall of Bevanism*, p. 37.
51 Miliband, *Parliamentary Socialism*, p. 327; Nairn, 'The Nature of the Labour Party – 2', p. 49.
52 Leach, *Political Ideology in Britain*.
53 Bevan, 'Being very, very practical', p. 4
54 Aneurin Bevan, 'Coalition of the left', *Tribune* (18 June 1943), pp. 6–7; Aneurin Bevan, 'Trade unions and the Labour Party', *Tribune* (23 July 1943), pp. 6–7; Aneurin Bevan, 'The block vote', *Tribune* (31 December 1954), p. 1.
55 Foote, *The Labour Party's Political Thought*, p. 273.
56 Foot, *Aneurin Bevan: 1945–1960*, pp. 622–7.
57 Francis, *Ideas and Policies under Labour 1945–1951*, p. 24.
58 Ellison, *Egalitarian Thought and Labour Politics*, p. 47.
59 Campbell, *Nye Bevan and the Mirage of British Socialism*, p. 213.
60 Bevan, *In Place of Fear*, p. 19.

Appendix: *Tribune* Articles by Category

A CENTRAL task of this book has been to reconstruct Bevan's voluminous writings. This Appendix collects Bevan's articles in *Tribune* under his own name and under his pseudonym 'M.P.'. The purpose of this Appendix is to enable future scholars studying Bevan to identify which articles discuss a particular subject. Therefore, they have been organised according to the topic under which they provide the most insight. It is inevitable that a number of the articles collected here could be included under more than one category and often cover other related topics. Nonetheless, they have been assigned to their most relevant category.

Economic Power

CAPITALISM AND PRIVATE ENTERPRISE

These articles are the most focused that Bevan wrote on capitalism, although Bevan's critique of capitalism remained central to the vast majority of his writing.

Date	Title	Page no(s)
12 February 1937	Government offers dumb-bells to children who want food (M.P.)	7
23 April 1937	Prim Neville takes his bow for state profiteering (M.P.)	7

Date	Title	Page no(s)
18 June 1937	Softening soap for workers and convicts (M.P.)	6
5 November 1937	Cabinet's witch-doctor remedy in 'war on slump' dilemma	5
3 December 1937	On babies unborn and fish that's too dear	7
9 September 1955	Society and your pay packet	4–5
23 September 1955	Government by the bankers	4
11 November 1955	Beware of this Tory trap	1
19 July 1957	Spectre over Europe	1 and 3
30 August 1957	Back to free markets – and the jungle	5
7 March 1958	The slump and the summit	5
30 January 1959	The decline of capitalism	9

CLASS CONFLICT

Bevan's analysis of class conflict, as outlined in this book, underpins his writing throughout his career.

Date	Title	Page no(s)
29 January 1937	Baldwin's retreat from freedom in case of the five men (M.P.)	7
5 February 1937	Deportation – the old Tory cure for unemployment (M.P.)	7
19 February 1937	John Simon takes brief from the factory employer (M.P.)	7

Date	Title	Page no(s)
26 February 1937	Grenfell and Cripps put the mineowners in dock (M.P.)	7
16 April 1937	£40 a week for our ex-premiers – 10s for Brain workers (M.P.)	7
30 April 1937	MPs pack commons to listen to rich men's sad woes (M.P.)	7
4 June 1937	The clergyman departs and now the undertaker takes over (M.P.)	6
25 March 1938	Class war in Commons committee 'A'	7
14 April 1938	A bad break for our Dr Goebbels	7
2 February 1940	The means test	1
18 October 1940	The Tories' prisoner	12–13
8 November 1940	Means test dead and damned	12–13
18 April 1941	The cow, the farmer and the MP	12–13
22 March 1957	A declaration of class war	4

TRADE UNIONS AND INDUSTRIAL ACTION

Bevan's attitudes towards the trade union movement, inside and outside of the Labour Party, as well as the power of direct action are collected here.

Date	Title	Page no(s)
2 April 1937	It wants more than words to end arms racketeers (M.P.)	7
7 May 1937	'Peace in our time' Baldwin sings his swan-song, sighing for a quiet coronation (M.P.)	7

Date	Title	Page no(s)
22 July 1938	Wanted – a new drive for wages	7
12 August 1938	Big wage problem faces the TUC	3
18 November 1938	Workers fight dictatorship plot in France	13
23 December 1938	For national service make terms – or be tricked	11
17 February 1939	The police were out	5
23 August 1940	A job for the trade unions	12–13
23 July 1943	Trade unions and the Labour Party	6–7
26 May 1944	The Labour Party and the trade unions	6–7
20 May 1955	Why Winston Churchill has been gagged	2 and 8
17 April 1959	The budget and the unions	1 and 9

Political Power

PARLIAMENT AND DEMOCRACY

Bevan's insights into the functions of Parliament and his advocacy of the House of Commons as a vehicle for social change.

Date	Title	Page no(s)
1 January 1937	When kings and commons meet in medieval tourney (M.P.)	7
12 March 1937	Storm meets Baldwin's efforts to save democracy for the rich (M.P.)	7

Date	Title	Page no(s)
9 April 1937	Why Mr Ernest Brown infuriates opposition and Tory members alike (M.P.)	7
9 July 1937	After prayers, when our MPs become curious (M.P.)	7
29 October 1937	People versus privilege lock in combat as Parliament reassembles	7
12 November 1937	Tory benches cheer white-headed boy of reaction	7
17 December 1937	Ernest Brown heads for dangerous waters	7
11 February 1938	People versus property	7
18 February 1938	When the burglar invests in state bonds	7
13 May 1938	How the landowner pays for the experts	7
29 July 1938	MPs recall days of August 1914	3
17 March 1939	Make the government act	10–11
10 November 1939	Attempt to muzzle MPs	5
23 February 1940	Hitler – the bogeyman	1
19 July 1940	Watchdog of liberty	7
15 November 1940	We get a dirty deal from the press	12–13
21 March 1941	MPs tongues must be loosed	6–7
2 May 1941	Hope and new strength	12–13
20 August 1943	Rubber stamp MPs	11

Date	Title	Page no(s)
18 May 1951	Wanted – a minister for social services	5
26 November 1954	Can Parliament do it?	1
18 January 1957	Save democracy – have a general election now	5
6 June 1958	How long will it last?	7
5 June 1959	Bevan on Parliament	12

THE STATE

Bevan's most insightful and sophisticated analyses of the state. Although, as highlighted in the book, his pre-1945 critique of the state was not substantially developed.

Date	Title	Page no(s)
8 July 1938	Highwaymen in the upper house	7
13 October 1944	The T.U.C.'s two voices	6–7
30 September 1955	Burgess and Maclean	8

PUBLIC OWNERSHIP AND ECONOMIC PLANNING

Bevan's advocacy of public ownership is evident in other writings, but his arguments for it are most clearly stated in these articles.

Date	Title	Page no(s)
26 November 1937	When a mines minister wished he wasn't	7
10 December 1937	Labour takes honours in Commons coal battle	7
1 April 1938	The struggle behind the coal bill	7

Date	Title	Page no(s)
3 June 1938	This cabinet of incompetents	7
31 May 1940	The way to win through	12–14
11 October 1940	Blind men are leading us!	10–11
25 October 1940	Next steps to a new society	6–7
13 December 1940	End the great coal muddle	12–13
28 February 1941	All is not well	1
29 December 1944	Who wants controls?	9–10
31 January 1947	Ten years of *Tribune*	7
3 February 1950	The people's coming of age	3–4
13 June 1952	The fatuity of coalition	1–2
2 January 1953	The truth about Harold Macmillan	4
30 October 1953	Steel ramp exposed	1–2
18 June 1954	Now will Labour learn?	1
29 October 1954	Rationed – or 'free'?	1–2
12 November 1954	Nationalisation and tomorrow	1 and 12
17 December 1954	Why scrap the bob?	1
24 December 1954	The Coal Board loss	1
21 January 1955	Should we plan wages?	1
4 February 1955	No jam today	1
8 April 1955	Britain without Churchill	1
8 July 1955	Automation: the socialist answer	2
13 January 1956	Facts and taxes	5
10 January 1958	Who has to hold the baby?	5

Date	Title	Page no(s)
7 November 1958	Tory gamblers pour £1,500 million down the drain	1 and 3
9 January 1959	Private enterprise vs public ownership: the moon and the £	5
11 December 1959	How to avoid shipwreck	5

LABOUR PARTY

Despite being a consistent advocate for the Labour Party as *the* vehicle to achieve socialism, Bevan had a troubled relationship with its leaders and many of its key figures. These articles contain Bevan's criticisms of the party, his thoughts on its links with the trade union movement and his views on its attitude and approach to socialism.

Date	Title	Page no(s)
23 December 1937	Attlee, Cripps, Morrison and Greenwood	7
6 May 1938	When Attlee spoke for united party	6
7 October 1938	Call a Labour conference at once	16
25 November 1938	You will want to attack me for this	11
2 December 1938	Sham fight for the workless	9
10 February 1939	They've said it!	13
10 March 1939	End this party tyranny	16
26 May 1939	An open letter to conference delegates	10–11
19 January 1940	Neville's meat is poison for the Labour Party	6–7

Date	Title	Page no(s)
5 March 1943	Labour must stay in the government	6–7
11 June 1943	To any Labour delegate	6–7
18 June 1943	Coalition of the Left	6–7
5 October 1951	Destroy the Tory challenge	2–3
26 September 1952	All set for a new thrust forward	4
17 October 1952	Build Labour unity, says Nye Bevan	1–2
3 December 1954	Why we lost West Derby	1
31 December 1954	The block vote	1
1 April 1955	Bevan's statement to the NEC	1
3 June 1955	Aneurin Bevan gives his verdict	1–2
7 October 1955	The struggle for socialism: why I am standing for treasurer	1–2
16 December 1955	Clement Attlee	5
24 February 1956	Being very, very practical	4
2 March 1956	Labour must believe in freedom	4
12 October 1956	Now – let's give a socialist lead	5
7 June 1957	Labour takes the lead	5
21 February 1958	Are they working for another 1931 coalition?	6

CONSERVATIVE PARTY

Bevan saw the Tories as the representatives of the capitalist class. Although he criticised the party throughout his writing, these articles focus particularly on his condemnations of Conservatism and its leading figures.

Date	Title	Page no(s)
15 July 1938	Fox and hounds in Sandys case	7
16 December 1938	Premier's future depends on Rome	4
12 January 1940	Hore-Belisha	1
7 June 1940	Guilty ministers must go	12–13
30 August 1940	Portrait of Churchill	12–13
1 August 1941	The problem of Mr Churchill	12–13
8 March 1957	The Tories on the rocks	5

Military Power

SPAIN

Bevan was actively involved in the Popular Front campaign in support of the Republicans in Spain. His writings on the Spanish Civil War contain his critique of war, capitalism and fascism. Bevan's description of his trip to Spain in 1938 – 'Inside Teruel' – is a stark insight into the destruction and fear that engulfed Spain during the war and the struggle of the Republicans.

Date	Title	Page no(s)
25 March 1937	When Labour's front benchers gave up ghost on Spanish policy (M.P.)	7
2 July 1937	Spain and the big guns go booming (M.P.)	6
23 July 1937	Eden shows white flag at Gibraltar battle in commons (M.P)	6
21 January 1938	Inside Teruel	8–9 and 11

Date	Title	Page no(s)
18 March 1938	Spain: Labour's challenge	3
3 February 1939	Spain: does Parliament know what the people really think?	17
3 March 1939	The blackest page in Britain's history	5
25 April 1941	Stop fooling with Franco	12–13

WAR AND CAPITALISM

These articles demonstrate Bevan's attitude towards the Second World War and potential conflict post-1945. They show how Bevan related war to the destructiveness of capitalism.

Date	Title	Page no(s)
19 February 1937	Giant strides to the next war: we must oppose arms plan root and branch	8–9
5 March 1937	Tories join merrily in the Chancellor's death dance (M.P.)	7
19 March 1937	Why benches empty when Labour speaks on arms estimates (M.P.)	7
25 June 1937	Neville's tax hoax: will Labour put its own house in order? (M.P.)	6
30 July 1937	MPs doubts and fears as they depart for their holidays (M.P.)	6
19 November 1937	The man who cried out with a loud voice	6
11 March 1938	Labour and arms	7
29 April 1938	Simon's hand in the worker's pocket	3

Date	Title	Page no(s)
20 May 1938	Britain's 1,700,000 forgotten men	8–9
27 May 1938	Honours in air debating – but	3
24 February 1939	Eight hundred million pounds go up in smoke	9
14 July 1939	What is happening to the people's food?	9
29 December 1939	War on your wages: big business plan explained	1
9 February 1940	Britain's food peril	1
9 August 1940	Beaverbrook: and what next?	12–13
6 September 1940	A plan for air raid warnings	12–13
20 September 1940	This gross negligence must be punished	12–13
6 December 1940	Why are there still idle men?	12–13
4 July 1941	Now is our chance to strike	12–13
8 August 1941	Coal muddle – who is to blame?	12–13
22 May 1942	Labour must lead now	6–7

FASCISM

Although Bevan's account of the rise of fascism is apparent in his writings on the Second World War more generally, these articles are focused on analysing its features and reasons for its rise.

Date	Title	Page no(s)
2 December 1938	If Lady Astor had her way	5
24 May 1940	Are you a traitor? – answer now	12–13
26 July 1940	Freedom is not enough	12–13

WAR, LIBERTY AND SOCIETY

Bevan's defence of liberty during the war and his arguments for democracy to be upheld even during wartime.

Date	Title	Page no(s)
3 November 1939	A bandage for wounded liberty	4–5
24 November 1939	End the political truce!	6–7
1 December 1939	Labour should turn on the heat	6–7
15 December 1939	The mental black-out	8–9
5 January 1940	Challenge – or die!	3
8 March 1940	The fate of the 'Daily Herald'	5
15 March 1940	It's time Labour was tough	12–13
5 April 1940	Set the Commons free	12–13
14 June 1940	Incompetents: the danger within	12–13
28 June 1940	Bevan letter to local Labour Party secretary	12–13
2 August 1940	The voice of the White Knight	12–13
16 August 1940	Let us deserve our fighters	12–13
27 September 1940	The morale of the people	12–13
7 February 1941	Choose now, to live or die	1–2
14 February 1941	Workers in Britain and America unite!	8–9
10 October 1941	The people demand action	12–13
24 October 1941	These men are paralysed	12–13
11 December 1942	Labour and the Coalition	1–2

POST-WAR SOCIETY

Bevan's vision for society after the war is contained in these articles. Some of them include references to the need for public ownership as part of a wider call for socialist principles to be applied post-war.

Date	Title	Page no(s)
8 September 1939	Our duty! (with Stafford Cripps)	1 and 3
21 June 1940	The end of retreat	12–13
5 July 1940	Editorial board manifesto (with others)	12–13
4 October 1940	War aims begin at home	12–13
10 January 1941	Gentlemen, do read Hansard!	8–9
25 June 1943	We and the Germans	6–7
3 September 1943	The politics of strategy	6–7
11 February 1944	A Labour plan to beat the Tories	6–7
17 March 1944	Are miners different?	6–7
14 April 1944	What Eden cannot do	6–7
10 November 1944	Shall they cheat you again?	6–7

ARMS

After the Second World War, rearmament was a major concern in international politics, particularly the threat of nuclear weapons.

Date	Title	Page no(s)
1 March 1940	Holes in the blockade	1
12 January 1945	How do we keep Germany disarmed?	6–7
31 July 1953	No settlement of the German problem unless we disarm	4 and 8

Date	Title	Page no(s)
1954	It need not happen: the alternative to German rearmament (*Tribune* pamphlet to which Bevan contributed)	All
12 February 1954	We must not despair	1–2
28 January 1955	Western double-talk	1
18 February 1955	Why did Labour change its mind?	1 and 8
25 February 1955	American bases in Britain	1
11 March 1955	Churchill confesses	3
19 August 1955	We can't leave it all to the Russians	8
2 December 1955	The H-bomb: now there's a new chance for sanity	1 and 12
23 December 1955	The second Cold War	4
6 April 1956	Arms: there is real hope now	1
11 May 1956	The disarmament breakdown	5
24 May 1957	Destroy the bombs before they destroy us!	1
31 May 1957	Cut arms to save peace – not to balance the budget	7
21 June 1957	Is MacMillan a candidate in the German elections?	5
2 August 1957	A Western conspiracy in favour of Adenauer!	5
31 January 1958	Arms and the slump	5
7 February 1958	Khrushchev's cocktail	5

Date	Title	Page no(s)
9 May 1958	Polish plan could bridge the way to real peace talks	5
30 May 1958	H-tests: Russia should accept Eisenhower's new offer	5
31 October 1958	Tests: don't throw this chance away	1–2
14 November 1958	A nuclear free zone in Europe would be a benediction	12
10 April 1959	Now we know	5

POWER POLITICS

The conflict between the United States and the Soviet Union was the dominant feature of post-war international relations. These articles represent Bevan's attempts to find solutions to the conflict in order to ease international tensions. Also included is an article from 1938 where Bevan discussed a similar situation of power politics before the First World War.

Date	Title	Page no(s)
8 April 1938	Schoolmates cheer a slapstick act	7
23 February 1950	Britain's policy for peace	9–11
1951	Going our way (*Tribune* pamphlet for which Bevan wrote the introduction)	3
1951	One way only: a socialist analysis of the present world crisis (*Tribune* pamphlet for which Bevan wrote the foreword)	3
18 September 1953	We asked for it	1 and 6

Date	Title	Page no(s)
19 November 1954	America: a warning	1
15 July 1955	Aneurin Bevan attacks radioactive nonsense	4–5
18 November 1955	Russia and the Middle East	6–7
27 January 1956	Which nation drew back?	4
20 April 1956	Welcome to B & K	6-7
4 May 1956	What happened to Eden's plan?	1–2
1 June 1956	When Eden sold out to the soldiers	4
23 November 1956	The last chance for statesmanship	1 and 12
23 August 1957	The clash of the giants	5
6 September 1957	Statesmanship is the only answer to the rockets	7
8 November 1957	Talk with Russia on the Middle East: Bevan tells America	8–9
29 November 1957	Here's a real peace policy for Europe	7
3 January 1958	An open challenge must be openly met: Yes, there must be a summit meeting	5
17 January 1958	Someone must tell Eisenhower the whole truth	7
20 June 1958	Mr Khrushchev's new letter shows – the West is stalling on summit talks	5
5 December 1958	A hundred words that could spell real peace for Europe	6–7

Date	Title	Page no(s)
8 May 1959	Mr Nehru, China and the Russians	5
22 May 1959	Britain in the Middle East	12
19 June 1959	The new spectre that haunts Europe	4
28 August 1959	Eisenhower and Khrushchev	12

INTERNATIONAL ORGANISATIONS

Bevan's solution to rising international tensions was for principles of democracy to be enshrined in the UN. As well as detailing Bevan's advocacy of the UN, these articles also contain Bevan's reflections on national sovereignty and the plight of exploited nations.

Date	Title	Page no(s)
4 September 1953	Labour and the United Nations	1–2
1 January 1954	The year of hope	4
16 September 1955	Uneasy peace	8
6 January 1956	The United Nations should send aid	4
5 October 1956	Give the United Nations a real job to do	4
19 October 1956	It's naked and brutal imperialism	12
16 November 1956	Wanted: a new bold policy for peace – that will save Hungary	1
21 December 1956	How Ike can take the lead	1 and 12
4 January 1957	Dollar diplomacy? That's no answer	1–2
11 January 1957	A war for holy oil?	5

Date	Title	Page no(s)
1 February 1957	Crisis time for United Nations	5
15 February 1957	When the two guilty men meet in Bermuda	5
15 March 1957	No double standards at UN	5
12 July 1957	At last the Socialist International wakes up!	12
1 November 1957	Patch up NATO – that's the new Anglo-U.S. plan	6
13 December 1957	Platitudes won't save mankind	5

SOCIAL REVOLUTIONS AND WORLD DEVELOPMENT

Bevan placed great emphasis on social revolutions throughout the world and on the need for larger nations to help in the development of poorer nations. These articles also reveal Bevan's understanding of the materialist conception of history.

Date	Title	Page no(s)
7 August 1953	Here is a real plan to put the war machine in reverse	4 and 8
16 April 1954	America must be told: 'You go it alone'	1 and 3
29 July 1955	Verdict on Geneva	1–2
17 February 1956	Eisenhower's greatest blunder	4
10 May 1957	Needed – a sane world policy to take the place of hate	6–7
11 April 1958	Russia's proposals put Eisenhower on the spot	5

Date	Title	Page no(s)
5 September 1958	We must save India – or lose democracy's hope	5
1 January 1960	The biggest question for our century	6

EMPIRE AND IMPERIALISM

Many of the countries that were going through social revolutions were the victims of a history of empire and imperialism. These articles reflect Bevan's critique of imperialism and the effects of empire.

Date	Title	Page no(s)
4 March 1938	Britain's black empire put in the dock	7
17 June 1938	In the shadow of an empire's flag	7
9 December 1938	Our reply to Anderson	1
18 December 1953	Empire and the Tories	1–2
23 April 1954	Britain will not fight in Indo-China	1–2
25 May 1956	Bases: the plan that failed	12
24 August 1956	Bring back Makarios and talk peace	4
31 August 1956	'The times' gets a bad attack of nostalgia	5
9 November 1956	Two crimes we can never forget	12
28 June 1957	Tory financial policy could smash the Commonwealth	1
5 July 1957	My answer to Guy Mollet	1 and 12
25 July 1958	Bevan on the crisis	1 and 12

Date	Title	Page no(s)
10 October 1958	Has Macmillan sold out to the Turks on partition?	12
6 March 1959	After the peace settlement in Cyprus: Makarios and the future	5

NATIONALISM AND NATIONAL SOVEREIGNTY

Bevan understood the increase of nationalist sentiment throughout the world to be a result of Western imperialism. Although Bevan's analysis of nationalism and national sovereignty is contained in articles placed in other categories, these articles contain Bevan's most explicit accounts of this phenomenon.

Date	Title	Page no(s)
20 December 1940	Stop that nonsense now!	12–13
4 April 1941	Why is Duff Cooper so bad?	12–13
5 September 1941	Complacency will not win the war	12–13
18 September 1942	India: pride and prejudice	6–7
25 October 1957	Family, patriotism, religion!	5
23 May 1958	De Gaulle	5
21 November 1958	Independence – then hard work: how to maintain the frontiers of liberty	5

EGYPT

A number of the themes contained in previous categories can be illuminated by reading Bevan's dissection of the Suez Crisis in 1956. These articles saw Bevan reflect on the nature of social revolutions, nationalism, national sovereignty and international organisations.

Date	Title	Page no(s)
3 August 1956	It must be world control for all the commercial waterways	5
10 August 1956	It must not be all 'take', Colonel Nasser	12
17 August 1956	Don't risk one British life	1 and 12
14 September 1956	Aneurin Bevan asks: do they want to wreck the United Nations?	2
7 December 1956	Suez: the excuses are demolished	6
17 May 1957	Suez: now what?	1 and 3

Ideological Power

IDEOLOGICAL STRUGGLE

Bevan identified class conflict as fundamental to capitalist society. These articles contain Bevan's interpretation of the ideological conflict being waged between the working class and the ruling class.

Date	Title	Page no(s)
24 June 1938	A swastika nailed to England's mast	7
1 July 1938	This is how fascism is born	7
17 November 1939	Labour – the prisoner of the Tories	1
26 January 1940	Political black-out	1
5 December 1941	Conscription: why MPs revolted	12–13
1 December 1944	The parties' line-up in Parliament	6–7
21 November 1952	Baldwin and Butler	4

Date	Title	Page no(s)
28 September 1956	This minor Caesar	4
21 March 1958	Two faces of Macmillan	5

COMMUNISM

A materialist conception of history is evident in Bevan's writings on the ideology of communism. These articles contain Bevan's engagement with communism more broadly. Assessments of specific communist countries are categorised below.

Date	Title	Page no(s)
24 July 1953	The peasants who dictate to Moscow	4
25 November 1955	Russia must take her share of the blame	4
22 June 1956	What next for Western Communists?	1 and 12
29 June 1956	This may be the real chance for Italian socialism	5
6 July 1956	Will the Poles learn the real lesson of Poznan?	6–7
26 October 1956	Gomulka holds the aces	1–2
16 August 1957	A very dangerous game	1 and 12
27 September 1957	The world of Gomulka, Tito – and Djilas	6
14 March 1958	Communism or suicide? That's not the real choice	5
11 July 1958	The real arguments behind the Tito-Khrushchev row	6

Date	Title	Page no(s)
28 November 1958	The Communist failure in the West	8

SOVIET UNION

The Soviet Union takes a prominent place in Bevan's thought due to his hopes for its potential to develop into a representative democracy as a result of economic planning. Bevan's materialist grasp of economic development is apparent in these writings.

Date	Title	Page no(s)
18 July 1941	Meaning of the alliance	12–13
17 October 1941	Russia and ourselves	12–13
17 July 1953	In place of the Cold War	4
24 September 1954	My private talk with Malenkov	1–2
1 October 1954	Kremlin personalities	1–2
9 March 1955	Don't write off these Kremlin charges as just another 'plot'!	6–7
23 March 1956	After Stalin: the big test for communists	1
27 April 1956	Farewell to the Trojan Horse	5
11 October 1957	Why Russia wins space race	5
18 October 1957	Khrushchev has the trumps	7

CHINA

Bevan's writings on China, including his account of his trip there with a Labour Party delegation, also contain important pointers to Bevan's political thought.

Date	Title	Page no(s)
4 June 1954	Why we are going to China	1–2
3 September 1954	Do not dismiss our ideas of freedom	2
8 October 1954	Marx versus birth control	1 and 3
15 October 1954	I put a question mark against his judgement	4
22 October 1954	How much freedom in the new China?	4
10 December 1954	Will this mean war?	1
26 August 1955	Give China the help she needs	4
14 June 1957	Has America got a government?	5
15 August 1958	Dulles must be defied	7
24 October 1958	Quemoy: stumbling in the dark	6

IMMIGRATION

The article below appears to be Bevan's only explicit engagement with immigration.

Date	Title	Page no(s)
11 February 1955	Jamaicans: where the danger lies	2

HEALTH

Bevan did not often return to his achievements in establishing the NHS, but these articles include his advocacy for health policy within factories and his claims that his plans for the NHS had been vindicated by a 1956 report into the service.

Date	Title	Page no(s)
14 January 1955	Health in the factory	1
3 February 1956	This famous victory	1 and 12

DEMOCRATIC SOCIALISM

Bevan's vision for democratic socialist society can be discerned throughout the variety of his writings and appears very prominently in *In Place of Fear*. These articles contain noteworthy descriptions of what a democratic socialist society would look like for Bevan.

Date	Title	Page no(s)
2 July 1948	July 5th and the socialist advance	7
5 November 1954	Freedom and socialism	1
7 January 1955	Private schools	1
4 March 1955	Scrap this levy	1

REFERENCES

Allen, Geoff, 'Labour and Strike-Breaking 1945–1951', *International Socialism*, 2/24 (1984), 45–73, *www.marxists.org/history/etol/newspape/isj2/1984/isj2-024/ellen.html* (accessed 10 January 2024).

Anderson, Perry, 'Origins of the Present Crisis', *New Left Review*, 1/23 (1964), 26–53.

Arblaster, Anthony, 'The Old Left', in Raymond Plant, Matt Beech and Kevin Hickson (eds), *The Struggle for Labour's Soul: Understanding Labour's Political Thought since 1945* (London: Routledge, 2004).

Balls, Ed, 'Labour's Greatest Hero: Nye Bevan', *The Guardian*, 19 September 2008, *www.theguardian.com/commentisfree/2008/sep/19/labour.labourconference2* (accessed 10 January 2024).

Bealey, Frank, *The Social and Political Thought of the British Labour Party* (London: Weidenfeld & Nicolson, 1970).

Beckett, Clare, and Francis Beckett. *Bevan* (London: Haus Publishing, 2004).

Bevan, Aneurin, 'Socialist Classics: The Communist Manifesto', *The Plebs*, 13/1 (1921), 19–21.

— 'Giant strides to the next war: we must oppose arms plan root and branch', *Tribune* (19 February 1937), pp. 8–9.

— 'The man who cried out with a loud voice', *Tribune* (19 November 1937), p. 6.

— 'People versus property', *Tribune* (11 February 1938), p 7.

— 'Schoolmates cheer a slapstick act', *Tribune* (8 April 1938), p. 7.

— 'A bad break for our Dr Goebbels', *Tribune* (14 April 1938), p 7.

— 'How the landworker pays for the experts', *Tribune* (13 May 1938), p. 7.
— 'Britain's 1,700,000 forgotten men', *Tribune* (20 May 1938), pp. 8–9.
— 'A swastika nailed to England's mast', *Tribune* (24 June 1938), p. 7.
— 'This is how fascism is born', *Tribune* (1 July 1938), p. 7.
— 'Highwaymen in the Upper House', *Tribune* (8 July 1938), p. 7.
— 'M.P.'s recall days of August 1914', *Tribune* (8 July 1938), p. 3.
— 'Big wage problem faces the T.U.C.', *Tribune* (12 August 1938), p. 3.
— 'Our reply to Anderson', *Tribune* (9 December 1938), p. 1.
— 'Premier's future depends on Rome', *Tribune* (16 December 1938), p. 4.
— 'Eight hundred million pounds go up in – smoke!', *Tribune* (24 February 1939), p. 9.
— 'The blackest page in Britain's history', *Tribune* (3 March 1939), p. 5.
— 'Make the government act!', *Tribune* (17 March 1939), pp. 10–11.
— 'What is happening to the people's food?', *Tribune* (14 July 1939), p. 9.
— 'A bandage for wounded liberty', *Tribune* (3 November 1939), pp. 4–5.
— 'Freedom is not enough', *Tribune* (26 July 1940), pp. 12–13.
— 'Beaverbrook: and what next?', *Tribune* (9 August 1940), pp. 12–13.
— 'A job for the trade unions', *Tribune* (23 August 1940), pp. 12–13.
— 'A plan for air raid warnings', *Tribune* (6 September 1940), pp. 12–13.
— 'War aims begin at home', *Tribune* (4 October 1940), pp. 12–13.
— 'Blind men are leading us!', *Tribune* (11 October 1940), pp. 10–11.
— 'The Tories' prisoner', *Tribune* (18 October 1940), pp. 12–13.
— 'Next steps to a new society', *Tribune* (25 October 1940), pp. 6–7.
— 'We get a dirty deal from the press', *Tribune* (15 November 1940), pp. 12–13.
— 'Stop that nonsense now!', *Tribune* (20 December 1940), pp. 12–13.
— 'Gentlemen, do read Hansard!', *Tribune* (10 January 1941), pp. 8–9.
— 'Choose now, to live or die', *Tribune* (7 February 1941), pp. 1–2.
— 'All is not well', *Tribune* (28 February 1941), p 1.
— 'M.P.s' tongues must be loosened', *Tribune* (21 March 1941), pp. 6–7.
— 'Why is Duff Cooper so bad?', *Tribune* (4 April 1941), pp. 12–13.
— 'Hope and new strength', *Tribune* (2 May 1941), pp. 12–13.
— 'Meaning of the Alliance', *Tribune* (18 July 1941), pp. 12–13.
— 'Complacency will not win the war', *Tribune* (5 September 1941), pp. 12–13.

— 'Conscription: why MPs revolted', *Tribune* (5 December 1941), pp. 12–13.
— 'Plan for Work', in Fabian Society (ed.), *Plan for Britain: A Collection of Essays Prepared for the Fabian Society* (London: The Labour Book Service, 1943), pp. 34–52.
— 'To any Labour delegate', *Tribune* (11 June 1943), pp. 6–7.
— 'Coalition of the Left', *Tribune* (18 June 1943), pp. 6–7.
— 'We and the Germans', *Tribune* (25 June 1943), pp. 6–7.
— 'Trade Unions and the Labour Party', *Tribune* (23 July 1943), pp. 6–7.
— 'Rubber stamp M.P.s', *Tribune* (20 August 1943), p. 11.
— 'The Politics of Strategy', *Tribune* (3 September 1943), pp. 6–7.
— *Why Not Trust the Tories?* (London: Victor Gollancz, 1944).
— 'A Labour plan to beat the Tories', *Tribune* (11 February 1944), pp. 6–7.
— 'Are miners different?', *Tribune* (17 March 1944), pp. 6–7.
— 'What Eden cannot do', *Tribune* (14 April 1944), pp. 6–7.
— 'The T.U.C.'S two voices', *Tribune* (13 October 1944), pp. 6–7.
— 'The parties' line-up in Parliament', *Tribune* (1 December 1944), pp. 6–7.
— 'Who wants controls?', *Tribune* (29 December 1944), p. 9.
— 'Ten Years – *Tribune*, 1937–1947', *Tribune* (31 January 1947), p. 7.
— 'July 5th and the socialist advance', *Tribune* (2 July 1948), p. 7.
— *Democratic Values: First in the Series of Fabian Autumn Lectures* (Fabian Tracts, 1950).
— 'The People's Coming of Age', *Tribune* (3 February 1950), pp. 3–4.
— *In Place of Fear* (London: William Heinemann, 1952).
— 'The fatuity of coalition', *Tribune* (13 June 1952), pp. 1–2.
— 'All set for a new thrust forward', *Tribune* (26 September 1952), p. 4.
— 'Traitors or Heroes?', *In This I Believe*, CBS, 14/12/22 1953, *www.youtube.com/watch?v=hYSvt-9wgZ0&ab_channel=Tannhauser* (accessed 10 January 2024).
— 'In place of the Cold War', *Tribune* (17 July 1953), p. 4.
— 'No settlement of the German problem unless we disarm', *Tribune* (31 July 1953), p. 4.
— 'Here is a real plan to put the war machine in reverse', *Tribune* (7 August 1953), pp. 4 and 8.
— 'We asked for it', *Tribune* (18 September 1953), pp. 1 and 6.

— 'Steel ramp exposed', *Tribune* (30 October 1953), pp. 1–2.
— 'The year of hope', *Tribune* (1 January 1954), p. 4.
— 'We must not despair', *Tribune* (12 February 1954), pp. 1–2.
— 'America must be told: "you go it alone"', *Tribune* (16 April 1954), pp. 1 and 3.
— 'Britain will not fight in Indo-China', *Tribune* (23 April 1954), pp. 1–2.
— 'Why we are going to China', *Tribune* (4 June 1954), pp. 1–2.
— 'Do not dismiss our ideas of freedom', *Tribune* (3 September 1954), p. 2.
— 'My private talk with Malenkov', *Tribune* (24 September 1954), pp. 1–2.
— 'Kremlin personalities', *Tribune* (1 October 1954), pp. 1–2.
— 'How much freedom in the new China?', *Tribune* (22 October 1954), p. 4.
— 'Rationed – or "Free"?', *Tribune* (29 October 1954), pp. 1–2.
— 'Freedom and socialism', *Tribune* (5 November 1954), p. 1.
— 'Nationalisation and tomorrow', *Tribune* (12 November 1954), pp. 1 and 12.
— 'Can Parliament do it?', *Tribune* (26 November 1954), p. 1.
— 'Why we lost West Derby', *Tribune* (3 December 1954), p. 1.
— 'The Coal Board loss', *Tribune* (24 December 1954), p. 1.
— 'The block vote', *Tribune* (31 December 1954), p. 1.
— 'Should we plan wages?', *Tribune* (21 January 1955), p. 1.
— 'Western double-talk', *Tribune* (28 January 1955), p. 1.
— 'Churchill confesses', *Tribune* (11 March 1955), p. 3.
— 'Britain without Churchill', *Tribune* (8 April 1955), p. 1.
— 'Why Winston Churchill has been gagged', *Tribune* (20 May 1955), pp. 2 and 8.
— 'Aneurin Bevan gives his verdict', *Tribune* (3 June 1955), pp. 1–2.
— 'Automation: the socialist answer', *Tribune* (8 July 1955), p. 2.
— 'Verdict on Geneva', *Tribune* (29 July 1955), pp. 1–2.
— 'We can't leave it all to the Russians', *Tribune* (19 August 1955), p. 8.
— 'Give China the help she needs', *Tribune* (26 August 1955), p. 4.
— 'Beware of this Tory trap', *Tribune* (11 November 1955), p. 1.
— 'Russia must take her share of the blame', *Tribune* (25 November 1955), p. 4.

— 'The second Cold War', *Tribune* (23 December 1955), p. 4.
— 'The United Nations should send aid', *Tribune* (6 January 1956), p. 4.
— 'Facts and taxes', *Tribune* (13 January 1956), p. 5.
— 'This famous victory', *Tribune* (3 February 1956), pp. 1 and 12.
— 'Eisenhower's greatest blunder', *Tribune* (17 February 1956), p. 4.
— 'Being very, very practical', *Tribune* (24 February 1956), p. 4.
— 'After Stalin: the big test for communists', *Tribune* (23 March 1956), p. 1.
— 'Arms: there is real hope now', *Tribune* (6 April 1956), p. 1.
— 'Farewell to the Trojan Horse', *Tribune* (27 April 1956), p. 5.
— 'The disarmament breakdown', *Tribune* (11 May 1956), p. 5.
— 'It must be world control for all the commercial waterways', *Tribune* (3 August 1956), p. 5.
— '"The Times" gets a bad attack of nostalgia', *Tribune* (31 August 1956), p. 5.
— 'Aneurin Bevan asks: do they want to wreck the United Nations?', *Tribune* (14 September 1956), p. 2.
— 'This Minor Caesar', *Tribune* (28 September 1956), p. 4.
— 'Give the United Nations a real job to do', *Tribune* (5 October 1956), p. 4.
— 'Now – let's give a socialist lead', *Tribune* (12 October 1956), p. 5.
— 'It's naked and brutal imperialism', *Tribune* (19 October 1956), p. 12.
— 'Two crimes we can never forget', *Tribune* (9 November 1956), p. 12.
— 'Wanted: a new bold policy for peace – that will save Hungary', *Tribune* (16 November 1956), p. 1.
— 'How Ike can take the lead', *Tribune* (21 December 1956), pp. 1 and 12.
— 'Dollar diplomacy? That's no answer', *Tribune* (4 January 1957), pp. 1–2.
— 'Save democracy – have a general election now', *Tribune* (18 January 1957), p. 5.
— 'Crisis time for United Nations', *Tribune* (1 February 1957), p. 5.
— 'The slump and the summit', *Tribune* (7 March 1958), p. 5.
— 'No double standards at UN', *Tribune* (15 March 1957), p. 5.
— 'A declaration of class war', *Tribune* (22 March 1957), p. 4.
— 'Suez: now what?', *Tribune* (17 May 1957), pp. 1 and 3.
— 'Destroy the bombs before they destroy us!', *Tribune* (24 May 1957), p. 1.

— 'Cut arms to save peace – not to balance the budget', *Tribune* (31 May 1957), p. 7.
— 'Tory financial policy could smash the Commonwealth', *Tribune* (28 June 1957), p. 1.
— 'At last the Socialist International wakes up!', *Tribune* (12 July 1957), p. 12.
— 'A very dangerous game', *Tribune* (16 August 1957), pp. 1 and 12.
— 'The clash of the giants', *Tribune* (23 August 1957), p. 5.
— 'Back to free markets – and the jungle', *Tribune* (30 August 1957), p. 5.
— 'We must save India – or lose democracy's hope', *Tribune* (5 September 1958), p. 5.
— 'The world of Gomulka, Tito – and Djilas', *Tribune* (27 September 1957), p. 6.
— 'Why Russia wins space race', *Tribune* (11 October 1957), p. 5.
— 'Platitudes won't save mankind', *Tribune* (13 December 1957), p. 5.
— 'Arms and the slump', *Tribune* (31 January 1958), p. 5.
— 'Communism or suicide? That's not the real choice', *Tribune* (14 March 1958), p. 5.
— 'Two faces of Macmillan', *Tribune* (21 March 1958), p. 5.
— 'Russia's proposals put Eisenhower on the spot', *Tribune* (11 April 1958), p. 5.
— 'The real arguments behind the Tito-Khrushchev row', *Tribune* (11 July 1958), p. 6.
— 'Bevan on the Crisis', *Tribune* (25 July 1958), pp. 1 and 12.
— 'Dulles must be defied', *Tribune* (15 August 1958), p. 7.
— 'Tory gamblers pour £1,500 million down the drain', *Tribune* (7 November 1958), pp. 1 and 3.
— 'A nuclear free zone in Europe would be a benediction', *Tribune* (14 November 1958), p. 12.
— 'Independence – then hard work: how to maintain the frontiers of liberty', *Tribune* (21 November 1958), p. 5.
— 'The Communist failure in the west', *Tribune* (28 November 1958), p. 8.
— 'Private enterprise vs public ownership: the moon and the £', *Tribune* (9 January 1959), p. 5.
— 'The decline of capitalism', *Tribune* (30 January 1959), p. 9.
— 'Now we know', *Tribune* (10 April 1959), p. 5.

— 'The budget and the unions', *Tribune* (17 April 1959), pp. 1 and 9.
— 'Britain in the Middle East', *Tribune* (22 May 1959), p. 12.
— 'Bevan on Parliament', *Tribune* (5 June 1959), p. 12.
— 'Eisenhower and Khrushchev', *Tribune* (28 August 1959), p. 12.
Bevan, Aneurin, and Stafford Cripps, 'Our duty!', *Tribune* (8 September 1939), pp. 1 and 3.
'Bevan Plaque for NHS Anniversary', *BBC News*, 5 July 2008, *http://news.bbc.co.uk/1/hi/wales/7490391.stm* (accessed 10 January 2024).
Blackburn, Dean, 'Still the Stranger at the Feast? Ideology and the Study of Twentieth Century British Politics', *Journal of Political Ideologies*, 22/2 (2017), 116–30.
British Pathé, 'Labour Party Conference (1953)', 2014, *www.youtube.com/watch?v=RKhQRqRjnyk&t=555s* (accessed 10 January 2024).
Brome, Vincent, *Aneurin Bevan: A Biography* (London: Longmans, Green and Co., 1953).
Brown, Gordon, 'Power for a Purpose – Gordon Brown Speech: Sunday 16 August', 2015, *https://gordonandsarahbrown.com/2015/08/power-for-a-purpose-gordon-brown-speech-sunday-16-august/* (accessed 10 January 2024).
Callaghan, John, 'The Left: The Ideology of the Labour Party', in Leonard Tivey and Anthony Wright (eds), *Party Ideology in Britain* (London: Routledge, 1989), pp. 23–48.
— 'The Left and the "Unfinished Revolution": Bevanites and Soviet Russia in the 1950s', *Contemporary British History*, 15/3 (2001), 63–82.
— *The Labour Party and Foreign Policy: A History* (London: Routledge, 2007).
Campbell, John, *Nye Bevan and the Mirage of British Socialism* (London: Weidenfeld & Nicolson, 1987).
Castle, Barbara, 'A Passionate Defiance', in Geoffrey Goodman (ed.), *The State of the Nation: The Political Legacy of Aneurin Bevan* (London: Victor Gollancz, 1997), pp. 36–67.
Coates, David, *The Labour Party and the Struggle for Socialism* (Cambridge: Cambridge University Press, 1975).
Coates, David, and Leo Panitch, 'The Continuing Relevance of the Milibandian Perspective', in John Callaghan, Steven Fielding and Steve Ludlam (eds), *Interpreting the Labour Party: Approaches to*

Labour Politics and History (Manchester: Manchester University Press, 2003), pp. 71–85.

Corbyn, Jeremy. 'We Must Include Everybody and Exclude Nobody. They Were Nye Bevan's Values, They Are Labour's Values. #NHS70', *Twitter*, 3 July 2018.

Craik, William W., *The Central Labour College: A Chapter in the History of Adult Working-Class Education 1909–29* (London: Lawrence & Wishart, 1964).

Crosland, Anthony, *The Future of Socialism* (London: Constable, 2006).

'Dangers of Power Blocs', *The Times*, 2 March 1953, p. 7.

Davies, Nye (ed.), *This is My Truth: Aneurin Bevan in Tribune* (Cardiff: University of Wales Press, 2023).

Davis, Madeleine, '"Labourism" and the New Left', in John Callaghan, Steven Fielding and Steve Ludlam (eds), *Interpreting the Labour Party: Approaches to Labour Politics and History* (Manchester: Manchester University Press, 2003).

Demont, Susan E., 'Tredegar and Aneurin Bevan: A Society and Its Political Articulation 1890–1929' (PhD, University of Wales, College of Cardiff, 1990).

Desai, Radhika, *Intellectuals and Socialism: 'Social Democrats' and the Labour Party* (London: Lawrence & Wishart, 1994).

Diamond, Patrick (ed.), *New Labour's Old Roots: Revisionist Thinkers in Labour's History 1931–1997* (Exeter: Imprint Academic, 2004).

Drucker, Henry M., *Doctrine and Ethos in the Labour Party* (London: Allen and Unwin, 1979).

Edgerton, David, *The Rise and Fall of the British Nation: A Twentieth-Century History* (Milton Keynes: Penguin Books, 2019).

Editorial, 'Revenge or Reason?', *Tribune* (16 January 1942), pp. 1–2.

— 'What Churchill stands for', *Tribune* (30 January 1942), pp. 1–2.

— 'Labour has been tricked', *Tribune* (13 February 1942), pp. 1–2.

— 'Consider coal', *Tribune* (20 March 1942), pp. 1–2.

— 'Grigg's responsibility', *Tribune* (10 April 1942), pp. 1–2.

— 'The challenge of big business', *Tribune* (17 April 1942), pp. 1–2.

— 'The Palace revolt against Churchill', *Tribune* (24 April 1942), pp. 1–2.

— 'Big business at the wheel', *Tribune* (22 May 1942), p. 2.

— 'Coal owners *ueber alles*', *Tribune* (5 June 1942), pp. 1–2.

— 'No one is all alone', *Tribune* (24 July 1942), p. 2.

— 'What about Russia?', *Tribune* (7 August 1942), pp. 1–2.
— 'Let the dead past', *Tribune* (18 September 1942), pp. 1–2.
— 'The People versus the Prudential', *Tribune* (30 October 1942), pp. 1–2.
— 'Hatching vein empires', *Tribune* (13 November 1942), pp. 1–2.
— 'The art of political assassination', *Tribune* (27 November 1942), pp. 1–2.
— 'The old dealers return', *Tribune* (8 January 1943), pp. 1–2.
— 'Parliament on trial', *Tribune* (15 January 1943), pp. 1–2.
— 'Passports to insanity', *Tribune* (12 March 1943), pp. 1–2.
— 'The camouflaged saboteurs', *Tribune* (19 March 1943), pp. 1–2.
— 'Anglo-American back chat', *Tribune* (5 January 1945), pp. 1–2.
— 'Manchester – the real story', *Tribune* (10 February 1956), pp. 1 and 7.

Elliot, Gregory, *Labourism and the English Genius: The Strange Death of Labour England?* (London: Verso, 1993).

Ellison, Nicholas, *Egalitarian Thought and Labour Politics: Retreating Visions* (London: Routledge, 1994).

Favretto, Ilaria, '"Wilsonism" Reconsidered: Labour Party Revisionism 1952–64', *Contemporary British History*, 14/4 (2000).

Ferguson, Kate, 'Neil Kinnock Praises his "Political Hero" Nye Bevan as he Unveils Plaque in his Honour', *Wales Online*, 2015, *www.walesonline.co.uk/news/wales-news/neil-kinnock-praises-political-hero-10378669* (accessed 10 January 2024).

Fielding, Steven, and Declan McHugh, 'The Progressive Dilemma and the Social Democratic Perspective', in John Callaghan, Steven Fielding and Steve Ludlam (eds), *Interpreting the Labour Party: Approaches to Labour Politics and History* (Manchester: Manchester University Press, 2003), pp. 134–49.

Foot, Michael, *Aneurin Bevan: 1897–1945*, vol. 1 (London: Granada Publishing, 1975).
— *Aneurin Bevan: 1945–1960*, vol. 2 (London: Granada Publishing, 1975).

Foote, Geoffrey, *The Labour Party's Political Thought: A History* (London: Croom Helm, 1986).

Francis, Hywel, and Dai Smith. *The Fed: A History of the South Wales Miners in the Twentieth Century* (London: Lawrence and Wishart, 1980).

Francis, Martin, *Ideas and Policies under Labour 1945–1951* (London: MacMillan, 1997).

Freeden, Michael. 'The Stranger at the Feast: Ideology and Public Policy in Twentieth Century Britain', *Twentieth Century British History*, 1/1 (1990), 9–34.

— *Ideology: A Very Short Introduction* (Oxford: Oxford University Press, 2003).

Gallie, Walter Bryce, 'Essentially Contested Concepts', *Proceedings of the Aristotelian Society*, 56 (1956), 167–98.

Geddes, Marc, and R. A. W. Rhodes, 'Towards an Interpretive Parliamentary Studies', in Jenni Brichzin, Damien Krichewsky, Leopold Ringel and Jan Schank (eds), *Soziologie Der Parlamente: Neue Wege Der Politischen Institutionenforschung* (Wiesbaden: Springer VS, 2018), pp. 87–107.

Goodman, Geoffrey (ed.), *The State of the Nation: The Political Legacy of Aneurin Bevan* (London: Victor Gollancz, 1997).

Gramsci, Antonio, *Selections from the Prison Notebooks* (New York: International Publishers, 1992).

Griffiths, Robert, *S. O. Davies: A Socialist Faith* (Llandysul, Dyfed: Gomer Press, 1983).

Gwalchmai, Ben, 'Aneurin Bevan Killed My Sheep: Labour and Welsh Independence', *New Socialist*, 2019, *https://newsocialist.org.uk/labour-and-welsh-independence/* (accessed 10 January 2024).

Hannah, Simon, *A Party with Socialists in It: A History of the Labour Left* (London: Pluto Press, 2018).

Haseler, Stephen, *The Gaitskellites: Revisionism in the British Labour Party 1951–64* (London: MacMillan, 1969).

Haugaard, Mark (ed.), *Power: A Reader* (Manchester: Manchester University Press, 2002).

Healey, Denis, *The Curtain Falls: The Story of the Socialists in Eastern Europe* (London: Lincolns-Prager, 1951).

Healy, Gerry, 'The Way to Socialism: A Full Analysis of Bevan's New Book', *Labour Review*, 1/2 (1952), *www.marxists.org/history/etol/newspape/lr/vol01/v01n02-may-aug-1952-lr.pdf* (accessed 10 January 2024).

HC Deb (10 July 1933) vol. 280, col. 815.

HC Deb (4 December 1933) vol. 283 col. 1318–1319.

HC Deb (23 June 1944) vol. 401, col. 491–582.

HC Deb (6 December 1945) vol. 416, col. 2544.
HC Deb (6 March 1946) vol. 420, col. 377–463.
HC Deb (30 April 1946) vol. 422, col. 44–142.
HC Deb (15 February 1951) vol. 484 col. 733.
HC Deb (3 November 1959) vol. 612, col. 860–985.
Howell, David, *British Social Democracy: A Study in Development and Decay* (London: Croom Helm, 1976).
— *The Rise and Fall of Bevanism*, Labour Party Discussion Series 5 (Leeds, Independent Labour Party, 1982).
Hunt, Jeremy, 'Jeremy Hunt Speech: Party of the NHS', 2015 *https://press.conservatives.com/post/130944862065/jeremy-hunt-speech-party-of-the-nhs* (accessed 10 January 2024).
'Indian Initiative in Peace', *The Times*, 17 February 1953, p. 8.
Jackson, Ben, 'Revisionism Reconsidered: "Property-Owning Democracy" and Egalitarian Strategy in Post-War Britain', *Twentieth Century British History*, 16 (2005), 416–40.
— *Equality and the British Left: A Study in Progressive Political Thought, 1900–64* (Manchester: Manchester University Press, 2007).
Jeffries, Kevin, 'The Old Right', in Raymond Plant, Matt Beech and Kevin Hickson (eds), *The Struggle for Labour's Soul: Understanding Labour's Political Thought since 1945* (London: Routledge, 2004).
Jenkins, Mark, *Bevanism: Labour's High Tide* (Nottingham: Spokesman University Press, 1979).
Jones, Barry, and Michael Keating, *Labour and the British State* (Oxford: Clarendon Press, 1985).
Jones, Bill, *The Russia Complex: The British Labour Party and the Soviet Union* (Manchester: Manchester University Press, 1977).
Jones, Tudor, '"Taking Genesis out of the Bible": Hugh Gaitskell, Clause Iv and Labour's Socialist Myth', *Contemporary British History*, 11/12 (1997), 1–23.
Krug, Mark, *Aneurin Bevan: Cautious Rebel* (New York: Thomas Yoseloff, 1961).
Labour Party, 'Labour Party Annual Conference Report', 1949.
Lawson, George, 'A Conversation with Michael Mann', *Millennium: Journal of International Studies*, 34/2 (2006), 477–85.
Leach, Robert, *Political Ideology in Britain*, 3rd edn (London: Palgrave, 2015).

Lee, Jennie, *My Life with Nye* (Middlesex: Palgrave, 1981).

London, Jack, *The Iron Heel* (Marston Gate: Amazon, 1908).

Lüthi, Lorenz M., 'The Non-Aligned Movement and the Cold War, 1961–1973', *Journal of Cold War Studies*, 18/4 (2016), pp. 98–147.

M.P., 'Storm meets Baldwin's efforts to save democracy for the rich', *Tribune* (12 March 1937), p. 7.

— 'Why Mr Ernest Brown infuriates opposition and Tory members alike', *Tribune* (9 April 1937), p. 7.

— 'Prim Neville takes his bow for state profiteering', *Tribune* (23 April 1937), p. 7.

— 'M.P.s pack commons to listen to rich men's sad woes', *Tribune* (30 April 1937), p. 7.

— 'Softening soap for workers and convicts', *Tribune* (18 June 1937), p. 6.

— 'Spain – and the big guns go booming', *Tribune* (2 July 1937), p. 6.

— 'M.P.s' doubts and fears as they depart for their holidays', *Tribune* (30 July 1937), p. 6.

Macintyre, Stuart, *A Proletarian Science: Marxism in Britain, 1917–1933* (London: Lawrence and Wishart, 1986).

Mann, Michael, *The Sources of Social Power, Volume 1: A History of Power from the Beginning to A.D. 1760* (Cambridge: Cambridge University Press, 1986).

— *The Sources of Social Power, Volume 3: Global Empires and Revolution, 1890–1945* (Cambridge: Cambridge University Press, 2012).

Marquand, David, *The Progressive Dilemma: From Lloyd George to Tony Blair*, 2nd edn (London: Phoenix, 1999).

Marx, Karl, *Capital: A Critique of Political Economy*, vol. 3 (New York: International Publishers, 1959), *www.marxists.org/archive/marx/works/download/pdf/Capital-Volume-III.pdf* (accessed 10 January 2024).

— 'Theses on Feuerbach', in David Wootton (ed.), *Modern Political Thought: Readings from Machiavelli to Nietzsche* (Indianapolis IN: Hackett Publishing, 1996), pp. 798–9.

Marx, Karl, and Frederick Engels, 'Manifesto of the Communist Party', in *Marx Engels Selected Works* (Moscow: Progress Publishers, 1969), pp. 98–137.

Mason, Rowena, 'Owen Smith: Who is the Man Challenging Corbyn as Labour Leader?', *The Guardian*, 2016, *www.theguardian.com/*

politics/2016/jul/22/owen-smith-who-is-the-man-challenging-jeremy-corbyn-labour-leadership (accessed 10 January 2024).

McLellan, David, *The Thought of Karl Marx: An Introduction* (London: Macmillan, 1971).

Miliband, Ralph, 'Lenin's the State and Revolution', *Socialist Register*, 7 (1970), 309–19, *https://socialistregister.com/index.php/srv/article/view/5303* (accessed 10 January 2024).

— 'Poulantzas and the Capitalist State', *New Left Review*, 1/82 (1973), 83–92, *https://newleftreview.org/I/82/ralph-miliband-poulantzas-and-the-capitalist-state* (accessed 10 January 2024).

— *The State in Capitalist Society* (London: Quartet Books, 1973).

— 'Socialist Advance in Britain', in *Class War Conservatism and Other Essays* (London: Verso, 1983).

— *Parliamentary Socialism* (Pontypool: Merlin Press, 2009).

Morgan, Kenneth O., 'Nye Bevan', in Wm. Roger Louis (ed.), *Resurgent Adventures with Britannia: Personalities, Politics and Culture in Britain* (London: I. B. Tauris, 2011), pp. 181–95.

Morgan, Rhodri, 'Clear Red Water', *Socialist Health Association*, 11 December 2002, *www.sochealth.co.uk/the-socialist-health-association/sha-country-and-branch-organisation/sha-wales/clear-red-water/* (accessed 10 January 2024).

Myers, Matt, 'More Blair than Bevan', *Jacobin*, 19 September 2016, *www.jacobinmag.com/2016/09/aneurin-bevin-nhs-owen-smith-corbyn* (accessed 10 January 2024).

Nairn, Tom, 'The Nature of the Labour Party – 1', *New Left Review*, 1/27 (1964), 38–65, *https://newleftreview.org/I/27/tom-nairn-the-nature-of-the-labour-party-part-i* (accessed 10 January 2024).

— 'The Nature of the Labour Party – 2', *New Left Review*, 1/28 (1964), 33–62, *https://newleftreview.org/I/28/tom-nairn-the-nature-of-the-labour-party-part-ii* (accessed 10 January 2024).

— 'The Twilight of the British State', *New Left Review*, 1/101 (1977), 3–61, *https://newleftreview.org/issues/I101/articles/tom-nairn-the-twilight-of-the-british-state* (accessed 10 January 2024).

— 'The Crisis of the British State', *New Left Review*, 1/130 (1981), 37–44, *https://newleftreview.org/issues/I130/articles/tom-nairn-the-crisis-of-the-british-state* (accessed 10 January 2024).

Nuttall, Jeremy, '"Psychological Socialist"; "Militant Moderate": Evan Durbin and the Politics of Synthesis', *Labour History Review*, 68/2 (2003), 235–52.
— 'The Labour Party and the Improvement of Minds: The Case of Tony Crosland', *Historical Journal*, 46/1 (2003), 133–53.
— 'Tony Crosland and the Many Falls and Rises of British Social Democracy', *Contemporary British History*, 18/4 (2004), 52–79.
— 'Labour Revisionism and Qualities of Mind and Character, 1931–79', *English Historical Review*, 120/487 (2005), 667–94.
— *Psychological Socialism: The Labour Party and Qualities of Mind and Character* (Manchester: Manchester University Press, 2006).
— 'Equality and Freedom: The Single, the Multiple and the Synthesis in Labour Party Thought since the 1930s', *Journal of Political Ideologies*, 13/11 (2008), 11–36.
— 'Pluralism, the People, and Time in Labour Party History, 1931–1964', *Historical Journal*, 56/3 (2013), 729–56.
Palonen, Kari, 'Political Theorizing as a Dimension of Political Life', *European Journal of Political Theory*, 4/4 (2005), 351–66.
Petrović, Gajo, 'Praxis', in Tom Bottomore (ed.), *A Dictionary of Marxist Thought* (Oxford: Blackwell, 1983), pp. 384–9.
Pierson, Christopher, *Marxist Theory and Democratic Politics* (Oxford: Polity Press, 1986).
Poulantzas, Nicos, *State, Power, Socialism* (London: Verso, 2014).
Rawls, John, *Lectures on the History of Political Philosophy* (Cambridge MA: Harvard University Press, 2007).
Reid, Alastair J., 'Class and Politics in the Work of Henry Pelling', in John Callaghan, Steven Fielding and Steve Ludlam (eds), *Interpreting the Labour Party: Approaches to Labour Politics and History* (Manchester: Manchester University Press, 2003), pp. 101–15.
Riddell, Peter, 'The End of Clause IV, 1994–95', *Contemporary British History*, 11/ 2 (1997), 24–49.
Rodó, José Enrique, *The Motives of Proteus* (Delhi: Facsimile Publisher, 1928).
— *Ariel* (Austin TX: Texas University Press, 1988).
Saville, John, 'The Ideology of Labourism', in Robert Benewick, R. N. Berki and Bhikhu Parekh (eds), *Knowledge and Belief in Politics: The Problem of Ideology* (London: George Allen & Unwin Ltd, 1975).

— *The Labour Movement in Britain: A Commentary* (London: Faber and Faber, 1988).

Schneer, Jonathan, 'Hopes Deferred or Shattered: The British Labour Left and the Third Force Movement, 1945–49', *Journal of Modern History*, 56/2 (1984), 197–226.

Smith, Dai, *Aneurin Bevan and the World of South Wales* (Cardiff: University of Wales Press, 1993).

— 'Ashes to the Wind', in Geoffrey Goodman (ed.), *The State of the Nation: The Political Legacy of Aneurin Bevan* (London: Victor Gollancz, 1997).

Spalding, Roger, *Narratives of Delusion in the Political Practice of the Labour Left: 1931–1945* (Cambridge: Cambridge Scholars Publishing, 2018).

Strachey, John, *The Coming Struggle for Power* (London: Victor Gollancz, 1932).

Thane, Pat, *Divided Kingdom: A History of Britain, 1900 to the Present* (Cambridge: Cambridge University Press, 2018).

Thomas-Symonds, Nicklaus, *Nye: The Political Life of Aneurin Bevan* (London: I. B. Tauris, 2015).

Thompson, Steve, 'NHS was Not Solely Modelled on a Welsh Workmen's Medical Society', *The Conversation*, 3 July 2018, *https://theconversation.com/nhs-was-not-solely-modelled-on-a-welsh-workmens-medical-society-98024* (accessed 10 January 2024).

Thompson, Willie, *The Long Death of British Labourism: Interpreting a Political Culture* (London: Pluto Press, 1993).

Thorpe, Andrew, *A History of the British Labour Party* (Basingstoke: Macmillan, 1997).

Todd, Selina, 'Affluence, Class and Crown Street: Reinvestigating the Post-War Working Class', *Contemporary British History*, 22/4 (2008), pp. 501–18, *https://doi.org/10.1080/13619460802439382* (accessed 10 January 2024).

'Two "Giants"', *The Western Mail*, 17 February 1953, p. 1.

Unofficial Reform Committee, *The Miners' Next Step*, 1991.

Vickers, Rhiannon, *The Labour Party and the World, Volume 1: The Evolution of Labour's Foreign Policy 1900–51* (Manchester: Manchester University Press, 2003).

— *The Labour Party and the World, Volume 2: Labour's Foreign Policy since 1951* (Manchester: Manchester University Press, 2011).

Ward, Colin, *Social Policy: An Anarchist Response* (London: Freedom Press, 2000).

'Watch: Jeremy Hunt Compares Himself to Nye Bevan', *The Spectator*, 2016, *www.spectator.co.uk/article/watch-jeremy-hunt-compares-himself-to-nye-bevan/* (accessed 16 January 2023).

Waugh, Paul, 'Owen Smith Interview: On the "Likelihood" of a Labour Split, Politics of "the Street", and a "Real Living Wage"', *Huffington Post*, 3 August 2016, *www.huffingtonpost.co.uk/entry/owen-smith-interview-on-the-likelihood-of-a-labour-split-politics-of-the-street-and-a-real-living_uk_57a1e26ce4b0f42daa4ba666* (accessed 10 January 2024).

Wickham-Jones, Mark, 'An Exceptional Comrade? The Nairn-Anderson Interpretation', in John Callaghan, Steven Fielding and Steve Ludlam (eds), *Interpreting the Labour Party: Approaches to Labour Politics and History* (Manchester: Manchester University Press, 2003), pp. 86–100.

Williams, Daniel G., *Wales Unchained* (Cardiff: University of Wales Press, 2015).

Williams, Gwyn Alf, 'The Concept of "Egemonia" in the Thought of Antonio Gramsci: Some Notes on Interpretation", *Journal of the History of Ideas*, 21/4 (1960), 586–99.

— *The Welsh in their History* (London: Croom Helm, 1982).

Williams, Raymond, 'Base and Superstructure in Marxist Cultural Theory', *New Left Review*, 1/82 (1973), 3–16.

— 'Problems of Materialism', *New Left Review*, 1/109 (1978), 3–17.

— *Politics and Letters: Interview with* New Left Review (London: Verso, 1981).

INDEX